Praise for the first edition of *The Gos*

"Thoughtful and genuinely entertaining
— *Publishers Weekly*

"A seriously funny examination of the popular TV show."
— *Booklist*

"A straight-faced (yet unavoidably amusing) look at the program's treatment of faith, ethics, and, yes, 'family values.'"
—*Toronto Star*

"If you believe in the power of popular culture to teach Christian theology, ethics, and values, then Mark Pinsky's *The Gospel according to* The Simpsons needs to be at the top of your reading list."
—*Circuit Rider*

"*The Simpsons* is one of the most subtle pieces of propoganda around in the cause of sense, humility, and virtue. Mark Pinsky manages to decipher the code without deadening the humor, which is quite an achievement."
—The Most Reverend Rowan Williams, Archbishop of Canterbury

"I've never been much of a TV watcher. It's against my religion, as they used to say. But now Mark Pinsky's *The Gospel according to* The Simpsons has made me at least a partial convert. I was blind, but now I see that in *The Simpsons* anyway, there is goodness galore—intelligence, hilarious writing, insight, telling social criticism and commentary, and plenty of helpful hints for spiritually challenged people like me. Thanks to Pinsky and *The Simpsons* my conscience has been caught, my train of thought has finally left the station, and I've been thoroughly delighted without feeling guilty about it. Now when *The Simpsons* is on, I'm in the front row. I've even learned how to use the remote."
—Robert L. Short, author of *The Gospel According to Peanuts*

"This is a brilliant, witty, readable book, which every *Simpsons* lover will *want* to read, every parent *should* read, and every Christian *needs* to read immediately."
—Theodore Baehr, chairman of the Christian Film & Television Commission and publisher of *Movieguide*™

The Gospel according to *The Simpsons,* Bigger and Possibly Even Better! Edition

The Gospel according to *The Simpsons*, Bigger and Possibly Even Better! Edition

With a New Afterword Exploring *South Park, Family Guy,* and Other Animated TV Shows

MARK I. PINSKY

Westminster John Knox Press
LOUISVILLE • LONDON

Scripture quotations from the Revised Standard Version of the Bible are copyright
© 1946, 1952, 1971, and 1973 by the Division of Christian Education of the
National Council of the Churches of Christ in the U.S.A., and are used by permission.

Scripture quotations from *The Holy Bible, New International Version*
are copyright © 1973, 1978, 1984 International Bible Society.
Used by permission of Zondervan Bible Publishers.

Book design by Sharon Adams

Second Edition
Published by Westminster John Knox Press
Louisville, Kentucky

This book is printed on acid-free paper that meets the
American National Standards Institute Z39.48 standard. ∞

PRINTED IN THE UNITED STATES OF AMERICA

07 08 09 10 11 12 13 14 15 16—10 9 8 7 6 5 4 3 2 1

U.S. Library of Congress Cataloging-in-Publication Data

Pinsky, Mark I.
  The gospel according to the Simpsons, bigger and possibly even better! edition with a
new afterword exploring South park, Family guy, and other animated TV shows / Mark
I. Pinsky.—2nd ed.
    p. cm.
Includes bibliographical references and index.
ISBN 978-0-664-23160-6 (alk. paper)
  1. Simpsons (Television program)   2. Animated television programs—United States.
3. Television broadcasting—Religious aspects.   I. Title.
PN1992.77.S58P56   2007
791.45'72—dc22   2007006909

British Library Cataloguing-in-Publication Data
A catalogue record for this book is available from the British Library.

ISBN: 978-0-664-23265-8 (U.K. and Canada)

For
Sallie, Liza, and Asher
and
in memory of my parents,
Charlotte and Oscar Pinsky

Contents

viii   *Contents*

Introduction to the Second Edition: Epiphany on the Sofa

George Bush the Elder once denounced it; his wife, Barbara, called it dumb. Former Education Secretary William Bennett questioned its values. So the dilemma loomed: Should my wife, Sallie, and I allow our young kids to watch *The Simpsons*? Many considered the show to be abrasive, abusive—even abominable. We were concerned, as most parents are, that our children would grow up too quickly because of what they saw on the screen. When our son Asher (then 11) and our daughter Liza (then 8) took an interest in *The Simpsons*, I began to watch it with them—and was I ever surprised! At first, the popular program featuring a spikey-haired kid seemed to be the antithesis of *Leave It to Beaver*, a program my brother Paul and I watched with our parents in our suburban home. But the modern cartoon sitcom turned out to be family-friendly and full of faith. Even Barbara Bush and Bill Bennett eventually backpedaled. George Bush *pere*, who was able to embrace *Saturday Night Live* impersonator Dana Carvey, has not yet recanted his criticism of the series.

How did it happen? What made *The Simpsons* so popular and its popularity so durable? Would regular viewers be catching some glimpses of faith that the spiritually faithful have been trying to communicate for years? What lessons might the program have for viewers of varying spiritual, moral, political, and social stripes?

On Sunday nights, when America's best-known dysfunctional family is a fixture in millions of households, many Christians are in church. At home, the less devout were probably tuned to the long-time competition, *Touched by an Angel*, which usually won the ratings time period when the two shows went head to head. But a lot

1

of people *are* watching *The Simpsons*, and have been watching faithfully and, yes, religiously for nearly two decades. "*Simpsons* fans treat Sunday as a day of worship," wrote Jon Horowitz of Rutgers University in an unpublished paper. "Not early mornings at church; 8 P.M. in front of the holiest of holies, the TV tuned into the FOX network."[1]

In addition to the millions who watch the series each week, millions more tune in each week to watch reruns of the show in syndication (it was still rated first among all rerun shows in the 1994–1995 season). More than 180 Fox affiliates carry the new episodes on Sunday nights. Over 250 stations in the U.S. and Canada air the highly rated reruns, some twice a day or more. Around the world, it is more popular than *Baywatch*, reaching sixty million people a week in more than seventy countries (though not in Costa Rica or the Dominican Republic, where it is banned as an affront to family values, or in prime time in China, to avoid competing against local programs), dubbed in dozens of languages. A syndicated Sunday comic strip in 250 newspapers reaches an audience of fourteen million, and hundreds of thousands of copies of more than two dozen authorized books about the show have been sold—part of a billion-dollar *Simpsons* merchandise industry. By the 1990s there were more than a thousand *Simpsons* Web sites in cyberspace.

In July 2007 came the long-awaited feature film. "Our greatest hope is the movie winds up inspiring a lot of new audiences to actually come to the show," Peter Liguori, Fox's president of entertainment, told the *Orlando Sentinel's* Hal Boedeker at the Television Critics' meeting in Hollywood in January 2007. "The show is about as creatively fertile as it's ever been." Asked if there is too much *Simpsons* material in circulation, Liguori replied, "The answer is no. . . . In this current environment, given the paucity of comedy, an audience is going to show up to a really funny show. I think it can go on for a long time." Series creator Matt Groening told the critics that the reason for the film's July release was that "We're coming up on the twentieth year of the show, we're coming up on the four hundredth episode, and if we're ever going to do it, we should do it now. . . . I thought it would really be neat to do a movie while the fans are still clamoring for it." Added *Simpsons* codeveloper James L. Brooks,

"For our animators to have this kind of scope and this stuff to play with for the first time, I can't tell you what that means to them."

In prime time, the series has ranged from the fringes of the top 15 in the Nielsen ratings to the 30s, doing best among males ages 18–49. In the 2000–2001 season, eleven years after it began, the show actually *gained* in the ratings, and its 2000–2001 premiere pulled sixteen million viewers. The series ended the 2000–2001 season ranked 21 of 150 network shows, but was still the third most watched show on Fox. Through the first half of the 2006–2007 season, *The Simpsons* dropped to number 47 overall in rankings by Nielsen Media Research, while still maintaining an average of 9.5 million viewers a week. Among 18–49-year-old viewers coveted by advertisers, it rated a respectable number 20. As important to Fox as the show's ratings success was *The Simpsons'* continued critical acclaim, superlatives that rained on Rupert Murdoch's fledgling network like manna from heaven. In its first dozen years, the show was nominated for thirty-four Emmys and has won twenty-three, including nine for best animated series. It has also won a Peabody award, which recognizes distinguished achievement in radio and television. *Time* magazine called *The Simpsons* the twentieth century's best television show, and the entertainment industry took note of the series' tenth anniversary with a star on Hollywood Boulevard. The show has made the cover of *TV Guide* a dozen times. During the same two-week period in early 2001, the Simpsons appeared on the covers of both *Christianity Today* and *The Christian Century*, two magazines at opposite ends of the Christian theological spectrum. *Life* magazine, in a cover titled "The Shows That Changed America: 60 Years of Network Television," called *The Simpsons* the "millennium family unit: struggling, skeptical, disrespectful, ironic, hopeful. . . . The Simpsons verify our country's strength: If they can make it in today's America, who can't?"[2] In the words of cultural guru Kurt Andersen, it is "smarter, sharper and more allusive than any other show on television."[3] Robert Thompson, founding director of the Center for the Study of Popular Television at Syracuse University, said in a newspaper interview that the series "doesn't compare just with other television programs, but with the best of American humor. Will Rogers,

Mark Twain and *The Simpsons* can happily occupy the same stratosphere of respect in the annals of American humor."[4]

The Simpsons has exerted an ongoing influence on American culture, high and low. "D'oh!" Homer's expression of consternation, has been added to the *Oxford English Dictionary*. Bad boy Bart became a giant, sixty-foot balloon in the Macy's Thanksgiving Day parade. The *New York Times* predicted in its millennium edition, perhaps with tongue in cheek, that *The Simpsons* would still be a top-rated show in 2025, and suggested that one of the show's characters, the avaricious nuclear plant owner Montgomery Burns, was a better-known exemplar of capitalism than Ayn Rand. A 1999 survey conducted by Roper Starch Worldwide found that 91 percent of American children between the ages of 10 and 17, and 84 percent of adults, could identify members of the Simpson family. In each case, this was a greater percentage than knew that the vice president of the United States was Al Gore—a man who later identified himself as a fan of the show to a high school crowd in Concord, New Hampshire.

This influence may be nearly as great outside America. In Britain, where in recent years the show has rated higher than in the United States, former Prime Minister Tony Blair revealed himself to be a fan of the series. Campaigning for reelection in May of 2001 in the city of Norfolk, he confessed that he "is a bit of a Simpsons addict." His wife, Cherie, rolled her eyes in embarrassment and confirmed that the English leader is devoted to the show. The prime minister appeared as himself in a 2005 episode.

All this began in 1987 with 30 two-minute, animated vignettes that ran between segments of *The Tracey Ullman Show* on the Fox Television Network. The family was created by cartoonist Matt Groening, then best known for a comic strip called *Life in Hell*, which appeared in alternative weekly newspapers.

The Simpsons are a lower-middle-class family living in the town of Springfield, in an unidentified state. They consist of:

> Father—Homer, bald and overweight, with a weakness for beer, pork chops, television, and donuts. Employed as a safety inspector at the local nuclear power plant. Named

for character of the same name in Nathaniel West's Hollywood classic, *Day of the Locust.* Also shares first name with Groening's father.

Mother—Marge, a long-suffering, stay-at-home mom with a towering beehive of blue hair. Same first name as Groening's mother.

Son—Bart (an anagram for "brat"), a ten-year-old with a world-class attitude. Stand-in for young Matt.

Daughter—Lisa, a good-hearted and gifted eight-year-old, usually dressed in a strapless red frock and a strand of Barbara Bush pearls. Name of one of the Groening sisters.

Baby—Maggie, who does not speak and is rarely seen without her pacifier. Name of another Groening sister.

So popular were *The Simpsons* snippets on *The Tracey Ullman Show* that in 1990 the family got its own half-hour series on Fox. In the ultimate counterprogramming move, Fox first put their edgy new series into what was considered a suicide slot on Thursday nights, opposite the wholesome and high-flying *Cosby Show*, then number one in the ratings. The contrast between the two family comedies could not have been more stark, and *The Simpsons* caused a sensation, sparking denunciations throughout the nation over the next few years as the animated show moved to Sunday nights and became even more popular. Across the country, merchandise featuring Bart Simpson and his disrespectful catch phrases such as "Don't have a cow, man," and "Eat my shorts" caused outrage. In April 1990, the principal of Cambridge Elementary School in Orange County, California, banned students from wearing the Bart shirts to school. In June, Mayor Sharpe James of Newark, New Jersey, asked retail stores and street vendors in his city to stop selling the shirts, according to the Associated Press. "Just at a time when we are trying to get our young people to develop their abilities to the fullest, we get a tee-shirt with a popular cartoon character saying he is proud to be an underachiever," James told the Associated Press.[5] J.C. Penney halted sales of the offending shirt.

Nowhere was the initial uproar more vigorous than in America's pulpits. Upset by his child imitating Bart at the dinner table, an outraged member of Willow Creek Community Church near Chicago complained to one of the ministers, Lee Strobel, who in turn preached a widely reprinted sermon titled "What Jesus Would Say to Bart Simpson." A Baptist pastor, Dan Burrell, recorded an educational audiotape entitled "Raising Beaver Cleaver Kids in a Bart Simpson World," instructing parents how to rear their children with "value and character."

America's moral leaders thundered that this nuclear but troubled family was the latest evidence of the fall of Western civilization. When drug czar and former education secretary William Bennett visited a rehabilitation center in Pittsburgh in 1990, he spotted a Bart Simpson poster on the wall with the caption, "Underachiever and Proud of It." Bennett then asked, "You guys aren't watching *The Simpsons*, are you? That's not going to help you any." Bennett later retreated from his criticism, acknowledging that he didn't watch the show. Making the best of the backlash, he retorted several days later, "I'll have to sit down and have a talk with the little spike head."[6]

From his own bully pulpit, President George H. W. Bush told the National Religious Broadcasters in 1992, "We need a nation closer to the Waltons than the Simpsons." Not to be outdone, Bart responded in an episode that followed three days later. The segment featured the family watching the president's attack on them on TV, puzzled. Noting the sharp economic downturn attributed to the Bush administration, Bart cracked, "We're just like the Waltons. We're praying for an end to the depression too." Barbara Bush shot back, "*The Simpsons* is the dumbest thing I've ever seen." Then, and in much the same fashion as Bennett, she backpedaled. In a letter to "Marge Simpson," the First Lady called the animated family "charming" and complimented them for "setting an example for the rest of the country."[7] The series returned this conciliatory gesture with the back of its hand, portraying the First Lady in the White House bathtub. Several years later, *The Simpsons* took an episode-length shot at the former president in retirement, in which the otherwise genial Bush was driven to spank Bart, infuriating Homer, whose preferred form of corporal punishment is strangulation.

These early controversies branded the series in the minds of many—especially some Christians—as negative and juvenile. In the years that followed, this impression obscured a fundamental shift in *The Simpsons*, as the narrative focus of the episodes moved from rebellious son Bart to his hapless dad, Homer. The show was delving deeper in the issues it tackled and was friendlier to faith, but many viewers who might have appreciated this dimension had tuned out or had never tuned in.

You can find God in the funniest places. "Humor is a prelude to faith, and laughter is the beginning of prayer," Reinhold Niebuhr observed.[8] Or as Conrad Hyers wrote in *The Comic Vision and the Christian Faith*, "If humor without faith is in danger of dissolving into cynicism and despair, faith without humor is in danger of turning into arrogance and intolerance."[9] Tuning in nearly a decade after the series premiered, I found God, faith, and spirituality in abundance on *The Simpsons*. Like most of the show's episodes, my involvement with the series began on the family couch. I had been vaguely aware of the series since its debut, but I was not a fan or even a regular viewer; the hype and the controversy put me off. If I happened to see an episode every now and then, I enjoyed it, but I would never rearrange my schedule to watch. It was only during the summer of 1999, when my young son and daughter became interested in the program, that I started to tune in regularly. In light of the show's reputation for rude behavior, bad language, and sexual innuendo, I insisted on sitting with them. Watching the weekly episodes—supplemented by a double dose of nightly reruns through the summer—led to valuable discussions with the kids about moral issues, and I was relieved to see that most of the naughty stuff sailed over their heads (I hope).

The real epiphany for me, as a longtime religion writer for daily newspapers, was the surprisingly favorable way religion, in its broadest sense, was presented in the series, and what a central role faith played in the lives of the characters. In many ways, Simpson family members were both defined and circumscribed by religion. The family attended church every Sunday, read the Bible, and said grace before meals. Their next-door neighbors were committed evangelical Christians. When faced with crises, the Simpsons turned to God and prayed aloud. God often answered their prayers and intervened in their world. Here was a complete (if inconsistent) cosmology—God, the devil, angels—and a fully realized universe of faith. Characters believed in a literal heaven and hell, and, like most Americans, they ridiculed cults. Clearly, Christians and Christianity were more a part of *The Simpsons* than of any other prime-time network sitcom or drama, excluding shows specifically devoted to religion such as *Touched by an Angel* and *7th Heaven*.

The Simpsons, wrote Jim Trammell in a 2000 master's thesis for the University of Georgia's Grady School of Journalism and Mass Communication, "proves it is possible to produce a profitable, respected program that credits religion as a part of the American lived experience. In an industry where spirituality is either absent or merely glossed over for a cheap, dispensable laugh, this cartoon proves religion can be featured as a theme without isolating the audience."

Still, no one would mistake Homer Simpson and his family for saints. In many ways, in fact, they are quintessentially weak, well-meaning sinners who rely on their faith—although only when absolutely necessary. *The Simpsons* is consistently irreverent toward organized religion's failings and excesses, as it is with most other institutions and aspects of modern life. And Bart is still Bart. He is not the youngster of whom the prophet Isaiah said "a little child shall lead them"; with Bart, it is literally a case of "suffer the little children" (Mark 10:14 KJV). Homer's grasp of theological complexity is, at best, fuzzy. Asked by Bart what the family's religious beliefs are, his father answers, "You know, the one with all the well-meaning rules that don't work in real life. Uh, Christianity." Inexplicably, along with Catholics, Unitarians have been the butt of most denomination-specific jokes ("If that's the one true faith, I'll eat my hat," Homer cracks), although Lutherans, Mormons, and Jehovah's Witnesses come in for stray shots.

The gift of *The Simpsons* is that the characters' fundamental beliefs are animated but not caricatured. God is not mocked, nor is God's existence questioned. Springfield, where the family lives, possesses a rich spiritual life, according to Gerry Bowler, professor of history at University of Manitoba and founder of the Centre for the Study of Christianity and Contemporary Culture. (Like me and many others, he had been drawn to the show by the requests of his children to watch.) "The satiric *Simpsons* program takes religion's place in society seriously enough to do it the honor of making fun of it," he later wrote. "As satires go, these criticisms are not overly harsh and indeed most Christians would find much truth in them. . . . If this is a show with attractive Christian characters, where good usually triumphs, where the family virtues are always affirmed in the end, why are Christians put off by it? It's a case of where if you're a mature Christian and you get all the jokes, you could watch it."[10]

William Romanowski, author of *Pop Culture Wars: Religion and the Role of Entertainment in American Life*, found that *"The Simpsons* is not dismissive of faith, but treats religion as an integral part of American life." At the same time, the Calvin College professor said, "Episodes generally leave the matter of God and religion open to multiple interpretations, perhaps so as not to potentially alienate audience members, but also as a reflection of American attitudes."[11] The Reverend David Bruce, webmaster of hollywoodjesus.com, which uses popular culture to spread the gospel, put it more simply. He called the Simpsons "the best Christian family on television."

This aspect of the series was spotted very early on, in a 1992 master's thesis written by Beth Keller at Pat Robertson's Regent University. While "it is safe to say that the Simpson clan does not represent an ideally religious family," she wrote, and "it may not completely resonate with the evangelical Judeo-Christian belief system, *The Simpsons* does portray a family searching for moral and theological ideals. . . . I believe religion is viewed positively, overall."[12]

In retrospect, the opening seconds of *The Simpsons* should have tipped me off: harp strings accompany a heavenly choir as the clouds part and the show's title appears on the screen and the camera swoops down over Springfield. As my summer viewing with my children wore on, I found myself watching the show with my reporter's notepad, scribbling feverishly. Then I bought a copy of *The Simpsons: A Complete Guide to Our Favorite Family* and read through a decade of episode summaries, which confirmed my initial impression of religion's role in the series. Interviews with media experts, academics, and the show's executive producer led me to write a lengthy essay that appeared in the Sunday "Insight" section of the *Orlando Sentinel*, a piece reprinted widely in newspapers around the country. Fans of the show sent me e-mails referring me to other newspaper articles and academic papers on the show's spiritual side. The more I saw in the show, the more I wanted to understand this dimension. Since very little of what appears on television and in the movies is there by accident, I wanted to know why religion was treated the way it was.

Mike Scully, at the time the series' executive producer and "show-runner," explained to me that the series wanted to reflect through its characters the fact that faith plays a substantial part in many families' lives, although it is seldom portrayed on television. "We try to represent people's honest attitudes about religion," he said in another interview. "You see the Simpsons and all the townspeople in church together, just like real life. You're in church giving the sign of peace to somebody and then in the parking lot afterward, you're giving them the finger because he's blocking your way. It's just human nature," he told another interviewer.[13] Scully's successor, Al Jean, told me in 2005 that the show was simply mirroring the reality that, during the first Bush administration, religion had become a more prominent part of American life than it had been fifteen years before. Integrating more religion into *The Simpsons* wasn't "really something we did consciously." As creator Matt Groening put it in a 1999 interview with the Associated Press, "You're inviting yourself into someone's home when you do a TV show. . . . For all of *The Simpsons'* darker strains of satire, ultimately it's a celebration of America and the American family in its exuberance and absurdity."[14]

And its faith. Some in the religious world have recognized this phenomenon, making *The Simpsons'* beliefs the subject of at least half a dozen favorable academic journal articles and Web sites. According to one study by a theologian (and fan), fully a third of all the episodes include at least one religious reference. Another study of randomly chosen episodes, by John Heeren of California State University at San Bernardino, found that there was some religious content in 70 percent of these episodes and that 10 percent of the episodes surveyed were constructed around religious themes. Religion was more prominent in the show in the jaded, decadent decade of the 1990s than in other programs in the more religious 1950s, he said. *Simpsons'* writers and producers, Heeren said, "think religion is important in people's lives, and that's why they put it in the center of the work they do."[15]

The accolades have continued to pour in: Christian humor magazine *The Door* said, "There is more spiritual wisdom in one episode of *The Simpsons* than there is in an entire season of *Touched by an Angel.*"[16] David Dark, writing in the Christian monthly *PRISM*, published by Evangelicals for Social Action, called the series "the most pro-family, God-preoccupied, home-based program on television. Statistically speaking, there is more prayer on *The Simpsons* than on any sitcom in broadcast history."[17] David Landry, a theologian and New Testament scholar at the University of St. Thomas, a Catholic college in St. Paul, Minnesota, agreed. "This is not the be-all and end-all of theology on TV, but the most consistent and intelligent treatment of religion on TV is on *The Simpsons*," he told a newspaper interviewer.[18]

Paul Cantor, professor of political science at the University of Virginia, was not willing to go that far. "*The Simpsons* is not pro-religion—it is too hip, cynical and iconoclastic for that," he wrote in the journal *Political Theory*. Yet, "even when it seems to be ridiculing religion, it recognizes, as few other television shows do, the genuine role that religion plays in American life. . . . [I]n Homer Simpson it also suggests that one can go to church and not be either a religious fanatic or a saint."[19]

As a journalist, I have covered religion in the American Sunbelt, from Orange County, California, to Orlando, Florida, for the better part of twenty years. The cultural disconnect in the United States over faith and values, which began in the 1980s and was manifest in the 2000 and 2004 presidential elections, is such that I can think of few groups with as little in common as committed evangelical Christians and hard-core fans of *The Simpsons*. Many of the former are no more likely to watch the show than they would be to turn on a boombox and dance naked in front of the church—which Homer actually did when he thought he was the lone survivor after Springfield was wiped out by a neutron bomb launched by France.

Dedicated fans of *The Simpsons*, I have learned in researching this book, miss very little of what goes on in the series, and they analyze the show's minutiae with the intensity of committed Talmudists. There are Web sites devoted to religion in the series and to Springfield's pastor, Reverend Lovejoy, yet I suspect that even most of these fans have not noticed the consistent fabric of belief that the show's writers and producers have been weaving over the years.

If this little book can in some way create a common ground for these two groups—and the many between them—I will be happy. And there is evidence that this has already begun.

"*The Simpsons* is one of the most important common experiences in the American home," said Stewart Hoover, a religion and media scholar at the University of Colorado. In a study funded by the Lilly Foundation, Hoover found that "*The Simpsons* consistently comes up in our interviews as a subject for family discussion and family interaction around issues of values and morality and religion. It's kind of a meeting place for families. The show has quite a cross-generational appeal and effect," he told me.

This was true in the Tilley household in Orlando. Mike Tilley works for Campus Crusade for Christ as the worldwide evangelical organization's national director for U.S. expansion. His son, Jonathan, began watching *The Simpsons* when he was 11 or 12, he recalled, probably behind his parents' backs. But he became convinced the show was not something to hide after watching an episode called "Homer vs. Lisa and the Eighth Commandment." In that show there was an extended discussion involving Simpson family members and their pastor about whether an illegal cable television hookup was theft, as defined by the Bible. Jonathan approached his dad and, as a result, watching the show together on Sunday evenings became a ritual for father and son.

"I saw it as a time to get into my son's world," Mike said. "It was a chance for us to connect. It was a great bridge, a relationship-building thing. Sometimes I think Christians are a little too uptight to share a good laugh. I wanted to do something together with him that was fun; I didn't want him to see his Christian upbringing as overly serious." Jonathan, now a college graduate, agreed. "It was humor I would relate to then and can relate to now," he said, acknowledging that in the early years of their viewing his father probably understood some of the humor that he did not. Still, "it was a special time. My dad and I like to do things [together]. It's cool when we find something that is truly enjoyable for both of us."

One episode in particular, in which Homer resists the temptation to commit adultery, rang a bell with father and son, and provoked a conversation both recall vividly years later. "That show won me over," Mike said. "These guys—the show's writers—despite the fact they were exposing the apparent idiosyncrasies of religious people, they obviously had a moral message they wanted to reinforce." Said Jonathan: "He liked the fact that Homer was able to turn it down. The value of a long-lasting loving relationship was there. Marge said she would always love him. My dad said he liked that."

For years, Mike and Jonathan talked about *The Simpsons*, usually via e-mail or by phone. Jonathan, who wants to be a missionary, found the show valuable in his relationships with his classmates at Florida State University, even in those episodes when the foibles of organized religion and religious people are the targets of humor. "Pretty much everyone watches *The Simpsons* at college, and it's important for me in my faith to have common ground with everyone."

This book is a distillation, an interpretation and analysis of material about God, faith, and religion contained in close to 400 episodes of *The Simpsons*. In that sense it is a magnification, but I hope it is not a distortion. As Neil Postman wrote in 1985 in *Amusing Ourselves to Death: Public Discourse in the Age of Show Business*, religion on television, "like everything else, is presented, quite simply and without apology, as . . . entertainment." I'll be discussing concepts like prayer, the Bible, sin, and grace, and examining the ways in which Catholics, Jews, Buddhists, and Hindus are portrayed in *The Simpsons*. The evidence I present here notwithstanding, the series is not a television show *about* religion, and I would not want uninitiated viewers tuning in thinking it is.

The Simpsons is a situation comedy about modern life that includes a significant spiritual dimension; because of that, it more accurately reflects the faith lives of Americans than any other show in the medium. Why is this important? "TV and mass media in general are the conduit by which most people get their information and form their opinions," especially young people, Andi Zeisler, cofounder of *Bitch* magazine, told the *New York Times Sunday Magazine* on August 6, 2006. From my own experiences lecturing at prep schools and college campuses since this book was first published, I have found that when young people sit in a sanctuary or a lecture hall to consider faith and religion, a veil of skepticism descends in their minds. Yet, sitting in the comfort of a living room or commons room, watching cartoon characters in a half-hour comedy, they will consider these issues with a more open mind. For that, we can all be grateful.

The Simpsons swung wide the door to portraying faith for other television writers and artists. For this reason, I have added a lengthy afterword to this second edition, exploring the impact *The Simpsons'* treatment of religion has had on other animated cartoon series. This afterword is composed of five "mini-gospels" in which I apply the same approach I have used in examining and analyzing *The Simpsons* to *Futurama*, *King of the Hill*, *Family Guy*, *American Dad*, and *South Park*, with some brief references to a few newer and edgier entries to the field. By and large, the treatment of religion in these other series is not as deep or subtle—or favorable—as it is in *The Simpsons*. Still, the congregation on the couch is growing.

One

Divine Imagery: "Perfect Teeth. Nice Smell. A Class Act All the Way."

God answers all prayers. The problem, ministers say, is that sometimes the answer is "no"—not a thundering denial but often a silence that implies that a request will not be fulfilled, for reasons best known to the Almighty. For Homer Simpson, this conundrum represents an opportunity rather than a reason to question the validity of prayer. In a flashback episode we see him at home, ostensibly thanking God for his life—his marriage, his two children, his job—a constellation in balance that is "absolutely perfect the way it is." Homer asks that everything be frozen in place. This is impossible, of course, sort of the equivalent of praying for a protective "hedge around him and his household and everything he has," as the book of Job (1:10) puts it. It is at this point that Homer, at best an imperfect believer, attempts to toy with God. He prays that if the Almighty agrees to keep everything exactly as it is, Homer won't ask for anything more. Confirmation of the deal, he prays, will come in the form of "absolutely no sign." There is no sign. In gratitude, Homer presents an offering to God of cookies and milk. Should God want Homer to eat the cookies himself, he asks again for "no sign." After a pause, Homer utters the benediction, "Thy will be done."

Homer's theological sophistry caught the attention of more than one Christian thinker. The incident appears in the opening lines of William A. Dembski's *Intelligent Design: The Bridge between Science and Theology*, a book designated one of the ten best of 1999 by *Christianity Today* magazine in the category of "Christianity and Culture." In a chapter titled "Recognizing the Divine Finger," Dembski argues that something very serious is going on in the dialogue. "What's the matter with Homer's prayer? Assuming God is the sovereign ruler of the universe, what is to prevent God from answering Homer's prayer by providing no sign? Granted, usually when we want God to confirm something, we look for something extraordinary, some sign that leaves no doubt of God's will. But presumably God could have made it thunder when Homer asked God to freeze everything and God could have made the earth to quake when Homer asked to eat those cookies and milk. Presumably, it is just as easy for God to confirm Homer's prayer with no sign as to disconfirm it with a sign."[1]

Dembski's answer is that the flaw in Homer's reasoning is that the prayer is self-serving. There is asymmetry in "tying a course of action to a sign and tying it to no sign" and of "seeking confirmation through the absence of a sign." Actually, the series writers may be providing a simpler answer, in the form of an underlying cosmic joke. Homer begins his prayer by brushing off his wife, Marge, who we later learn has been trying to tell him that she is pregnant with their third child, an event guaranteed to turn his life upside down. Even before Homer asks, God has already given him both a sign *and* an answer (no), if he will only listen.

"Right-wingers complain there's no God on TV," *The Simpsons'* creator Matt Groening said in a 1999 interview in *Mother Jones* magazine. "Not only do the Simpsons go to church every Sunday and pray; they actually speak to God from time to time. We show Him, and God has five fingers—unlike the Simpsons, who have only four."[2] *The Simpsons* is consistently irreverent toward organized religion's failings and excesses, as it is with most other institutions of modern life. However, God is not mocked. When *The Simpsons* characters are faced with crises, they turn to God. He answers their prayers, often instantaneously, and he intervenes in their lives. Mike Scully, the series' former executive producer, insists that God is not off-limits as a target, although there are considerable challenges. "It's more difficult to satirize something than to mock it," he says, and "it's hard to satirize something you don't see."

Characters in the series are admittedly a little hazy on the essence of the Almighty and His plan for humanity. When a character declares Homer a god, Homer corrects him, saying, "God has a white beard and invented *The Da Vinci Code.*" In another episode Homer mistakes a waffle stuck to his ceiling for God, and then compounds the error by eating the waffle and mocking Communion by describing the taste as "sacrelicious." "I don't know who or what God is exactly," says Lisa to her brother Bart. "All I know is, he's a force more powerful than Mom and Dad put together." Bart thinks the tooth fairy is God's daughter. In an attempt to con the neighbor boys, evangelical Christians Rod and Todd Flanders, Bart impersonates the voice of God. Mother Marge, the most faithful member of the family, believes that when she sings "You Light Up My Life," she is singing about God. And the sign outside Springfield Community Church offers multiple views, from "God, the Original Love Connection" to "God Welcomes His Victims." Another asks, "Is God Patriotic Enough?" Outside a downtown Springfield homeless shelter, yet another reads, "We Add God to Your Misery."

Predestination makes an appearance from time to time, where God's plan is used sometimes as an excuse, sometimes as an explanation. "Until this moment," says Bart, poised to buy a rare issue of *Radioactive Man,* "I never knew why God put me on this earth. But now I know . . . to buy that comic book." Informed that his house is teetering on its foundation, Homer says the situation is simply "all part of God's plan," and when he causes a traffic accident, he shouts, "Act of God, not my fault!" After a giant sturgeon falls to Earth from a Russian spacecraft and crashes onto his car hood, Homer complains, "God conned me out of sixty-five hundred dollars in car repairs." Criticized for using bad language, he says, "Maybe I curse a little, but that's the way God made me and I'm too old to stop now." Homer does a dance on top of a baseball dugout during a game, to the delight of the crowd. "We all have a calling, a reason the Almighty put us on earth, and yours might be to dance on dugouts," says Marge. Lisa equates her family's weekly menu with predestination: "Friday night. Pork chops. From cradle to grave, etched in stone in God's library somewhere in heaven."

It is Homer, however, who has the most personal relationship with God. Denounced by some as a simple-minded pagan, he is much more than that. According to the book *God in the Details: American Religion in Popular Culture,*

> Homer fulfills the role of the American spiritual wanderer. Though linked culturally (if unsteadily and unenthusiastically) to biblical tradition, he regularly engages a mosaic of other traditions, mythologies, and moral codes. In the face of these ever-shifting layers of meaning, he stumbles along, making the most of his limited understanding of their complexities. His comic antics remind us that the making of meaning (religious or otherwise) is ever an unfinished business, and that humor and irony go a long way toward sweetening and sustaining the endeavor.[3]

In their spiritual searching, neither Bart nor Homer is shy about going directly to the source and asking God for help in his daily life. When Bart sees a copy machine in the library with 199 free copies on it, he asks God for a sign. His pants fall down, so he makes 199 copies of his butt, which he later inserts in the church bulletin. Uncertain how to help his gifted daughter Lisa, Homer asks for a sign from God. Suddenly he sees a storekeeper putting a sign in his window, "Musical Instruments: The Way to Encourage a Gifted Child," that answers his question exactly, beginning her saxophone career. Over the years that the series has run, Homer has gone back and forth about God's fundamental nature: "He's always happy. No wait, He's always mad." Homer is not alone in this confusion. The Jewish philosopher and theologian Abraham J. Heschel, in his study of the prophet Amos, noted this stark duality of God. On one hand, he is "the Deity of stern, mechanical justice." On the other, he is the God who overlooks and forgives a faithless Israel.[4] So maybe *The Simpsons'* writers are after more than a cheap laugh.

Without question, this is also a jealous God that does not like to be challenged. Montgomery Burns, the richest man in Springfield and Homer's boss at the nuclear power plant, fancies himself divine when a cult sweeps the town. Likening himself to "The New God," he tells workers at the nuclear plant, "You may now praise me as the almighty"—whereupon his robe catches on fire and he is left standing naked before the people. Homer falls into a similar trap when he finds a six-foot Tiki statue in the trash, sets it up in his backyard, and runs a gas line to the idol so it can spew flames. "Can your god do that?" he asks Ned Flanders, the evangelical next door. Actually, his neighbor replies, "we worship the same God." Not so, says Homer, yelling "I am your god now!" as the Tiki drops from his hands and sets the yard afire. In another episode, Homer and a friend engage in a vicious competition for snowplow customers, one so intense that Homer uses an opportunity to read the Bible from the pulpit during Sunday service to plug his plowing service. After reconciling with his competitor, Homer proclaims, "When two best friends work together, not even God can stop them." The words "Oh, no?" then appear large in the sky, and the rays of sunshine instantly melt the accumulated snow. Sometimes fire and sometimes ice, but the result is the same.

Homer is never entirely certain of God's love, which he tests repeatedly. Driving the family car during a Halloween fantasy sequence, he flees a zombie—the undead Ned Flanders. "Dear God," he cries, "it's Homer. If you really love me, you'll save me now," after which, he runs out of gas. In a Christmas episode, Homer is horrified to discover the family's gifts and tree missing on Christmas morning, and he reaches an inescapable conclusion: "Kids, God hates us!"

In another episode, he struggles to express God's universality: "You're everywhere. You're omnivorous." He's also somewhat confused about God's sense of self and what he does when not conversing with Homer. "I feel this incredible surge of power," Homer says in one episode, "like God must feel when he's holding a gun." In another, after shaking up Springfield with revelations on his personal Web site, he believes he has changed the world: "Now I know how God feels." At the other end of the spectrum, in an annual Halloween fantasy episode, God is sucked into a black hole.

On a Pacific island, where he finds himself an accidental missionary, Homer is asked why an all-powerful Lord cares how or even whether he is worshiped. The question, profound and serious, is answered on this occasion with a disappointingly superficial quip.

"It's because God is powerful, but insecure," Homer replies, "like Barbra Streisand before James Brolin." Homer is on even shakier ground when he tries to explain God and heaven to the islanders. After overseeing construction of a primitive church, he explains why church bells have to be rung. "God's palace is way up on the moon. So if you want him to hear us, you have to crank up the volume."

Embroiled in an escalating feud with George H. W. Bush when the former president moves into the neighborhood, Homer asks himself, "What would God do in this situation?" The next scene shows Bart carrying a box of locusts. In another episode, after watching a biblical epic about Noah on television, Bart gets carried away, telling Homer that God is cool because he is so "in-your-face!" Homer agrees, sort of, saying that God is his favorite "fictional character." After being accidentally hit in the face with an ice cream cone while on a hunger strike in another episode, he snaps, "Nice try, God, but Homer Simpson doesn't give in to temptation that easily." For his part, the Almighty is not without a sense of humor, at least where Homer is concerned. He leaves Homer a note reading, "IOU one brain, God."

Like many biblical figures and religious mystics through the ages, Homer has his most intense encounters with the Divine while dreaming. A vivid and extended example of this takes place in the 1992 episode "Homer the Heretic," written by George Meyer, long a guiding force in the series. The episode is used in college and seminary classes on religion and popular culture around the country. On a cold Sunday morning, Homer splits his pants as he dresses for church, so he decides not to go. Again, he offers what he takes as a clever, if familiar, theological justification: What's the big deal about going to some building on Sunday, he asks his wife. "Isn't God everywhere?" What he is asking is, How does God want to be worshiped? It is a question people of most cultures have been asking for thousands of years. Homer believes that if God wanted people to worship him for an hour a week, he should have made the week an hour longer.

At Springfield Community Church, where the furnace has broken, the other members of the Simpson family shiver, warmed only by Reverend Lovejoy's sermon promising hell's fire and brimstone. Meanwhile, Homer luxuriates in a hot shower and a warm house, with loud music and fattening food. Thus, the dichotomy is established: The faithful suffer for their belief, while the prodigal father enjoys the sybaritic life. As if the point is not made well enough, the contrast deepens. Together with the rest of the congregation, Marge and the children are stuck in church *after* the service, since the doors have frozen shut, and are forced to listen to the minister fill time by reading from the bulletin. At home, Homer wins a radio trivia contest, then watches an exciting football game on television and even finds a penny on the floor. After the congregation is finally able to leave the building, Marge's car won't start, leaving the family cold and stranded. When his family finally trudges in with their tales of woe, Homer proclaims that he has been having a wonderful day, perhaps the best of his life. Based on his analysis of divine favor, he decides never to go to church again. Marge can't believe that her husband intends to give up his faith. At first, he denies that is his intention, but then he admits it.

Homer's decision to abandon church provokes a full-blown theological debate in the Simpson household, with Bart supporting his father's choice with call-and-response evangelical fervor. In his defense, Homer offers a corollary to the "one true faith" argument for abandoning worship: "What if we picked the wrong religion?" he asks. "Every week we're just making God madder and madder." That question, undermining as it is to more than one denomination, cannot remain unanswered. Before going to sleep that night, Marge kneels by her bed and prays for Homer to see the error of his ways, as he drifts off to sleep.

As so often in *The Simpsons*, God hears and answers. God comes to Homer in his dream, and provides as dramatic and direct an answer as can be imagined. Sitting on his couch, watching television, Homer feels the house begin to shake. A beam of light shines through the clouds and a large hand—with five realistic fingers—removes the roof. God is standing in the Simpsons' living room. In deference to several faiths, God's countenance is not shown. He is seen from the flowing beard down, wearing a robe and, it appears, Birkenstock sandals. At first, God is in no mood for pleas-antries: "Thou hast forsaken my church!" he thunders.

Homer is frightened, but is nothing if not quick on his feet: "I'm not a bad guy! I work hard and I love my kids. So why should I spend half my Sunday hearing about how I'm going to hell? . . . I figure I should try to live right and worship you in my own way." God seems won over, acknowledging that Homer has a point as God pets the family cat. God agrees with Homer's complaints about Reverend Lovejoy's sermons. Because the minister dis-pleases him, the Almighty will give him a canker sore. Here, truly, is God alive in the world. God agrees to let Homer worship him in his own way and departs, explaining that he has to appear in a tortilla in Mexico. Is this a dig at believers who report seeing reli-gious visions in unlikely places? Clearly not, because God says he will actually *be present* in the tortilla.

After waking, Homer dives wholeheartedly into his new reli-gion, donning a monk's robe and a mien of inner peace. In the manner of Saint Francis of Assisi, he attracts backyard birds and squirrels. Naturally, he decides his new religion needs holidays— what would a religion be without holidays? From the neighbor-hood bar, Moe's Tavern, Homer calls the nuclear power plant where he works to inform his employer that he will be out for a religious holiday. Asked the name of the holiday, he spies a sign on the wall of the bar and replies, "the Feast of Maximum Occu-pancy." Homer invites Moe to join his new religion, pointing out that it has the advantages of no hell and no kneeling. The bar-tender, a self-professed lifelong "snake handler," declines.

Lisa cautions against her father's apparent blasphemy, but Homer explains that he is covered. In his own variation of Pas-cal's wager, he says that if he is wrong he can always recant on his deathbed. Lisa does not remind him that this strategy may contain a fatal flaw, in light of the biblical warning that "no man knows when his hour will come" (Eccl. 9:12). Marge takes a more assertive approach to saving her husband from perdition by invit-ing Reverend Lovejoy to dinner. At the table, Homer describes to Bart how God appeared to him in the dream: "Perfect teeth. Nice smell. A class act, all the way." Under divine instructions, Homer tells the minister, he is seeking a new religious path. Lovejoy quotes Matthew 7:26 about the foolish man who built his house on sand. Homer replies with a bogus verse from Matthew, plucked out of the air, which is completely irrelevant.

How silly is Marge's concern with her husband's apparent loss of faith? Not silly at all, to judge from the numerous books, television, and radio shows that discuss the dilemma of spouses with different religions or different levels of religious commitment—what Christians call "unequally yoked." Homer's decision to abandon the church, and his persistence in this course, continue to have serious repercussions within his family. His wife makes an argument familiar to many households with divided beliefs: She has an obligation to raise the children with moral values, and church is a part of that obligation. Exasperated, Marge tells the children that Homer is wicked, and warns her husband not to force her to choose between him and God, because he will lose. At church the next Sunday, the sign out front reads "When Homer Met Satan." Inside, Reverend Lovejoy—who understands the struggle he is engaged in—preaches that the devil is at work among them, in a seductive incarnation. As he speaks, Homer is again at home enjoying himself, drooling over a pornographic magazine. Lovejoy continues from Exodus 20:8, "Remember the Sabbath day, to keep it holy," as Homer is seen buying beer and cigars at the convenience store. "Pride goeth before destruction," the minister intones, and once more Homer takes the opposite message, smoking his cigar and reading his magazine while concluding that "everyone is stupid except me." He's right; he has abandoned organized religion with no discernible consequence. What is the lesson? What does God say?

This time—with or without God's canker sore—Reverend Lovejoy is onto something with his warning about haughtiness going before a fall. Homer dozes off, and his lighted cigar starts a fire in the couch, setting the house ablaze. The volunteer fire department comes to his aid. Homer is saved—twice—by his next-door neighbor, Ned Flanders, the devout Christian. The fire is put out by Lovejoy and the other members of the ecumenical crew, including Krusty, the Jewish clown, and Apu, the Hindu convenience store operator. Homer, always quick to learn the wrong lesson, takes the fire as a sign of divine retribution for abandoning his traditional Christian faith for a self-indulgent, personal religion. Converted by what he takes to be God's vengeance, Homer falls to his knees and prays for new marching orders: "O Spiteful One, show me who to smite, and he shall be smoten!"

Here the Christians come through, validating the essence of their faith rather than pressing their advantage on a weak mind. Ned assures Homer that the fire was not God's vengeance. Lovejoy explains that God was "working in the hearts of your friends and neighbors when they came to your aid." The minister asks if Homer would like to give church another try, and next Sunday he is back in church, snoring in the front pew. He dreams that he resumes his dialogue with God, albeit God with only four fingers. God takes him under his arm and tells him not to worry about his unsuccessful foray into religion, since nine out of ten new faiths fail in their first year. Homer then asks God about the meaning of life, and God replies with an old joke. He can't reveal the meaning of life until Homer dies. When Homer says he can't wait that long, God asks, "You can't wait six months?" as the two are bathed in a heavenly glow.

This episode, said author and Calvin College professor William Romanowski, is instructive because "it tries to get at the role of God and religion in people's everyday lives." Like Romanowski, David Landry uses "Homer the Heretic" in his religion and mass media classes at the University of St. Thomas. Michael Glodo, professor of Old Testament and preaching at Reformed Theological Seminary in Orlando, said the series writers "have captured a very common understanding of who God is." The lesson of the episode, wrote David Owen in *TV Guide*, is disarmingly simple: "Going to church may not be a terrible idea."[5]

In *The Simpsons*, God is a cross between Mel Brooks's Twothousand-year-old Man and Charlton Heston's aged Moses, "a familiar stereotype with a humorous and not-too-blasphemous sting," according to one book on religion and popular culture.[6] Having fun with the image of God the Father is one thing in *The Simpsons*; Jesus is another matter entirely or was, until recent seasons. When characters are in peril or crisis, they pray to "God" or "Lord" but rarely to Jesus. In one exception, Homer cries out, "Jesus, Allah, Buddha—I love you all!" Here the writers have tread lightly. Why? Is the series that is not afraid to satirize anything afraid of offending Christians? Or are they afraid that any reference to Jesus might offend people of other, non-Christian religions? Perhaps. Jokes about God can refer to any of the major monotheistic faiths, and so are less likely to offend any particular denomination. Homer doesn't think Jesus was that funny, even with his apostles. In another episode, he describes Jesus as "a dude [who] was born a million years ago that most of us thought was magic."

Neil Postman, in *Amusing Ourselves to Death*, was as prescient on this point as he was on many others. "Christianity is a demanding and serious form of religion," he wrote. "When it is delivered as easy and amusing, it is another kind of religion altogether."

Each episode of *The Simpsons* begins with a fleeting sequence featuring Bart in the classroom after school, writing and rewriting an admonition on the blackboard, presumably punishment for some misbehavior that day. Sometimes the sentence refers to a theme of the story to follow, and sometimes it is a stand-alone gag, as in an episode in 2000 when Bart writes, "I was not touched by an angel"—a dig at *The Simpsons'* Sunday night competition. In the case of the Easter Sunday 1999 show, Bart writes, "I cannot absolve sins." Yet in the episode that follows, the context for which is an Easter Sunday service, there is no mention of crucifixion or resurrection, something that would never happen in any Christian church. Reverend Lovejoy drones on about other things, including a chocolate bunny. All of the biblical dream sequences that follow are from the Old Testament, except for a short, closing sequence about the rapture. This is no accident.

One of the few physical images of Jesus in the early history of *The Simpsons* is in the same episode, a quick *People's Court* parody, "Jesus Christ vs. Checker Chariot," depicting a silent, bearded Jesus in a business suit and neck brace. In other, later episodes, Jesus appears with children on the cover of the comic book *Easy to Believe Tales* and is seen, without dialogue, sitting on a chair. When Homer gets his first computer, he calls up a real Web site, "Dancing Jesus."

There are offhand and throwaway references to Jesus in a dozen
or more episodes, some just this side of sacrilege. As a winter
storm approaches Springfield, neighbor Ned Flanders takes down
his manger scene because "if Baby Jesus gets loose, he could really
do some damage." A Sunday school teacher assures one of the
children that Jesus "did not have wheels." Barney, the town drunk,
suggests at one point that Jesus "must be spinning in his grave."
Jesus is also used as a way to take a shot at an easy target—com-
mercialism and Christmas. A store sign proclaims, "In honor of
the birth of Our Savior, Try-N-Save is Open All Day Christmas."
Bart believes that "Christmas is the time when people of all religions come together to worship Jesus Christ." Explaining a
Christmas buying spree, Homer says, "I'm not looking for glory
or wealth. I'm just buying that stairway to heaven that Jesus sang
of," confusing Jesus with Led Zeppelin.

More specific references are oblique or problematic. Upon
reading his Bible, Homer says, "Everybody's a sinner, except this
guy," without naming "this guy." Flying into Rio de Janeiro with
the family, Homer spots the massive statue known as *Christ the
Redeemer* atop the city's Corcovado and observes, "It looks like he's
on the dashboard of the whole world." Bart asks why he has to
wear shoes to church since Jesus wore sandals. Homer replies that
"maybe if he had better arch support they wouldn't have caught
him." In Sunday school, Bart says he learned that lepers were
cured by "a bearded dude." When the boy, reacting to drugs he
takes for attention deficit disorder, steals a tank and aims the can-
non at the church, Reverend Lovejoy shouts, "Not the church!
Jesus lives there!" Outside the sanctuary building in the same 1999
Easter show, the sign reads, "Christ Dyed Eggs for Your Sins." At
times, even Lovejoy is a little unclear on the concept of Jesus. "I
remember another gentle visitor from the heavens," he says. "He
came in peace and then died, only to come back to life. And his
name was E.T., the extraterrestrial. I loved that little guy." In a
Treehouse of Horror fantasy, Homer's coworker Lenny says that six
leprechauns are "better than Jesus." His friend Carl agrees, but
says the wee Irish fairies are "a lot harder to catch."

If anything, Homer is even hazier on the nature of Jesus and Christianity than he is about God. While walking through the Springfield Airport, he and Bart cross paths with a Christian evangelist holding a Bible and quoting the Golden Rule: "Do unto others as you would have them do unto you" (Matt. 7:12). Homer replies sarcastically, "That'll work."

Homer has the unsettling habit of comparing himself to Jesus, often under trivial circumstances. "Kids, let me tell you about another so-called wicked guy," he says in his defense in "Homer the Heretic." "He had long hair and some wild ideas. He didn't always do what other people thought was right. And that man's name was . . . I forget. But the point is . . . I forget that too." After bowling a perfect game, Homer is briefly the center of Springfield's attention, only to have the spotlight inevitably fade. "They did it to Jesus and now they're doing it to me," he tells his wife, who is shocked. "Are you comparing yourself to Our Lord?" Marge asks. "In bowling ability, yes," Homer replies blithely. In a Halloween fantasy, Homer dies and can only get into heaven if he returns to earth to do a good deed. Marge offers his hovering spirit a simple list of choices, which her husband rejects, saying, "I'm not running for Jesus!" Driven to delirium during a hunger strike to protest the move of Springfield's minor league baseball team to another city, Homer tells the crowd that he is, himself, "kind of like Jesus, but not in a sacrilegious way." When Homer climbs a mountain, in triumph, he orders the young thugs around him to bow, because "your king commands it." One of the teenagers, Jimbo, replies, "Jesus is our only king."

In the extreme, Homer even gets Jesus' name wrong. In one episode, he becomes involved in a madcap comedy of errors involving an unpaid pledge to a PBS telethon that leaves Homer trapped on a Christian relief flight heading for a remote Pacific island. He runs to the cockpit and begs the pilots to stop the plane and let him off, sounding a lot like Peter before the cock crowed. "I don't even believe in Jebus," he pleads, using the ancient name for Jerusalem before it was conquered by King David. Yet when the plane takes off, the desperate Homer knows where to go for help. "Save me, Jebus!" he cries. Sacrilege has its costs: Homer attributes part of the fall of his popular barbershop quartet, the Be Sharps, to the group's decision to name their second album "Bigger Than Jesus," a play on John Lennon's celebrated boast.

Homer thinks Ned Flanders is "holier than Jesus" and so turns to him in the mistaken belief that he and Bart have been afflicted with leprosy. Bart wonders aloud why God would punish a kid with such a disease, most particularly "an American kid." Homer correctly identifies the divine figure in question as Jesus but tells his son not to hope for a similar miracle because "I think we're on the outs with him." Even this may be changing. Twice in a single episode in May 2001, Homer says, "Christ be with you," once as a way of expressing gratitude and once expressing irony.

There have been surprises regarding Jesus. In the same 2001 episode where Homer starves himself to keep the baseball team in Springfield, Duff Man—the superhero mascot of the team's owners, the Duff Beer Company—is torn between helping Homer do the right thing and the orders of his boss. Uncertain, Duff Man (who we learn in a later season is actually Jewish) asks himself, "What would Jesus do?" In what is arguably a loose interpretation of the biblical Jesus, Duff Man tosses his employer out of the stadium.

Salvation by grace is never mentioned in *The Simpsons*. Crucifixion and resurrection, essential elements of Christianity, are also not often referred to in the series because neither is "a big laugh getter," according to former executive producer Mike Scully. The writers would use such imagery only if there were some point in doing so, he said, although in a May 2001 episode Reverend Lovejoy is seen serving "Cruci-fixins" ice cream toppings at a church social. More particular Christian concepts like the Trinity or the Holy Spirit can be difficult enough for believers to grasp, so it is not surprising that *The Simpsons* makes little effort to bring them into the series. Yet there is something more at work in this reluctance of *The Simpsons* to deal with Jesus as divine, as well as the refusal to deal with the other specific details of Christianity in the series.

In her 1992 master's thesis at Regent University, "The Gospel according to Bart: Examining the Religious Elements of *The*

Simpsons," Beth Keller provided an in-depth context for the presentation of religion in popular culture. She analyzed five episodes from the first few seasons, not including "Homer the Heretic," which had not aired at the time of her research. She concluded, perceptively, that the theological construct that informs the series and the churchgoing Simpsons is actually the Old Testament.

> The show seems to promote the idea that following the law, or being ethically good, is all that is required to gain entrance to heaven. While this is theoretically true, the evangelical believes that "keeping the law" is impossible. That is why grace by faith in Jesus Christ is understood to be the way to stand before God in the afterlife. . . . However, the viewer is given the strong impression that the Simpsons represent a Protestant Christian family, so there is a dichotomy between the full truth from an evangelical perspective and the "truth" that is represented in *The Simpsons.*[7]

In the years of episodes that have followed, this dichotomy has been reinforced time and again, much like the one between a vengeful God and a loving God. Homer and Bart watch a television movie about Noah's ark, which ends with God telling Noah, "Remember, the key to salvation is. . . ." Just then, a news story interrupts the show. But this poses no problem for most monotheists. "After the key to salvation remains ambiguous," writes Trammell, "the Simpsons still pray to God."

Gerry Bowler, of University of Manitoba, has a simpler explanation: "Though he claims to be a Christian, Homer is essentially a pagan. Religion for him consists of placating or bribing an angry god or gods."[8] And in one episode, Homer actually prays, "God bless those pagans." In a 2007 episode, cast adrift on a stormy sea after his fishing boat has been crushed by a giant wave, Homer calls on the sea god, Poseidon, for deliverance. Support for the position that Homer is satanic came in an episode in the show's 2000–2001 season, when Homer shapes a snow angel with his body. Getting up, all that remains is a dark outline of a devil with pitchfork, something Homer says happens whenever he tries to be an angel.

Another reason Jesus may be largely off-limits for *The Simpsons* is the problem many Christians have associating their Savior—or any aspect of the New Testament—with humor. (The Hebrew Bible offers more opportunities, as Psalm 2:4 notes: "Who sits in the heavens laughs.") This subject has drawn the attention of numerous authors over the years, who have produced works such as *Laughing Out Loud and Other Religious Experiences* by Tom Mullen, *Humor: God's Gift* by Tal Bonham, *Serve Him with Mirth* by Leslie Flynn, and *The Ontology of Humor* by Robert Parrott.

A book on this subject preferred by many evangelicals is *Humor of Christ*, by the late Elton Trueblood, a slim volume first published in 1964 and now out of print.[9] At the outset, Trueblood acknowledges that many Christians, perhaps a majority, believe that finding humor in the person of Jesus is at least inappropriate and may be sacrilegious. "Religion, we think, is serious business, and serious business is incompatible with banter." He agrees that some elements of the gospel, such as the crucifixion, are so tragic as to be "intrinsically unhumorous." Still, he argues, humor is a fundamental part of Jesus' message and method. He wrote his book to "help overcome an almost universal failure to appreciate an element in Christ's life which is so important that, without it, any understanding of Him is inevitably distorted." Trueblood is determined "to do something to challenge the conventionalized picture of a Christ who never laughed. . . . If Christ laughed a great deal, as the evidence shows, and if He is what He claimed to be, we cannot avoid the logical conclusion that there is laughter and gaiety in the heart of God."

The humor of Jesus is ironic, sardonic and, occasionally, sarcastic, according to Trueblood. Thus, Jesus dubs the inconstant Peter his rock, or "Rocky," as Trueblood puts it. His wit is sly and wry, the absurdist imagery most evident in the parables and paradoxes: the beam and the mote, the gnat and the camel, the camel and the eye of the needle. Trueblood believes that even more of Jesus' humor was probably lost in the transcription, if not in the translation. Examples from the Gospels, when properly analyzed, "are luminous once we become liberated from the gratuitous assumption that Christ never joked." In Matthew 24:28, for example, Jesus explains his ability to draw a crowd by observing, in apparent self-deprecation, that, "Wherever there is a carcass, there the vultures will gather."

But a joking Jesus is not the same as a Jesus joke, which may be why, in the end, *The Simpsons'* writers treat Jesus so gingerly. There is a great tradition of gentle Christian humor, much of which centers around the clergy, the inconsistencies of church life, and getting into heaven. Portraying Jesus as a humorous character in an animated comedy may simply be too much to ask of a network sitcom audience. Here, Trueblood offers some useful—if unsolicited—advice to the show's writers: "The only kind of laughter which can be redemptive is that which goes beyond scorn to recognition of a common predicament."

Two

Personal Prayer: "Dear God, Give the Bald Guy a Break!"

In the Simpson household, prayer most frequently takes the form of blessings at mealtimes, including grace over take-out fast food and, on at least one occasion, in a restaurant. Often, the prayers are perfunctory, as in Bart's "Rub a dub, dub, thanks for the grub" or Homer's equally succinct but barely more reverent, "Good drink, good meat, good God, let's eat." On one occasion, Bart seems to speak the unspeakable: "Dear God, we paid for all this stuff ourselves, so thanks for nothing." In the early 1990s, the young child of a member of Willow Creek Community Church, the megachurch in South Barrington, Illinois, offered a version of this grace at the family table, shocking his father. The man complained to a minister, Lee Strobel, saying that the child was prohibited from watching *The Simpsons* but had picked up the prayer from a commercial advertising an upcoming episode.

Strobel, a former journalist at the *Chicago Tribune* who became a teaching pastor at Willow Creek, used the incident to introduce a sermon titled "What Jesus Would Say to Bart Simpson." Strobel explained that the episode's grace was "an exaggerated look at life from a kid's perspective, with a kernel of truth at its core." Because Bart is so uninhibited, he

> says things that other people only think. When he prays, "Why should we thank you, God—we bought this ourselves," people recoil in horror. Yet isn't he just expressing a sentiment that a lot of people secretly harbor? They'd never *say* it, but don't many people live their lives with the attitude that they've earned what they've received and that God really

had nothing to do with it? So, in ways, Bart is merely more honest than most.[1]

Grace at mealtime is far more common than prime-time television would suggest. A 1999 Gallup survey found that 51 percent of Americans says a blessing over food always or frequently. In *The Simpsons*, such prayers can express a larger gratitude, beyond simple sustenance. Next door to the Simpsons, at the home of the evangelical Flanders family, father Ned prays, "Dear God, thanks for *Ziggy* comics, little baby ducks, and 'Sweatin' to the Oldies' volumes one, two, and three."

The Simpsons are "a family where God has a place at the table," said Robert Thompson of Syracuse University in a newspaper interview.[2] Homer gives thanks for his job. One evening he takes the opportunity to thank God "most of all for nuclear power, which has yet to cause a single, proven fatality, at least in this country." And at Thanksgiving he prays, "We especially thank you for nuclear power, the cleanest, safest energy source there is, except solar, which is just a pipe dream." Yet the family sometimes acknowledges during grace that its blessings are mixed and, this being *The Simpsons*, things simply spin out of control. After one particular Thanksgiving turns into a disaster, Homer loses it, offering thanks "for the occasional moments of peace and love our family's experienced . . . well, not today. You saw what happened. O Lord, be honest! Are we the most pathetic family in the world, or what?" (His sister-in-law Selma comments, "Worst prayer yet.") By the conclusion of the episode, the conflicts are resolved and, as the soundtrack plays "We Gather Together," the family eats turkey sandwiches. "O Lord," Homer says, "on this blessed day, we thank thee for giving our family one more crack at togetherness."

On another occasion, Homer gives way to exasperation. "Dear Lord, thank you for this microwave bounty, even though we don't deserve it," he says. "I mean . . . our kids are uncontrollable hellions. Pardon my French, but they act like savages! Did you see them at the picnic? Of course you did; you're everywhere, you're omnivorous, O Lord! Why did you spite me with this family?"

As in all aspects of faith, belief, and religion, Homer has a fundamental misunderstanding of the nature of prayer. Beginning a contest with his neighbor, he notices that Ned has his hands folded and his eyes closed. "Hey, Flanders," Homer shouts, "it's no use praying. I already did the same thing, and we can't both win." Yet on another occasion, Homer muses, "God does so much for me, and he doesn't ask anything in return." Usually more in tune with the Word, Marge can also get a little wobbly about prayer. When a series of family cats die, Marge loses her temper at one of the funerals, saying, "Lord, you better stop killing our pets." She explains her threats to God to her family by saying, "There's only one way to deal with a bully." In another episode, she says, "If I believe hard enough, sometimes God cuts us a break. After all, we pay his salary." (Homer and Marge give thanks before marital sex, even though they acknowledge in their prayer that God will be watching.)

Prayer at the Simpsons' is fervent in the face of disaster, like a hurricane or a comet bearing down on their cartoon town. It often comes in the form of a bargain: "Dear God, this is Marge Simpson. If you stop this hurricane and save our family, we will be forever grateful and recommend you to all of our friends"; likewise, during a nuclear meltdown begun at Homer's workplace, Marge prays, "Dear Lord, if you spare this town from becoming a smoking hole in the ground, I'll try to be a better Christian. I don't know what I can do. Ummm . . . oh, the next time there's a canned food drive, I'll give the poor something they actually like, instead of old lima beans and pumpkin mix." In desperation, Homer can even forget the exact nature of the divine: "I'm not much of a praying man, but if you're up there, please save me, Superman." And the Simpsons are not unique in this respect. In the face of these and other imminent disasters, all of Springfield is seen praying, in church, at the nuclear power plant, and even on a hillside where a divine apparition seems to have appeared. In a fantasy sequence about the Puritans' voyage to America, Reverend Lovejoy is the chaplain who thanks God for the abundant wind and rain, in an obsequious and transparent effort to abate a storm that is buffeting the *Mayflower*. It has no effect, so he gives up. "Kissing your ass is getting us nowhere," the minister says to God. Even lesser primates pray. When Mojo, Homer's abused pet monkey, is dropped off at the Animal Assistants Program, he frantically taps out on a keyboard the message: "Pray for Mojo."

Intercessory prayer is rare in the series. Characters pray directly to God for what they want. Imprisoned in the Tower of London for insulting Queen Elizabeth II while on a family visit to England, Homer prays for release, which comes in the form of a secret passage out. Between the extremes of grace for meals and appeals for physical survival come appeals for some of the simple—sometimes trivial and absurd—things for which most people pray. Bart promises to build a church if God will stop Homer from embarrassing him. When the Simpsons' television reception goes out, Homer prays, "Dear God, just give me one channel!"

When God responds favorably to pleas like these, there is often a twist. Larry Dossey explores this issue in *Be Careful What You Pray For . . . You Just Might Get It*. He discusses the notion of "toxic prayer," which can do damage to the petitioner or others. For example, Homer and Marge approach the houseboat of a judge he has been feuding with. Homer tosses a large chunk of concrete, praying, "Lord, guide this cinder block." Homer wants a hair-restoring formula to work: "Dear God, give the bald guy a break!" It does work, but only for a time, and it turns Homer's life upside down. Desperate to attend the big football game, Homer prays, "God, if you really are a God, you'll give me tickets to that game." As soon as the words are out of his mouth, the doorbell rings and it is his next-door neighbor, Ned Flanders, whose company he does his best to avoid. Ned has tickets to the game and asks Homer to join him. Homer slams the door and cries out, "Why do you mock me, O Lord?"

In another episode, Homer is jealous when Ned's prayer at a WNBA game enables him to win $50,000 in a contest for making a half-court shot at halftime. Flanders announces he is going to donate the money to "Bibles for Belgians," an act of charity that prompts the town's rich Texan to give Ned another $100,000. "How come all the good things happen to Jesus H. Nice," Homer asks, "by which I mean Flanders? He's got some secret, and I'm going to find out what it is." Always willing to share his faith, Flanders explains that his secret is prayer. Homer is doubtful, but the next day, while searching for the TV remote and on his knees anyway, he gives it a try. Praying for divine direction, he spies the remote sticking out from under the couch. He is quick to draw the wrong—or at least the exaggerated—conclusion: "From now on, I'll pray till my hands are chapped and bleeding." At work, he sets up a prayer station, complete with votive candles, pleased to know that prayer is not only for professional athletes and Grammy winners. On his console, Homer has one of those pictures that changes when tilted, a version of Michelangelo's *Creation of Adam*, and is tickled at the way it alternates between the images of a vengeful God and a loving God.

Driving home from the nuclear plant, he prays for "a delicious new taste treat," clapping his hand as if commanding some genie. He also closes his eyes, causing a collision between a tanker carrying fudge and another truck loaded with precooked bacon. Again, he assumes that the fresh, hybrid bounty is the result of divine intervention. Increasingly carried away, Homer prays at the kitchen table for help for Bart and his homework, as organ music plays. Marge, the voice of sanity, cautions her husband, "God isn't some sort of holy concierge. You can't keep bugging him for every little thing." Homer disregards her, kneeling at the clogged sink. Nothing hapens, so Marge calls the plumber. As nimble as any medieval theologian, Homer interprets this, too, as divine intervention, "working through Marge, thy imperfect vessel." His wife retorts, "Most people pray silently," to no avail. The plumber is no help either, and, in fact, sets off a chain of destructive events that renders the Simpsons' house uninhabitable.

Undeterred, Homer remains hooked on prayer. As the family walks into church on Sunday morning, he is so distracted by his devoted praying for a new place to live that he stumbles into a shallow hole being built for the congregation's nativity display. Lying in the dirt, his leg broken, Homer looks up to see that an ambulance-chasing lawyer has walked by, which he interprets as another sign from heaven. Folding his hands, Homer replies to

God: "That's your answer. I'll sue the church." Marge is opposed, fearing the congregation will make fun of her husband in the church bulletin. But as Homer points out, it wouldn't be the first time. Near him, in the hole, is a crumpled bulletin from the previous week, with a picture of Homer on the cover, asleep and drooling, sprawled on a pew. The headline reads, "Jesus Died for This?" Despite Ned's pleas, Homer sues the church and is awarded a million dollars. "We don't have that kind of money," Reverend Lovejoy says, then adds with typical ecumenical sensitivity, "We're not a synagogue." Instead, Homer gets the deed to the church, which he insists is an answer to his prayer. Lisa suggests it might be the work of Satan, whom she doesn't normally believe in.

In a scene reminiscent of the episode of the golden calf in Cecil B. DeMille's *The Ten Commandments*, Homer moves into the church and turns it into a scene of abject debauchery, possibly the most blasphemous portrayal in the series' history. He drinks beer from the Communion chalice and plays air guitar with a large cross that once hung on the wall. (Al Jean, the season's executive producer, later told a college audience at the Museum of TV and Radio in New York that Fox censors objected to the air guitar sequence and insisted that several seconds be cut.) The Alcoholics Anonymous group is expelled from the church's outreach center to make room for the Simpsons' dog; Marge observes that this does not seem very Christian. Homer says he will make it up by throwing a combination beer bash and housewarming party, welcoming guests at the door in the minister's robes and serving popcorn from a wicker collection basket, as the hymn "Bringing in the Sheaves" plays. Increasingly disturbed, Marge leaves as the party begins to attend ad hoc services at the bowling alley, which is providing a home for the displaced congregation. Dodging stray bowling balls and gibes from nearby teams, Reverend Lovejoy urges the faithful to keep their hearts pure, but he soon concludes that there is no place for him in the community. He loads his station wagon outside the alley and drives off with his wife. "Looks like God packed up and left Springfield," Marge tells Ned.

The minister's departure is worthy of a local television report, at least on an admittedly slow news day, as anchor Kent Brockman intones, "Local Bible nut leaves Springfield." Brockman then asks a correspondent how the town is coping with the spiritual vacuum. Just fine, apparently, is the answer. At the former church, Homer's party is into its second day and is still going strong. From a distance, Ned surveys the scene through binoculars and declares that revelers have broken every commandment but one—which is unnamed—although it is then apparently broken. Flanders prays with his two young sons in the backyard, before a cross made of two pool cues tied together. "Wherever we are," he prays, "you'll have your church"—that is, wherever two or three are gathered. Rod and Todd begin speaking in tongues and rolling on the ground, "slain in the spirit" in a way not typical of a mainline congregation. But Ned is proud of this expression of Pentecostal fervor. "What great kids," he says.

Back at the church, a steel beer keg comes flying out of the sanctuary, crashing through the upper reaches of a large stained glass window and interrupting an all-male, outdoor game of strip poker around a picnic table. Nearby, Homer, Lenny, and Carl are roasting raw steaks on sticks, over a roaring bonfire and under a clear blue sky. Naturally, the talk turns theological and, very quickly, sacrilegious. "It's hard to believe that one God came up with all this," Lenny marvels. His friend Carl agrees. "There's probably a lot of gods." Lenny thinks that some of these deities must be women, and Carl speculates that at least one must have "a thousand boobs." Lenny says that's the one he'd worship, while Carl prostrates himself in the parking lot before a stuffed deer's head in the back of Lenny's car. Clearly, without the discipline of organized religion, it's a slippery slope to paganism in Springfield. Dark smoke from the bonfire wafts up, mingling with black storm clouds, as ominous music plays.

The moment of reckoning is coming, and at least one person at the party senses it. "Aren't you afraid you might be—I don't know—incurring God's wrath?" Marge asks her husband, who is still blithely sipping brew from the sacred cup. He insists that "God's cool," but she disagrees. "I don't know that he is," Marge says. "In the Bible, he's always smiting and turning people into salt." Just then a pelting rain begins to fall. Homer insists it is just a little shower, and he jumps up on the picnic table, thanking God for the much needed rain. Then he takes one step too far, telling God to turn the rainwater into wine. Homer is in the wrong testament for what is coming: a prolonged lightning strike that lifts him off his feet and sends everyone else fleeing in terror into the church. As the waters rise, Flanders recognizes the impending, earth-cleansing flood. He pulls out of his driveway, pulling his boat loaded with pairs of animals. The deluge has forced people onto the church roof, and the rain shows no sign of abating. Homer is again on his knees, praying, but frankly perplexed at the extent of God's wrath. "Surely this has proved whatever point you had," he pleads. Apparently not, as the water continues to rise. "Oh, God's ignoring me," Homer wails. Bart has an intriguing theological suggestion: "Dad, maybe you should *stop* praying. See if that makes it happy." Others on the roof are less conciliatory. Sideshow Mel denounces Homer as a heretic who has doomed them all. Moe the bartender suggests the crowd, which by now is transforming itself into a mob, skin Homer alive and set him on fire, which Carl agrees should appease God.

From above, a voice booms: "Leave that man alone!" It is not the Almighty but God's (imperfect) man on earth, Reverend Lovejoy, using a loudspeaker while perched in the door of a hovering helicopter. The minister calls on his congregation to pray. "Lord, please spare this sinful town," he says. "They were misled by a demon in blue pants," a clear reference to a cringing Homer. Suddenly, the rain stops, the clouds part, and a dove flies by with an olive sprig in its beak, as the floodwaters suddenly recede and the congregation cheers. "I guess I learned something here," Homer says. "God is capable of great anger and great mercy. But mostly, great anger." The lesson, of course, is not to confuse plausible (or even implausible) coincidence with answered prayers—as some believers do in real life. Or to become so intoxicated by prayer that divine supplication becomes a demand.

This illustrates a fundamental and very thorny theological issue presented by *The Simpsons*. For hundreds of years, Jewish sages have debated whether a God who is truly kind and compassionate would grant prayer requests that are not in the best interests of the petitioners. "What limitations or controls does God put in place to prevent us from experiencing our destruction?" asks Rabbi Sholom Dubov of Maitland, Florida. "Faith drives an inner mechanism." But in the Judeo-Christian tradition that has free will at its core, there is no guarantee that faith will not drive human beings in the wrong direction. The Roman philosopher Juvenal, a pagan, wrote of "enormous prayers which heaven in vengeance grants." Thus, Bart gives spontaneous thanks to God "for all the bad things adults do, which distracts attention from the stuff I am doing." (His protective mother, overhearing, adds a postscript: "He's also thankful for your bounty, Lord.") When the boy discovers a cache of lethal police equipment in a closet while playing at the home of the chief's son, Bart voices gratitude "for this bounty I am about to receive." Why thank God? Would a merciful God put murderous paraphernalia in the hands of children? Bart has it right when he voices his appreciation for discovering the keys to the school's steam tunnels: "Thank you, Satan."

On several occasions, characters ask for things so clearly beyond the pale that they are called on it. Bart prays for God to kill his nemesis and tormenter, Sideshow Bob, only to have Marge separate his praying hands and explain that such a prayer is wrong. When it comes to tasks like that, his father tells him, "you do your own dirty work." In another episode, Homer and Bart hatch a typically hare-brained money-making scheme to steal a load of kitchen grease from the elementary school kitchen. As the two are preparing to pump out the grease, Homer pauses to recognize the power of the Almighty. "All right, son," he says, "we're about to embark on a most serious mission. Let's bow our heads in prayer. Dear Lord, if you help us steal this grease tonight, I promise we'll donate half the profits to charity." To which Bart responds, "Dad, he's not that stupid." Homer agrees but is undissuaded from his course. "Screw it," he says. "Let's roll!"

"Bart Gets an F" offers the most detailed portrayal of the dynamic of prayer on *The Simpsons*. After the boy blows an oral book report of *Treasure Island* (which he neglected to read) and fails a test in colonial American history, Marge and Homer are called in and told by the teacher and the district psychologist that Bart is in danger of failing fourth grade. The boy pledges to do better, yet he fails to prepare for the next, crucial test and engineers a reprieve only when he fakes an illness. A makeup test, using cribbed answers, is a disaster. Time runs out the night before the test that will determine whether Bart has to be held back. He squanders his study time and faces a dire future.

At this point, Bart, kneeling by his bed, turns to God. "Well, Old Timer, I guess this is the end of the road," he says. "I know I haven't always been a good kid, but if I have to go to school tomorrow, I'll fail the test and be held back. I just need one more day to study, Lord. I need your help!" (His sister Lisa overhears and scoffs, "Prayer, the last refuge of the scoundrel," echoing the sentiments of many in recent years who have seen criminal defendants enter the courtroom with their Bibles and newfound faith.) Bart continues, listing God's alternatives: "A teachers' strike, a power failure, a blizzard. . . . Anything that'll cancel school tomorrow. I know it's asking a lot, but if anyone can do it, you can! Thanking you in advance, Bart Simpson." And God delivers. After Bart turns out the light, the first flakes of snow begin to fall as the strains of the "Hallelujah" chorus from Handel's *Messiah* are heard—the series' standard signal of divine intervention. A deep snow covers Springfield the next morning, prompting the closing of school. Bart, forgetting everything and reverting to type, prepares to head out for a day of carefree fun—until he encounters Lisa. "I heard you last night, Bart," she says. "You prayed for this and your prayers have been answered." Bart acknowledges his obligation: "I asked for a miracle, and I got it. I gotta study, man!" Bart passes the test by a single extra-credit point, and he tells his father, "Part of this D minus belongs to God."

"I like to think that Bart Simpson is in line with Abraham and Moses in that he talks to God directly," says Robert Thompson.[3] In his previously discussed Willow Creek sermon, Lee Strobel deconstructs this exercise and finds that this example is also theologically consistent with the New Testament concept of prayer. In Matthew 6:6, believers are advised, "When you pray, go into your room, close the door and pray to your Father, who is unseen. Then your Father, who sees what is done in secret, will reward you." In Philippians 4:6, they are told, "In everything, by prayer and petition, with thanksgiving, present your requests to God." And Proverbs 28:13 instructs, "He who conceals his sins does not prosper, but whoever confesses and renounces them finds mercy."

Bart does most things a praying Christian should do, Strobel says. He speaks directly and personally to God from the heart. He confesses his powerlessness. He admits his sinfulness. He voices faith in God's ability and power to grant his petition, and he expresses gratitude before *and* after it is granted. "Maybe—as outrageous as it sounds—we can come away with a few good ideas about how to notch up our own interaction with God," says Strobel, taking a lesson from *The Simpsons'* bad boy.[4]

While, as Trammell notes, prayer serves the narrative purpose of exposing characters' feelings and furthering the plot, "prayers are also used as quick, cheap, dispensable jokes." Thus Bart also prays to Santa on Christmas Eve: "If you bring me lots of good stuff, I promise not to do anything bad between now and when I wake up." The boy is a fervent believer in holiday miracles, despite his father's skepticism. In the original Christmas episode, titled "Simpsons Roasting on an Open Fire," Bart says, "Aw, come on, Dad. This could be the miracle that saves the Simpsons' holiday. If TV has taught me anything, it's that miracles always happen to poor kids at Christmas. It happened to Tiny Tim, it happened to Charlie Brown, it happened to the Smurfs, and it's going to happen to us!"

The mutual hostility between the secular culture and religion—in the context of the national conflict over moral values—pops up frequently on *The Simpsons*. An inmate performing in a prison rodeo is booed after being identified as having been convicted of erecting a nativity scene on city property. In another episode, Bart's elementary school teacher excuses two students, obviously Christian, when a sex education film is shown in class. "Ezekiel and Ishmael," she says, "in accordance with your parents' wishes you may go out into the hall and pray for our souls." The authors of a chapter on the show in *God in the Details: American Religion in Popular Culture* ask, "Does *The Simpsons* reflect our attitudes—particularly toward religion—or does it shape them? Does television act as a mirror to show us ourselves as we really are, or as we ought to be? As the reactions to *The Simpsons* suggest, it is an important debate."[5] How different, for example, is the personal prayer life of characters in *The Simpsons* from that of most Americans? John W. Heeren, professor of sociology at California State University at San Bernardino, writes that the series is "not a reflection of religious reality, but a pop culture version of religion. As the postmodernists say, it is a 'copy of a copy.'"[6]

I am not so sure that when it comes to religion, faith, and prayer that *The Simpsons* shapes, reflects, or copies our attitudes; it may simply portray our practice. The 1999 Gallup survey alluded to earlier found that 90 percent of Americans pray, and 75 percent pray on a daily basis. Ninety percent said that religion was very important or fairly important in their lives, although that reality is rarely evident in other series on prime-time television. By contrast, a 1994 study that surveyed the portrayal of religion on prime-time television found that it was "a rather invisible institution." Religion was infrequently the focus of the narrative in the one hundred episodes studied over a five-week period, and fewer than 6 percent of 1,462 characters had a recognizable religious affiliation. Through this fiction, the study's authors found, religion is "delegitimized" by television.

As with all things demographic in the United States, the trend toward prayer was strongly influenced and accelerated by the baby boom generation. By the end of the twentieth and the beginning of the twenty-first century, increasing numbers of the generation that believed it would be, in Bob Dylan's words, "forever young" were coming face-to-face with mortality, if not their own then that of their parents. And—some would say at long last—they began to shift their attention from themselves to their children, the generation that will succeed them. This happened to me in much the same way as it has to others of my peers. During one Jewish High Holiday service, around the time my son was three and my daughter was an infant, our rabbi at Temple Israel in Long Beach, California, Howard Laibson, suggested in his sermon one small way to get in touch with the divine: reciting the *Sh'ma* ("Hear, O Israel, the Lord is my God, the Lord is one") each night with the children before bed. When I heard those words they took me back to my own childhood when I would say the prayer with my parents and my younger brother. From that day on, evening prayers became a part of our home life. In religion, one thing has a tendency to lead to another. Some years later, at the suggestion of my wife, Sallie, we began to observe the arrival of the Sabbath on Friday evening, lighting the candles and blessing the braided challah bread, which she learned to bake herself. More recently, we have added grace before dinner, holding hands while we recite the Hebrew blessing for breaking bread and sing a simple Girl Scout grace my wife sang with her own family at dinner ("For health and strength . . .").

Something seismic was at work in this look to the heavens by Americans, and I believe, at a deeper level, that "something" is reflected in the way the supernatural is portrayed in *The Simpsons*. Season after season, the Simpsons have continued to pray, especially Marge. Despite a "No Praying" sign in her husband's hospital room, she asks for divine intervention. Faced with the latest in a never-ending series of sanity hearings endured by family members, she calls on God (in a soft but audible voice) to help her as she pleads her case to three psychiatrists. They ask her if she is praying, and she acknowledges that she is. Concerned by what they consider obvious evidence of mental instability, they inquire whether she thinks God is in the room. She replies that, yes, He's pretty much everywhere. Case closed: Marge is certifiably nuts.

Of course, there is a downside to this new spiritual consciousness and openness to the supernatural that is also reflected in the series. New Age beliefs are consistently mocked and disparaged. But two green, slimy beings from another universe (the planet Rigel-4), Kang and Kodos, visit Springfield from time to time in Halloween fantasy episodes for typical alien undertakings: either to abduct, breed with, or probe Simpson family members, or to conquer or destroy the earth. The aliens' presence in *The Simpsons* universe is as "real"—which is to say as unquestioned—as that of God. Characters on the show have no difficulty accepting both unconditionally.

Books such as Joel Achenbach's *Captured by Aliens: The Search for Life and Truth in a Very Large Universe* and Wendy Kaminer's *Sleeping with Extra-Terrestrials: The Rise of Irrationalism and Perils of Piety* explore this puzzling coexistence of belief in God and UFOs by many Americans. "No religion can simply be trusted to balance faith with reason," Kaminer writes, "but regular social rituals, like attending church or New Age lectures, and private rituals, like prayer, or maybe watching *Touched by an Angel* once a week, can provide people with the opportunity to compartmentalize their beliefs, so as not to be consumed by them."[7]

Unlike the regular characters on *Touched by an Angel*, the extraterrestrials on *The Simpsons* are in no way divine. To a degree, the difference between the irrationality of faith and the irrationality of extraterrestrials in Springfield is quantitative. Prayer and appeals to God are a much more routine and regular part of the Simpson family's life and the lives of their friends than are the appearances of Kang and Kodos on the show. In one episode, the two extraterrestrial siblings reveal that they too are creatures of faith (sort of): They identify themselves as "Quantum-Presbyterians," but only because Homer mistakes them for Mormons.

Three

The Evangelical Next Door:
"If Everyone Were like Ned Flanders, There'd Be No Need for Heaven."

On American college and high school campuses today, the name most associated with the word "Christian"—other than Jesus—is not the pope or even Billy Graham. Instead, it's a goofy-looking guy named Ned Flanders. Homer Simpson's next-door neighbor is the evangelical known most intimately to nonevangelicals. Flanders's mustache, thick glasses, sweater, and irrepressibly cheerful demeanor have made him an indelible figure. There are an estimated 50 million adult evangelical and fundamentalist Christians in the United States—one in every six Americans. Although heterogeneous in their beliefs, politics, and lifestyles, they are easily recognizable to one another, and they would have no difficulty in recognizing Ned and his family as their own. Gerry Bowler, professor of history at University of Manitoba and founder of the Centre for the Study of Christianity and Contemporary Values, calls Flanders "television's most effective exponent of a Christian life well-lived," while conceding that may be a mixed blessing. "We may have to make do with Ned Flanders as our televised spiritual mentor," says Bowler, who characterizes himself as a "mainstream evangelical."[1]

In society at large, however, evangelicals are subject to other, unflattering stereotypes, the most infamous of which was Michael Weisskopf's designation in the *Washington Post* as a group of people that is "largely poor, uneducated and easy to command."[2] Flanders is the antithesis of Weisskopf's cliché, and he has eclipsed it, offering the fairest and most sympathetic portrayal of an evangelical Christian in American popular culture. *The Simpsons'* popularity and longevity account for much of this, but there is more.

Throughout American history, the chief undermining sin of Christian character, in fiction and fact, has been hypocrisy. This strain runs from Reverend Dimmesdale in *The Scarlet Letter* to the title character in *Elmer Gantry* to televangelists Jimmy Swaggart and Jim Bakker. On this count, Ned Flanders is exemplary; his Christianity is unassailable. He may be a good-natured doofus, but he struggles mightily not to be a hypocrite. "American evangelicalism needs a good dose of demythologizing," says Christian Smith, professor of sociology at the University of Notre Dame and author of *Christian America? What Evangelicals Really Want*. "In the American media, in the popular imagination and often in academic scholarship, American evangelicals are routinely cast as either angels or demons."

Not Ned Flanders. Like many of the series' characters, he is the object of satire and sustained ridicule. An Oral Roberts University graduate who is never without a Bible and a large piece of the "True Cross" of Jesus (which saved his life in one episode when he was shot), Ned believes that one of the essential elements of a good life is "a daily dose of Vitamin Church." Harry Shearer, the actor who provides the voice for Flanders, said in a Texas magazine interview, "His spirituality is probably slightly deeper than the plaques that are on sale in the Dallas/Fort Worth Airport that have various spiritual slogans printed on them."[3] But Steve Tompkins, who wrote for the series in the mid-1990s, including several episodes that focused on Ned, has a somewhat different view. "He's a great character. He appeals to a lot of people in the audience. But he also appeals to a lot of the writers. They have a great affection for Ned Flanders, and that's probably why he gets so many great jokes. He's so funny." Ned, named for Flanders Street in Matt Groening's hometown of Portland, Oregon, represents most of the television viewing audience—white, Christian, and middle class. Al Jean, a longtime writer for the series who took over as executive producer and "show-runner" for the 2001–2002 season, agrees. "We don't mock Ned's faith," says Jean, who, like Tompkins, is a Christian. "We actually think he's a guy with a lot of wonderful qualities. . . . We can never get enough Flanders. If people accuse us of being anti-Christian, we just ask whether they'd rather have Flanders as their neighbor or Homer." Jean's longtime writing partner, Mike Reiss, a self-described "atheist Jew," says he is gratified that "some religious, good-hearted people could see the humor in this character and not be offended by it."

Despite (or perhaps because of) the comic exaggerations, Ned's portrayal as a character is complex and nuanced, enabling him to raise serious issues on a regular basis. Consider his journey of faith. The root of Flanders's turn toward a structured religious framework—probably a conservative, mainstream form of Presbyterianism—is a traumatic childhood. When Ned suffers a breakdown and is institutionalized, he experiences flashbacks of his child psychiatrist, who employed eight months of sustained, "therapeutic" spanking to control the obstreperous little boy. Before the "Spankological Program," his parents were "freaky beatniks" who raised their son with no rules at all. Ned's reaction to this chaotic and unstructured environment mirrors many studies of those who came of age in the 1960s and 1970s and, finding the freewheeling lifestyle unsatisfying or repugnant, gravitated to religion.

Religion and morality inform nearly every aspect of Flanders's life, from the doorbell that alternates chimes of "A Mighty Fortress Is Our God" and "Bringing in the Sheaves," to his air horn that blares the "Hallelujah" chorus at football games. At Yuletide, he answers his cell phone, "Christ is born, who's on my horn?" Together with his family, he prays at meals and before bed. He attends his church three times a week and tithes, contributing to seven other congregations just to be on the safe side. In church, Ned always has an emergency sermon in his back pocket. On one Christmas, Lovejoy doesn't appear for services, so Ned is drafted. But he gives himself a paper cut and passes out. Ned sometimes takes modesty to extremes. For example, he wants culottes banned in schoool, and he wears swimming trunks while taking a bath. "So I can't see my own shrinky-dink," he tells Homer. He belongs to a Bible study group and keeps notes stuck on his refrigerator with a fish magnet, and he turns his basement into a Christian youth hostel from time to time. Like many believers, he thanks God often for his blessings, for things as small as a beautiful day. He calls on the Almighty for everything from a better performance of

Guys and Dolls at the local dinner theater to the backstage players—those who work behind the scenes to make the production work. At the dinner table, he gives thanks for the middleman responsible for inflating the price of the food on his table and for the "humane but determined guys at the slaughterhouse." The family carves Bible dioramas out of pumpkins at Halloween and gives out hugs instead of candy to trick-or-treaters. Vacation destinations include Verbal Johnson's "Praying Hands" ("America's Most Judgmental Religious Theme Park!") and Sunday Bob Picker's "America, U.S.A." ("Nuclear Warhead Museum and Religious Arts Center").

Sometimes the series writers have turned more playful than usual with Ned's character and have used him as a transgressive figure. Dream and fantasy sequences, as you might expect, have featured Ned as God, the pope, a cardinal, and a Puritan witch burner; in others, as the devil, a werewolf, and a zombie. When Homer is shocked to see that Flanders is Satan, he replies that it's always the one you least expect. There are great extremes of belief and revelation in these fantasy sequences. In a tall tale, told by Lisa during an interminable wait for their food order to arrive, Ned is a prissy Puritan on the *Mayflower* who flagellates himself—pouring salt into the bloody wounds—when he accidentally sins, like composing a poem. In a Halloween episode, Flanders believes his life is ending. "I'm dying!" he exclaims. "And there's heaven! Who's that? Confucius? . . . And Milton Berle! Boy, have I been barking up the wrong tree!" In another *Treehouse of Horror* episode, Ned has a brain tumor removed, which enables him to see death claiming his friends. "God, why did you give me this power?" he asks. Ned unconsciously runs a riff of naughty double entendres. His sons Rod and Todd wear jerseys 66 and 6 on their football team, so when they stand together the shirts read 666, the mark of the beast in the book of Revelation.

Ned believes in the second coming, certain that Jesus will return to earth at any moment. He mistakes Lisa's backyard saxophone practicing for the sound of Gabriel's trumpet and the arrival of judgment day, and an escaped elephant from the Springfield Zoo for one of the four horses of the Apocalypse. An episode set thirty years in the future has a dissolute Bart Simpson ringing Ned's doorbell, intending to ask for money. Flanders, who has lost his sight (but not his vision), hears the bell, taps his cane to the door, and asks matter-of-factly, "Is that you, Jesus?" In his RV with his boys and near death from fumes, Ned sees Jesus. "Jesus wouldn't let us die this way."

Yet Ned is also deeply immersed in the good works of the social gospel, beginning with the random (and typically improbable) donation of one of his kidneys and a lung for anyone who might need them. For a time, his elderly grandmother lived with the family, and Ned volunteers at a foster home, hospitals, soup kitchens, and a homeless shelter. He is a scoutmaster and Pee Wee football coach, recycles, is active in the PTA and the neighborhood association (but not, for some unexplained reason, Neighborhood Watch), and volunteers for the marital stress hotline. Wednesday is tithe day at the Flanders house, when the family tries to join together to do good deeds. A homeless man arrives at their front door on tithe day, the family bathes him and treats his sores, gives him a new suit and sends him on his way, singing "Onward, Christian Soldiers." When British billionaire Richard Branson, of the Virgin empire, hands Ned a dollar at the grand opening of his Springfield Mega-Store, Flanders says it is going straight to the poor box. This is a family Jesus would have no trouble recognizing as one of his own.

Nominally a member of the religious right, Ned is politically active, at least at the local level. Some fans have suggested that, reflecting the rise of the Christian Right on the political and cultural fronts in recent years, Ned has become more overtly conservative. He explains to Lisa that he is so well informed, presumably by scripture, that it is unnecessary for him to read the newspaper's editorial page: "I don't need to be told what to think—by anyone living." Yet his is not an angry activism. To be sure, he belongs to the Citizens' Committee on Moral Hygiene, and he has picketed against cartoon violence. His most overt political act is one many Christians would consider inadvertent, and so ends in disaster. Homer objects to Ned's tenure as interim principal of Springfield Elementary School. Instinctively, Flanders says "Let's thank the

Lord" over the intercom and, for this offense, is fired on the spot by the superintendent. "God has no place within these walls, just like the facts have no place within organized religion! Simpson, you get your wish. Flanders is history."

Ned's Christianity plays a major part in the way he raises his sons Rod and Todd, and, predictably, he often goes to extremes. A typical bedtime story has the father reading that Harry Potter and all his friends "went straight to hell for practicing witchcraft." Ned doesn't allow the kids, one of whom is gay, to use dice when playing board games because dice are wicked. However, while attending the Springfield Animation Festival, he permits the boys to watch "The New Adventures of Gravy and Jobliath," a clay-mation show produced by the "Presbylutherans" in which a boy builds a pipe bomb to blow up a Planned Parenthood center. He is hesitant to buy the children Red Hots candy because there is a lascivious caricature of the devil on the package. The kids' favorite games are Good Samaritan, Clothe the Leper, and Build the Mission ("Finally the villagers have a place to pray"). Their preferred video game is "Billy Graham's Bible Blaster," in which the goal is to zap nonbelievers into converts (those hit only by glancing shots become Unitarians). Another game the Flanders boys play is "Christian Clue," where one solution to the murder is "The secular humanist in the schoolhouse with misinformation!" Cursing poses another problem, when Homer's foul language is picked up by one of the Flanders boys. Todd uses the word "damn" at the table and is punished by Ned, whose decree, "No Bible stories for you tonight!" sends the boy crying from the room. Later, Todd is seen wearing a tee-shirt with the name of the punk band "Butt-hole Surfers," which he finds in the church's donation bin after a disaster destroys their clothes.

The young Flanders boys are total innocents: They believe they are getting closer to God when they jump on the Simpsons' trampoline. The brothers believe Bart when he imitates the voice of God and tells them to walk into a wall, promising to remove it if they do. Of course, they crash, and—their faith thus tested—they balk when the voice of God/Bart tells them to take cookies to the

Simpson household. "Look," the voice intones sternly, "do you want a happy God or a vengeful God?" The boys complain to their parents that they *only* get to go to church three times a week, and they decide to stop watching reruns of the Lutheran Church's original *Davey and Goliath* animated series because they think that the idea of a talking dog is blasphemous. In a *Simpsons* comic book, Bart convinces the boys to dress up as a Druid priest and a sacrificial lamb when the Simpsons' basement is turned into a medieval dungeon. When Ned walks in on them he is outraged, saying the game smacks of "multiculturalism."

Ned is not immune to the familiar conflict between parental instruction on morality and the exigencies of modern life, especially when it comes to lying. Rod and Todd overhear Ned tell Homer that he can't come over to their house because the Flanderses are visiting relatives. The boys know it's untrue, though told to spare Homer's feelings. "Lies make Baby Jesus cry," Rod reminds his father. One Christmas, momentarily overcome by the holiday spirit, Homer walks arm in arm with Reverend Lovejoy. Todd asks his dad if the sight makes him feel "jealous of Brother Homer," and Ned answers, "Just a tad." Ned gets away with a borderline fib when he tells the boys that the blood of a mangled cartoon character is really jam. Ned acknowledges that he has a temper, and his own language approaches the mildly blasphemous, including "crap," "hell," and "heckaroonie." Once, he gets halfway to taking the Lord's name in vain before catching himself. When Ned slips, and says "bitchin'" in front of his children, they notice that he said a curse word. What really sets his temper off, he tells a counselor, is his wife's habit of underlining passages in *his* Bible.

Even Ned's various sideline businesses, some part of Flancrest Enterprises, reflect his faith. He sells religious hooked rugs on the Internet and Bible trading cards at the swap meet. Flanders is honorable in his business, sometimes to his detriment. His major plunge into the entrepreneurial world occurs when he gives up his job in pharmaceutical sales to open the Leftorium, a boutique in the mall for all things left-handed, including tee-shirts reading "The Lord Loves a Lefty." Asked once if his store is open, he replies,

"Open as a tomb on Easter!" His morality and good nature nearly do him in. He spends the day ignoring shoplifters and chasing down a customer he inadvertently shortchanged, and becomes known for validating parking for nonpatrons. Unbeknownst to Ned, Homer has wished failure on him and steers business away from his neighbor. Lisa accuses her father of *schadenfreude*, of taking joy from the misfortune of another. The Leftorium nearly goes broke, and Flanders has to sell everything he owns to pay off his debts. "At times like these, I used to turn to the Bible for solace," he tells Homer, "but the Good Book can't help me now." He hasn't lost his faith; it's simply that his neighbor picked up his Bible for seven cents at Flanders's desperation yard sale. In the end, Homer helps save the business and Ned forgives him for sabotaging the effort, preferring to thank him for warning him about the dangers of niche retailing. The warning is prescient; no sooner does the Leftorium recover than a competitor called Leftopolis moves next door. When economic times are tough at the Flanders home in December, they still celebrate, but with an "imagination Christmas."

Ned admits that most of the time he is "about as exciting as a baked potato." Yet for all his sweetness, he does have an unpredictable side. A part of him yearns to fit in with his worldly friends, even when his efforts are outlandish. Given his muscular physique, Flanders is selected to play the role of Stanley Kowalski in the community production of *A Streetcar Named Desire*, a musical version called *"Oh Streetcar!"* The director instructs him to play it as if he were "pulsating with animal lust." His video collection includes "Girls Gone Mild" and "Debbie Does Penance." At a Phish concert, he proclaims, "May the grace of the Lord Jesus be with God's people." When his middle-aged friends decide to form an outlaw motorcycle gang, Ned goes along. He reluctantly accepts the name "Hell's Satans"—such blasphemy might send him to hell—only after hearing the alternative, "Christ Punchers." Still, he frets when the gang begins to pitch pennies on the sidewalk. In another episode, after asking Homer the "secret of your intoxicating lust for life," he sins on a grand scale, going with his neighbor to Las Vegas for a wild weekend, during which he goes on an all-night bender and (apparently) marries a cocktail waitress. In the casino, he tells Homer that gambling is forbidden by Deuteronomy 7, so naturally Homer bets the number on roulette and wins. Ned looks up and asks God if he should gamble, and is assured that he should by the voice of a security guard speaking from a camera in the ceiling, which Ned assumes is God.

Ned grapples with other temptations of popular culture in various incarnations and, on those rare occasions when he succumbs to temptation, is quick to see divine retribution. He angrily runs off a shady cable installer who offers an illegal hookup. Instead, he turns to satellite television, which enables him to view more than two hundred channels—almost all of which he then locks out for offensive content. Mostly, Ned watches the Church Channel and says he feels he's spending all his money on "PPV"—pray per view. Straying from his usual screen fare, such as reruns of the *Jim Nabors Show*, he once watched *Married . . . with Children* (on the same network that produces *The Simpsons*). He insists he is afflicted with the flu for this lapse: "Oh, the network slogan is true! Watch Fox and be damned for all eternity!"

Ned's relationship with the church and his pastor is ambivalent, although he tries to stand by the congregation, come what may. When Bart becomes a faith healer and holds weeknight services in a backyard tent, drawing away most of the congregation, only the Flanders family remains faithful to Springfield Community Church. (However, vigilant keepers of *The Simpsons* Archive Web site note Ned's absence in at least four panning shots of the church's pews. Family vacation, perhaps?) Ned is so quick to consult Reverend Lovejoy with his theological concerns, large and small, that he puts the minister's church and home telephone numbers on his speed dialer. As a younger man, Ned worried about coveting his own wife, and he admits to the minister that, while he's pretty meek, he could be meeker. Like many clergy in these situations, Lovejoy doesn't always appreciate this devotion. Interrupted during dessert or in the middle of the night over a seemingly trivial issue, the minister curses Flanders out of earshot.

At a church picnic, Ned's questions about whether it's proper to engage in sports on Sunday prompts the exasperated minister to curse him to his face. Once, in the middle of the night, Ned is so upset his wife suggests he call Lovejoy. When the minister's wife wakes him with the news of Ned's call, he grumbles that Ned's crisis probably involves his stepping on a worm. Lovejoy tells him, "A gentle answer turneth away wrath," and then slams down the phone. When Ned suggests that a barbershop quartet might not be appropriate for a worship service, the pastor gets rid of him by sending him off to see an oil stain in the parking lot that looks "just like Saint Barnabas." Lovejoy's revenge is the perverse pleasure he takes in urging his dog do his "dirty sinful business" on Flanders's front lawn. The minister even suggests Ned try another denomination, since "they're all pretty much the same." Yet when Ned is in real trouble—held captive by angry, carnivorous baboons at the Springfield Zoo—it is the pastor who risks his life to save him.

For all his admirable qualities, Flanders occasionally exhibits the zealousness and narrow-mindedness that for many represent the darker side of evangelical Christianity. He distributes pamphlets titled "You Will Die in Hell" during an outdoor community movie showing. When Ned looks up at the night sky and sees a Jewish star, he rubs his eyes in disbelief. Homer has brain surgery that lifts his IQ fifty points and turns him into a genius. One of his accomplishments is writing a proof that there is no God, which he presents to Ned one Sunday when his neighbor is on his way to church. At first Ned scoffs at such proof, written on a single page, but he reads it through and agrees that it is airtight. "Can't let this get out," he says, burning the paper. Proselytizing is another touchy issue. Some true believers interpret the imperative of evangelism's Great Commission to mean never taking "no" for an answer. Homer's decision to stop going to church prompts Ned to show up at Moe's Tavern, complete with his guitar and his family, to bring his neighbor back to the fold. For their trouble, the door is slammed in their faces. Later, the Flanderses pursue Homer by car, as Todd calls out, "Dad, the heathen's getting away!"

After another typical misadventure costs Homer and Marge custody of their children, Bart, Lisa, and Maggie are placed in the

Flanderses' temporary care. Lisa observes to Bart that the house has a "creepy, Pat Boone-ish quality about it." A family parlor game, "Bible Bombardment," first reveals that Bart and Lisa have no grasp of the scriptural arcana that is common knowledge to the Flanderses. The Simpson offspring then let slip that, through their parents' neglect (or design), they have never been baptized. So, rather than consulting Homer and Marge, who are taking court-ordered parenting classes, Ned dresses the Simpson children— who voice neither interest nor acquiescence—in white robes for baptism. At the Springfield River he prepares to immerse them and asks if they reject Satan.

This situation is not as far-fetched as it may appear. As often happens in *The Simpsons*, the scenario illustrates a serious and historic theological issue, in this case involving religious commitment and free will. Conversion at the point of the sword and the threat of the stake were staples of medieval Europe, by both Christians and Muslims. In a case that became a world controversy, a six-year-old Jewish boy named Edgardo Mortara was taken from his parents in Rome in 1858 and raised as a Catholic after a servant girl claimed to have secretly baptized the boy when he was an infant. Closer to home and the present, parents in Central Florida in the late 1990s sued a Christian day care center for baptizing their children without their consent.

In Springfield, the involuntary rite is interrupted just at the moment of immersion by Homer, who saves Bart from being saved by being baptized himself. "Wow, Dad, you took a baptismal for me," says a startled Bart. "How do you feel?" Put another way, the curious boy is asking, "What is the spiritual impact of this practice?" At first, the effect seems to be transcendent. Homer, visibly aglow, replies, "Oh, Bartholomew. I feel like Saint Augustine of Hippo after his conversion by Ambrose of Milan." Ned, a world-class believer, is flabbergasted. It's not clear whether or not Flanders is familiar with this reference to one of Christendom's most famous turnarounds, by a self-proclaimed reprobate of epic proportions. In any event, Ned is dumbstruck by the transformation of his neighbor: "Homer, what did you say?" As any modern theologian can explain, this is not what Christian conversion is about, and it cannot stand. "You don't force your faith on anybody," says Reverend Matthew Gibbs, a young Southern Baptist preacher from Orlando who watched the episode, even though his wife doesn't normally let him. Bill Merrell, former vice president of the Southern Baptist Convention, agrees. "We believe that coercion cannot support faith. It completely erodes the value of any such profession."

James A. Smith, editor of the *Florida Baptist Witness*, the official weekly journal of the state's Southern Baptists, points out that even with the best intentions, manipulative evangelism "is really not evangelism at all. True evangelism is telling the Good News that God saves sinners and how human beings can be reconciled to Him. True evangelism does not happen when people are tricked." Sure enough, Homer's glow subsides and he returns to his natural state, snapping, "I said, shut your ugly face, Flanders!" For his part, Ned makes no apology or explanation for this breach, as he has in the past for lesser faux pas.

At times, Ned seems to have a direct pipeline to God. While making a movie based on the story of baby Moses for the first Springfield Film Festival, his son is swept away in a basket in a rushing river. "Flanders to God, Flanders to God, get off your cloud and save my Todd!" he shouts. Immediately, a bolt of light-ning drops a tree across the river, catching the basket and saving the boy. Ned thanks God, who responds with a huge hand (with five fingers) making the OK sign through the clouds and, in a deep version of "Flanders-speak," says, "Okily dokily."

Like some pious Christians, Ned is guilty of praying for trivial things. He and his wife, Maude, and Reverend Lovejoy and his wife comprise a bowling team called the "Holy Rollers." They arrive at the alley decked out in monks' robes and bathed in heavenly light, suggesting that there is more at stake in this league play than purely secular concerns. This is confirmed at one tournament when the Holy Rollers play Homer's team which is sponsored by Mr. Burns, the owner of the nuclear plant where Homer works. Burns asks, "Who's ready to kick some Christian keister?" As Ned leaves one pin standing after a frame, Homer mocks him and his religious faith, asking him where his God is. Flanders ignores the jibe and, again, turns his eyes above. "It's me, Ned," he says simply, and the lone pin drops. As a divine exclamation point, an electric charge from the machine that returns the bowling balls strikes Homer. His unfair appeal to the Almighty is troubling to Homer, and he says so when he sees Flanders praying, presumably to win a bet the two men have made on another occasion. Flanders replies that he is praying only that no one gets hurt in the contest.

Above all, Ned is the good neighbor, his basic role in the series. "Affordable tract housing made us neighbors," he tells Homer, "but you made us friends." In fact, the opposite is true. Homer does everything short of mayhem to abuse Flanders, and at one point Marge admonishes her husband: "You shouldn't be so hard on Ned. He's been a good neighbor ever since we moved here." Homer is unmoved and asks, "What has he ever done for us besides lend us things, do us favors, and save our children from the occasional house fire?" It is only by repeatedly turning to Matthew 19:19, Jesus' admonition to "love your neighbor as yourself," that Ned is able to survive the largely one-sided relationship, returning uncon- ditional love for sustained abuse. Well, maybe not unconditional love. Because Ned is human, his acceptance has limits, a trait that reinforces his believability. Homer steps over the line when he rips out the Flanderses' air conditioner during a heat wave. Discovered between their houses, Homer knows Ned well enough to try a bib- lical defense: "Haven't you ever heard, 'Let he who is without sin cast the first stone'?" Whereupon one of the Flanders boys lets fly with a rock that boinks Homer on the head. There are other times when Homer goes over the line with Ned. Lisa wins four tickets to an obscure foreign film in a public radio contest and coerces her family into going with her. So there is a sudden need for a babysit- ter for Maggie, and Homer barges into Flanders's house and asks Ned. At first his neighbor begs off, saying he has to rewind video- tapes for the homeless. "Doesn't that Bible of yours say, 'Love thy neighbor'?" Homer demands. "Why won't you love me?" The coercion works, and soon Ned is showing Maggie around his house. He starts with part of his collection of saccharine porcelain figurines and, opening the cabinet to the larger collection, he finds a note from Homer apologizing for smashing the others into shards. Maggie joins Rod and Todd on the carpet, playing the Last Supper with their stuffed animals. Ned won't take any money from Marge after the movie, but he admits that business is off at the Leftorium and he is strapped for cash. Marge suggests he rent out a room, which sounds like a good idea to him. "It might be fun to be a landlord," he says, quickly correcting himself to avoid inadvertently breaking a commandment. "Landfella," he says. "There's only one Lord." Ned's flyer—"Room for Rent. No Pagans"—draws two attractive young women who claim to be community college students. In fact, they operate a soft-core webcam site. Bart and his friend Milhouse stumble onto the site, and soon Homer has discovered it too. Homer spreads word around town that Springfield's most righteous citizen is inadvertently hosting a pornographic Web site. The only person he doesn't tell is Ned himself. "No one is telling him," Homer says gleefully. "Not even his good buddy, God." At church the next Sunday, Ned and his boys are greeted with gales of snickers, smirks, and laughter. Finally learning he has been duped, Ned goes home and expels the young women for sullying his good name.

Not withstanding this betrayal, Ned's faith is constant, and in the end it is always affirmed. Yet like most Christians, his faith is not perfect: God's will sometimes baffles him. Encouraged by the artist Jasper Johns, Homer floods Springfield one night as a conceptual art project. Ned wakes up the next morning and looks out of his second-story bedroom window. "It's a miracle!" he says to his wife, Maude. "The Lord has drowned the wicked and spared the righteous." Then he spies Homer in a rowboat and extends his leap to the wrong conclusion. "Looks like heaven is easier to get into than Arizona State." Maude grapples with the same conundrum but reaches her own conclusion: "I don't judge Homer and Marge. That's for a vengeful God to do."

Most frequently and most fervently, Ned prays for the strength to remain a good neighbor, which is his burden. Where Homer is concerned, Matthew 19:19 is never far from his mind. While Ned never suffers martyrdom for his faith, he comes in for more than his share of scorn, and it begins the day the Simpsons move into the neighborhood. Ned welcomes them and says cheerily that his friends call him by his first name; Homer immediately addresses him as "Flanders." Homer considers Ned "a big, four-eyed lame-o" who wears the same sweater every day, except to attend church. Homer tells Ned to shut up on innumerable occasions, calls him a liar and a square, nearly runs him over, and dumps garbage on his head. Homer avoids having to invite Flanders to a backyard dinner for Marge by giving him a note that he is to meet "Jesus H. Christ" in a cave in Montana. (Naturally, Ned immediately heads West.) Even Marge, a believer, takes advantage of her neighbor, tossing a stray snake from their overgrown backyard into Ned's yard, where it bites him. Ever the long-suffering good sport, Flanders good-naturedly sings along when the Simpsons serenade him with a Christmas carol that mocks him.

Homer refers to Ned by a variety of derisive terms such as "Saint Flanders," "Charlie Church," and "Churchy La Femme." Flanders is actually the physical embodiment of muscular, masculine Christianity, a man who would be right at home at a Promise Keepers rally, except, as Harry Shearer points out, Promise Keepers is for backsliders. Ned roots for the "Punishing Pilgrim" in professional wrestling. He is a former fraternity man and a football fan. Ned works out to a buff build that belies his age, which he insists is sixty. The secret of his youthful appearance, he explains to Homer, is that he "resists all major urges." He identifies himself as a recovering alcoholic, yet early in the series, he would have a beer or a cocktail—he claims a degree in mixology—and he smokes a pipe. Ned has many of the accoutrements of the 1990s middle-class prosperity, such as a boat ("Thanks for the Boat, Lord II") and a summer beach house. On the other hand, he drives an uninspiring Geo station wagon, with a license plate reading JHN 143 (John 1:43, in which Jesus calls on the disciples to "follow me").

Homer's hectoring notwithstanding, Ned also takes literally Jesus' words in John 15:13: "Greater love has no man than this, that a man lay down his life for his friends." When Homer faces a triple bypass operation, his neighbor apologizes for not being able to donate his own heart for a transplant. A volunteer fire-fighter, Ned says a prayer as he risks his life to save Homer from a house fire, almost losing his own life in the process. Homer assumes the fire is God's will, a notion Ned instantly rejects. As the fire spreads to Ned's house, the instantly ungrateful Homer observes that, for all his piety and churchgoing, God is not sparing the Flanderses' roof from fire. Suddenly, a small wisp floating above the Flanders home becomes a rain cloud and douses the blaze. Just to make certain the lesson from above is clear, a rainbow frames Ned's house.

Flanders is altruistic enough to build a bomb shelter large enough for both his and the Simpson families. As a comet approaches Springfield, Ned invites his neighbors to join him. But so many other friends and neighbors force their way in that the shelter becomes too crowded, and one person has to leave. Nominated by Homer as the most useless individual in the group, Ned is ejected, a verdict he cheerfully accepts. In the event he goes mad as the comet approaches, he asks Todd to "shoot Daddy if he tries to get back in."

Like any sitcom neighbor, Homer borrows things from Flanders, ranging from a TV tray, power tools, and a new sprinkler, to a camcorder—which he has no intention of returning. Once, this practice puts Ned in technical violation of the Eighth Commandment, when he steals back his own barbecue. Homer, who covets much of what he has not already borrowed or stolen from the Flanders household, also covets Maude Flanders from time to time, which causes her to make certain her blouse is buttoned to the neck whenever he is around. At times, Homer's view of his neighbor can become quite dark. "Life is just one crushing defeat after another," he says, "until you just wish Flanders was dead."

Flanders interacts with Homer on what appears to be a daily basis. However, it takes him eight years to invite members of the Simpson family into his home, a touch of suburban verisimilitude that reinforces the premise. Inside the recreation room, Homer notices the odd mixture of Ned's life: a tap featuring imported beer and a copy of Leonardo da Vinci's *Last Supper*. He owns a Shroud of Turin towel, which is later stolen, and a large collection of Bibles and holy writings, including the Septuagint in Aramaic, the Vulgate of Saint Jerome, the Living Bible, a Samaritan Pentateuch, Solomon's Song of Songs, and the "Thump-Proof Bible." Not all objects of veneration in the Flanders home are religious. Ned is a big Beatles fan and has a shrine to them in his house. "They were bigger than Jesus," he explains. Outside the shrine is a sign reading, "Beware of God." Typically, it is on this first visit that Homer's feelings of inferiority lead him to make a lewd compliment about Maude that Flanders finds insulting. Angrily, and uncharacteristically, Ned orders his neighbor out of his house. Guilt-stricken, he consults Reverend Lovejoy and then asks Homer for forgiveness. "You are my brother and I love you," he writes in a note. "I feel a great sadness in my bosom." Bart and Homer totally miss the message and guffaw over the word "bosom."

There are times when Flanders's response to Simpson appeals for Christian charity is, at best, qualified. Homer and Bart, believing (incorrectly) that they have leprosy, come to Ned for help. At first, he panics and slams the door. But thinking (correctly) that this response is not Christian, Ned dons a high-tech biohazard suit and invites them in, acknowledging at the same time that the Flanders house is "not really set up for lepers." Homer asks if they are being shunned, which is manifestly close to the truth. No, says Ned, they are being sent to a better place—the leper colony on the Hawaiian island of Molokai, at the Flanderses' expense. Stripped of its Simpsonian excess, it is the kind of solution familiar to many modern believers. Just think about how our society treats elderly parents, severely disabled children, and the mentally disabled.

Ned Flanders has undergone three major crises of faith, each of which has shaken the belief that is central to his life. The circumstances range from the surreal to experiences shared by many.

1. Love. For all his unrequited neighborly love, too much gratitude from Homer turns out to be a deadly thing. Again, prayer plays a central role as a plot device. No sooner does Homer pray for a ticket to a sold-out local football game than Flanders knocks on the Simpsons' door with an offer to take him. Ned buys him refreshments and even gets him the game ball (the quarterback had been converted through the efforts of Ned's Bible group). Homer decides that he has been unfair to his neighbor, in light of his many kindnesses, and he determines to show his love. Alas, the love is the oppressive, smothering variety, and before long it is Ned who is praying—for the strength to survive Homer's friendship.

Feeling trapped, Ned dreams of climbing the church tower, singing "Bringing in the Sheaves" while assembling an assault rifle and picking off people below—all of whom have Homer's face. He wakes, distraught, telling his startled wife that he thinks he hates his neighbor, something he must know is wrong and unchristian. Still, the next day he makes an excuse to avoid Homer and drives off with his family. In his haste to shake Homer, Ned is stopped for speeding by Springfield Police Chief Wiggum, who loudly (and erroneously) accuses him of driving under the influence of drugs—just as a church bus full of horrified members rolls past the scene. "Where's your Messiah now?" the chief asks in his best Edward G. Robinson accent. It's a good question for Flanders, who has rejected Homer's sincere, if irritating, efforts to be a good neighbor. For a man who puts his faith at the center of his life, where *is* his Jesus now?

On Sunday, Ned gets his answer. While driving to church, he is anxious about appearing at the one place, except for his home, where he feels most welcome and part of society. Maude assures him that the church is "a house of love and forgiveness." Sure enough, as Flanders enters the sanctuary people in the pews whisper that he is evil and "the fallen one." Reverend Lovejoy announces that the sermon topic is "What Ned Did." Distressed, Flanders has difficulty recognizing the irony of his situation. He is being condemned for something he did not do—taking drugs. But he is suffering for what he did do, which was to reject Homer's sincere neighborly love and gratitude. Ned then compounds this sin by cursing Homer for whistling through his nose during silent prayer, further inflaming the congregation against him. The role reversal is nearly complete, as Homer defends Ned, describing him—correctly—as a kind, wonderful, caring man who has "turned every cheek on his body" in the face of Homer's insults. "If everyone here were like Ned Flanders, there'd be no need for heaven. We'd already be there."

Reverend Lovejoy is convinced, acknowledging that Ned is owed an apology. Flanders has clearly learned his lesson and later thanks Homer for being a true friend. Homer reverts to type, telling him to get lost, and all is right again in the world.

2. Loss. A hurricane—an unusual occurrence in Springfield—bears down on the town. Typically, Ned again invites the Simpsons to share his shelter, only to be rebuffed by the neighbors, who prefer their own cellar to his company. Miraculously, the storm spares every house on the street *except* the Flanderses', which is reduced to rubble. Then looters single out the Leftorium, his business at the mall, for looting. Because Ned believes that insurance is a form of gambling, the losses are uncovered. His friends and neighbors come to his aid by rebuilding his home. Unfortunately, and despite their best intentions, the workmanship is shoddy and the new structure collapses immediately.

In the face of these trials, Ned takes the traditional, if not instinctive, path, going to his pastor, the intercessor. He tells the minister that he is beginning to feel a little like Job. Rather than sympathizing, Lovejoy suggests that Flanders is being melodramatic. The minister dissembles when Ned asks directly if God is punishing him, referring him to a book by Art Linkletter—hardly a source of theological solace. Unsatisfied, Ned goes directly to the source, praying, "Why me, Lord? Where have I gone wrong? I've always been nice to people. I don't drink or dance or swear. I've even kept kosher just to be on the safe side. I've done everything the Bible says, even the stuff that contradicts the other stuff." So, in the words of Rabbi Harold Kushner, why *do* bad things happen to good people? When Ned finds no satisfactory answer in his faith, he blows his top, denouncing his friends and going on a rampage that ends only when he drives himself to Calmwood Hospital, a mental institution, seeking a secular explanation and relief.

3. Love and loss. In early 2000, following a dispute over money with Maggie Roswell, the actress who provided the voice for Maude, the series writers killed Ned's wife in a freak accident, knocking her from the top of an auto racing stadium by a barrage of tee-shirts fired by air cannons. Although Homer is accidentally responsible, Ned blames himself, and is crushed to be bereft of his beloved "Popcorn Ball." After the funeral, the Simpsons do their best to comfort him and his boys by hosting a reception at their house. As guests come and go, Ned runs through a gamut of grieving emotions, sitting on the couch looking shell-shocked. Later, Moe the bartender makes a flattering but totally inappropriate remark about Maude, provoking a beating from Ned. Later, Flanders sits on the back swing with Homer and states the obvious, that he will just have to work through his own grief.

But Ned wouldn't be Ned if he didn't turn to God in his time of greatest need. Months later, still desolate, he prays, "Lord, I never question your will, but I'm wondering whether your decision to take Maude was, well, wrong—unless this is part of your divine plan. Could you please just give me some sign, anything?" Instead, there is only silence. Disappointed and angry with God, who has always been his rock, Ned turns a framed, bedside picture of a hoary, white-bearded God (albeit a Catholic one, not unlike the one in Michelangelo's *Creation of Adam* in the Sistine Chapel) to face the wall. The next morning, Sunday, he sleeps late and tells Rod and Todd to go to church with the Simpsons—an act so out of character that the boys back out of their father's bedroom, gasping. Ned vows not to attend church that day and says he might not go the next day as well, telling God he is not kidding.

In the scene immediately following, Flanders is speeding to church, repeating apologies for his momentary lapse of faith. He walks into the sanctuary to find a Christian rock group performing. The beautiful lead singer, later described as the "Christian Madonna," seems to be addressing him: "If you think [God] doesn't care, or maybe that he isn't there, it's not too late to see how wrong you are." Ned, still standing in the aisle, is transfixed. This is the sign he prayed for. Outside the church after the service, he introduces himself to the singer, saying, "My name is Ned Flanders and I'm here every week—rain or shine!" Later, when Ned wonders whether to remarry, he naturally consults his Bible.

In May 2001, three months after a Bible-based theme park called "The Holy Land Experience" opened with great fanfare in Orlando, *The Simpsons* aired an episode in which Ned builds a

"Christian amusement park" in memory of Maude. Like the Florida park, "Praiseland" is a tax-exempt attraction built with donated funds and volunteer labor, including that of the Simpson family. Ned's goal is to create "A shining beacon for the Lord," since he is convinced that "faith and devotion are the wildest thrill rides of all." But "King David's Wild Ride" turns out to be an enforced listening session of the entire book of Psalms. A pop-up game called "Whack-a-Satan" has no bat because, as Ned explains to a bewildered child, "You can stop Satan with your faith."

Customers soon lose interest and begin streaming toward the exit. Ned concludes that his memorial to his beloved wife is a failure, that his efforts to create an amusement park have resulted in a "bemusement park." Suddenly, a hidden gas leak at the foot of Maude's giant statute creates the illusion of a miracle, causing those who approach to speak in tongues and have comforting visions of heaven. Homer and Bart are quick to capitalize on the phenomenon. The entrance fee to the park does not include miracles, says the father; the son pipes up, "The power of Christ compels you to give Ned an extra ten bucks."

Ned objects, saying it would be wrong to exploit a divine manifestation, until he is convinced that the money could be used to help poor orphans. Even that justification is not enough to keep the park open when he realizes that the manifestation is not divine, and could be dangerous. Not even Homer's plea that Praiseland "has touched an entire town with its inspiring message" can keep Ned from padlocking the place.

Maude's death prompted Frederica Mathewes-Green, an author and former columnist for *Christianity Today* magazine, to write a love letter on Beliefnet.com to the suddenly available widower, called "Ned Flanders, My Hero." She wrote, "Ned is endlessly cheerful because he is pure in heart. He treats everyone around him with generosity and kindness, and can't imagine they wouldn't treat him the same way. He is incapable of cynicism or contempt," unlike most residents of Springfield. While he may be a fool, she observed, he is the kind of fool who makes the world a better place. Flanders, Mathewes-Green wrote, is Christlike, "a beam of light in a depressing little town," and the nicest person on the show.[4]

Not every academic observer is so unambiguous in praising Ned. Flanders's portrayal is "a cheap shot at fundamentalists— which is why I like it," says David Landry. Yet, at the same time, Landry says, Flanders's portrayal illustrates "the virtues of hard work and honesty. Flanders is very successful, with well-behaved children, an excellent marriage. He's not portrayed as a real nut. I mean, he's got a beer keg in his basement."[5] The Flanders family is portrayed "fallibly but sympathetically," says Michael Glodo, professor of Old Testament and preaching at Reformed Theological Seminary. "They are simple, sincere, earnest—a good package of virtue, especially in a postmodern culture where cynicism and irony and satire are the prevailing sentiments."

As Michael Weisskopf's *Washington Post* stereotype of evangelicals fades, another equally derogatory and inaccurate one may be emerging to replace it. In February 2000, a family named Scheibner was profiled on the cover of the *New York Times Magazine*. The cover line read "Inward Christian Soldiers: Fundamentalist families like the Scheibners are no longer fighting against the mainstream— they're dropping out and creating their own private America." In the article, author Margaret Talbot describes a family of nine fundamentalist Baptists, esconced in Pennsylvania's Lehigh Valley. On the surface, the Scheibners are similar to the Flanderses. There is no sports gear in the home because parents Stephen and Megan believe athletic competition is not Christlike. There are Christian board games that Rod and Todd Flanders might enjoy. Stephen Scheibner is a pilot for American Airlines and a commander in the Naval Reserve who, like his wife, found his Christian faith in his teens. But, apart from voting and paying taxes, he and his family have consciously opted out of a culture they believe is evil. Talbot, citing the Scheibners' plans to move to Maine and start a church, argue that they are typical of a modern counterculture being constructed by conservative Christians who, at the urging of activists like Paul Weyrich, are giving up on a hopelessly depraved society.

Yet the Scheibners may be more of a caricature than the Flanders family, whose members are fully engaged in the world. "We will exaggerate some of Ned's beliefs as a form of comic relief," says *The Simpsons'* Mike Scully. "I think everybody knows a family like the Flanderses." Stripped of their comedic excess and hyperbole, how fairly do Ned and his family represent evangelical Christianity to the world? As a committed Jew, raised in a Northeastern suburb, I may not be the best judge. Or maybe I am. For more than a decade, I have reported on the evangelical movement—locally and nationally—for the *Orlando Sentinel* newspaper. More to the point, fate and my Central Florida suburb put me into close contact with a family I see as a real-life Flanders family. Until I raised the issue with them, they had no basis for comparison; they didn't watch the show and did not allow their children to watch.

Dan and Lorraine Hardaway are an attractive couple in their forties. Each experienced some degree of dysfunction earlier in life before turning to Jesus. Dan, who has reddish blond hair and blue eyes, works full-time for Campus Crusade for Christ in Orlando. Lorraine, whose auburn hair frames a face brightened by a toothy smile, is a stay-at-home mom. Their four children, who range in age from twelve to nineteen, are as good-natured as Rod and Todd Flanders but considerably more worldly. The college-educated couple belongs to Northland Church in Longwood, Florida, a nondenominational, evangelical megachurch. They sing in the choir and listen to a contemporary Christian radio station in their cars and at home, and they hold conservative beliefs on social issues, although they disagree with some extreme positions and approaches of well-known leaders of the Christian right.

For the most part, they grapple with the same things our family does: balancing their stretched budget and busy schedules, deciding what television show or computer game is appropriate for the kids. They don't allow their children to watch *The Simpsons*, but, like their neighbors, they made an accommodation with cultural fads like Beanie Babies, Pokémon, and, after much soul-searching and consultation with Christian friends, the *Harry Potter* books. With their agreement, I frequently use them as a source, a sounding board, and a pipeline to ground-level believers for my newspaper reporting.

Are the Hardaways typical of evangelical Christians, as typical as the Flanderses? It's hard to say. We have gotten to know them pretty well in recent years. Our children attended the same public elementary school, were part of the same scout troops, and often attended the same birthday parties, which meant we were often in and out of each other's houses. They are sophisticated and generally open-minded, and never press their religious or political views on us or on our children. It is apparent, though, that they draw strength from their Christian faith, which they try to apply to every aspect of their lives. I met them before I started watching *The Simpsons*, but I cannot watch the Flanders family without thinking of the Hardaways.

So I showed them an early draft of this chapter and loaned them some tapes from the series and asked them what they thought. "All in all, it would be flattering to be associated with Ned Flanders, based on what I know about the person and how he lives out his faith," said Dan. "There's an element of unconditional love in his life that accurately portrays Christianity." There are Christians who might be put off by some of the idiosyncrasies associated with the character, like "nerdy behavior," he added.

Lorraine agreed that, as a family of believers, they are much closer to the Flanderses than to the Scheibners. "How else are people going to see Jesus' teachings lived out unless they see them in our lives? It's very important that we're part of the world, that others can see the difference he's made and the truth we believe he taught and shared."

Four

The Church and the Preacher: "We Don't Have a Prayer!"

The Hollywood Film Production Code of the 1930s mandated,

> No film or episode in a film should be allowed to throw ridicule on any religious faith honestly maintained. Ministers of religion in their characters of ministers should not be used in comedy, as villains, or as unpleasant persons. The reason for this is not that there are not such ministers of religion, but because the attitude toward them tends to be an attitude toward religion in general. Religion is lowered in the minds of the audience because it lowers their respect for the ministers.

While the code is long gone, the concern remains today. "When clergy are depicted on entertainment programming, their commitment to religion is either ignored completely, or is ridiculed," according to Jim Trammell, of the University of Georgia. "I am concerned that televised messages could influence false expectations and impressions of religiosity. Audiences whose only models of organized religion or spirituality are those depicted on television are perhaps more likely to assume such models are precise. Further, although spirituality is more closely regarded as a personal experience rather than a social function, the fact that television programs have been shown to influence audiences' perception of the social norms has particular ramifications for one's perception of spirituality." In *The Simpsons*, organized religion "is rarely depicted as helping to solve spiritual problems at all, another indicator of the inadequacy of the church."

And at first glance, it may seem that the portrayal of the Reverend Timothy Lovejoy and of Springfield Community Church in *The Simpsons* do stand the Hollywood Code on its head, to the exact effect feared by early industry censors. Although not a leading character in the series, Lovejoy is a major supporting player, presiding at most of the town's weddings and funerals and, in one *Simpsons* comic book, performing an exorcism when Lisa is possessed by the spirit of the pop singer Madonna. His name notwithstanding, this minister does not love joy. Because he is a foil in the series, personifying many of the failings of organized religion and Christian conservatism, he is usually portrayed as a shallow, intolerant, "pandenominational windbag," in the words of Steve Tompkins, who wrote for the series in the 1990s. As such, Lovejoy is a much less rounded character than the other prominent Christian in the series, Ned Flanders. Like other characters in the series, however, the minister has had an impact on the culture: There is a popular Norwegian rock group called "Reverend Lovejoy."

Sam Simon, who with Matt Groening and James Brooks shaped the show at its creation, was "very adamant that we not make [Lovejoy] a cartoony, hypocritical preacher," recalls Al Jean, a longtime writer for the series who became executive producer and "show-runner" in 2001. "He wanted a realistic person who just happened to work as a minister." Thus, the minister *is* hypocritical and occasionally venal, but he is not evil or immoral, merely human. Lovejoy has an interior life that includes a troubled family and a hobby—electric trains—and even a sense of humor. In a lighter moment, the minister snaps Homer in the rear with a towel when they end up in the winning locker room after the Super Bowl. He jogs with George Bush when the former president moves to Springfield, and he is the author of a cookbook, *Someone's in the Kitchen with Jesus.* Lovejoy mixes socially with his parishioners, and he drinks, but not to excess. He once had idealistic dreams for the ministry until, after decades in the pulpit, he came down with a classic case of preacher burnout. His sermons are boring, and he knows it. For the most part, the pastor provides an example of what a minister should *not* be.

What is fascinating about Springfield Community's congregation is the absence of significant internal strife and the overall support it gives its spiritual leader. In every congregation I have
covered as a journalist (or been a part of as a member) there has
been a "clergy party" and an "anticlergy party." Often, this division, or other issues such as biblical interpretation or the music of
worship, creates factions and divisions and, sometimes, splits. I
have come to believe that the reason this occurs so frequently and
can lead to so much bitterness and intense infighting is the depth
of feeling people have about spiritual matters. I think it may also
be a function of the powerlessness people experience in other
spheres of their lives: work, home, school, government bureau-
cracy, and the political system. This is an era of church "shoppers"
and church "hoppers." In their congregations, they can fight as
hard as they like and, if things don't go their way, they can walk
away and join another church down the street or around the corner. Regardless of how disappointed people in Springfield are with
Lovejoy, they don't fire him or leave the church.

However, from time to time, parishioners defect from the minister's flock, usually returning in subsequent episodes. The minister and members alike have voiced concern in recent years about
the Episcopal church next door. Lovejoy is worried that its vibrat-
ing pews are drawing away worshipers—and they are. The Hibbard family and Carl and Lenny are seen swaying blissfully among
the Episcopalians. When a model train wreck at home keeps the
Simpsons' minister from their Christmas service, Homer wonders
if Lovejoy is "cheating on us with the Episcopalians . . . with their
bright, airy narthex and their flaky Eucharist." Lovejoy holds a
church fund-raiser, featuring a distorting mirror to "see how
you'd look in hell" and a halo ring toss game aimed at religious
statues. Bart asks why God needs their money. The purpose of the
fair, Lovejoy explains, is to raise enough money to build a steeple
taller than the one the Episcopalians have.

In another episode, baby Maggie comes down with chicken pox
in the middle of a Sunday service, and Marge looks around for Dr.
Hibbert. When she can't find him, Lovejoy explains from the pulpit that the physician's family "now attends the more boisterous

house of worship." The scene then shifts to the "First A.M.E. Church of Springfield," where the all-black congregation—including all *The Simpsons'* African-American characters, plus boxing promoter Don King—are worshiping in the packed pews. The Simpson family walks in, searching for Dr. Hibbard, and finds the joyous service rocking and swaying. Bart is instantly enthralled, proclaiming, "This is awesome. Black God rules!" Marge apologizes to the congregation for interrupting "while you're rejoicing." Even Homer is swept up in the fervor, shouting, "I can walk again!" Given a sharp look by Marge, he explains that his foot had been asleep.

Reverend Lovejoy is an instantly recognizable and ludicrous character, with his jet-black pompadour and unctuous speaking voice. His office is that of a generic pastor, with painted cinder blocks on one wall and windows on the other. The décor includes a "praying hands" sculpture on the bookshelf and on his desk a set of three swinging, clacking metal balls. Lovejoy is so certain where he is going when he dies that, after a disastrous meal at the Simpsons', he tells Homer that he will see him in hell—"from heaven." The pastor's clerical garb makes it hard to pin down his denomination, probably by the writers' design, but it is probably somewhere between Presbyterian and Lutheran. His standard preaching attire is a plum shirt and tie, under a white robe with deep purple borders. He has been known to use sunscreen for anointing oil. In informal settings, he wears a black shirt and a white clerical collar, sometimes over black shorts, and once said he was considering pectoral implants. A *Simpsons* comic book suggests that in hot weather he wears only boxer shorts and garters underneath his robe. Like many of his colleagues, this preacher is both a writer and a broadcaster. His pamphlets include "Hell, It's Not Just for Christians Anymore" and "Satan's Boners." He cohosts a radio call-in show on Sunday nights with a rabbi and a priest, called "Gabbin' about God," sponsored by Ace Religious Supply, whose motto is, "If we don't got it, it ain't holy." Once, he invited a Mennonite minister to preach in his pulpit. (Groening's father was a Mennonite.)

Lovejoy is politically active, mostly on the local level. The minister belongs to two groups, Citizens' Committee on Moral Hygiene and Citizens for Tamer Television, and is a fixture in most mob scenes. He supports Springfield's ill-fated monorail but denounces the town's biosphere as the devil's playground. In addition to his battered Karmann Ghia, he drives a Book (Burning) Mobile, and in one episode leads a movement to destroy merchandise of the local children's television show host, Krusty, whom he describes as "the clown prince of corruption." At Easter, he refers to a chocolate bunny as a graven image. Lovejoy heads a drive to rid the town of its lone burlesque house when he learns that Homer has sent Bart there to work off a debt. Together with Ned Flanders, the preacher calls on the Simpsons to discuss the matter. Homer assumes their purpose is evangelistic. "Everything is about Jesus," the minister says, except this, which is about what Bart has been up to. Later, Lovejoy is in the crowd bent on destroying the burlesque house where, to his embarrassment, he spots his father in an upstairs window. (The critique of the minister can be even sharper in *The Simpsons* merchandise than it is in the television series. A CD-ROM called "Virtual Springfield" shows a book of Ukrainian erotica and a metal box labeled "hush money" hidden in the preacher's lectern.)

In a welcoming essay in *The Simpsons Guide to Springfield*, Lovejoy explains that the town "has a past steeped in faith and faith-related fund-raising activities."[1] This includes its founding by pioneer Jebediah Springfield, who left his home in Maryland with a band of misguided religious zealots in search of a place they called New Sodom, which later took the name of its founder. Newcomers to town are invited by the minister to worship at Springfield Community Church or, if they prefer, at the local Catholic church or synagogue. "A trip to Springfield can be informative, filling and even fun as long as you plan in advance to pacify our vengeful God . . . by attending church at least once while you are here." They are, however, warned away from local cults, secret societies, and, most of all, "from a small group of people who split off from the Presbyterians to worship an Inanimate Carbon Rod." One of the religious academies in town is Springfield Christian School, whose motto is "We put the fun in Fundamentalist dogma."

Springfield Community Church—or the First Church of Springfield, as it is sometimes called—is in many ways a quite successful congregation. The church is Springfield's central civic institution, second only to the town's community center. Each Sunday the pews are full. Worshipers represent every economic segment of the community, from Mr. Burns to "Cletus the Slackjawed Yokel." Children sit with their parents. African Americans, from Dr. Hibbert and his family to Carl, Homer's coworker at the nuclear power plant, are part of the congregation, as is Dr. Nick Riviera, an immigrant. Even Moe Szyslak, the bartender, who identifies himself as a lifelong snake handler and adherent of Santeria, attends. This is, in part, a plot device, and the lack of ecclesiastical competition may help; Springfield Community appears to be the main Protestant church in town, except for the Episcopalians. Still, many pastors would be happy to look out on such a Sunday morning vista.

The packed and diverse pews notwithstanding, there are serious problems at the church, problems familiar to many mainline churches in America. Worshipers sleep through services, sometimes with their eyes open. They are rarely moved or even involved in the worship experience. While sitting in the church basement, watching a screening of a biblical epic filmed by Flanders in his backyard, Homer's coworker Carl makes a suggestion to Lovejoy, who is sitting next to him. The minister, Carl says, could take a lesson from Ned and inject "a little razzle-dazzle" into his sermons. The preacher says he already does that, "if by 'razzle' you mean 'piety,' and by 'dazzle' you mean 'scriptural accuracy.'" Carl turns to his friend Lenny, who is sitting on the other side of him, and pronounces, "What a tool." The best advice Bart can give to a newcomer is to sit in the back row of the sanctuary. Often, the pastor himself seems to be going through the motions: he hangs a banner at the church's ice cream social announcing, "A Sundae Service You Can Swallow." On Super Bowl Sunday, the sanctuary is nearly deserted, despite the sign outside the church reading "Every Sunday is Super Sunday." *The Simpsons* "implicitly affirms an America in which institutional religion has lost its position of authority, and where personal expressions of spirituality have come to dominate popular religious culture."[2]

At least in respect to its packed, diverse pews, *The Simpsons'* mainline church reality is at variance with statistical reality. Why, in what is said to be an era of cynicism and skepticism, do millions of this edgy show's viewers accept this representation of faithful church attendance in a cartoon? The series' writers say it is because the faith is consistent with the characters. Faith has always been the belief in things unseen, and in that sense it is irrational.

Yet as America in the twentieth and twenty-first centuries became a more educated, prosperous, urban, and suburban society, its mainline religious denominations became more rational in their theology. As a result, their religious practices and rituals became more settled, staid, and, in the eyes of many experts, bloodless. There were two significant holdouts to this trend: African American churches and white Pentecostal congregations, both with roots in the working-class and rural South. These groups favored ecstatic and charismatic forms of worship, soul-stirring preaching and lively music, and throughout the century they continued to thrive.

Beginning in the 1960s, middle-class Americans outside these two traditions also began to seek more emotional release and fulfillment in their faith. They yearned to transcend the rational in their worship—to let go, to embrace an identifiably supernatural God. The result was a dramatic growth of invigorated strains of charismatic and evangelical Christianity—often in nondenominational megachurches—that has also proved attractive to a new wave of Third World immigrants to the United States. By the 1990s, some mainline Christian denominations whose memberships were static or declining recognized that they had to adapt to this change in spiritual consciousness or die. One by one, Catholic, Presbyterian, Southern Baptist, and Reform Jewish congregations, among many others, began to reexamine their practices and, where possible, to incorporate more expressive, mystical, and even ecstatic forms of worship, adding healing services, for example.

People continue to attend a mainline church in Springfield the way they do throughout the nation, and for some of the same reasons. "For most Americans, a preeminent benefit of faith is its capacity to improve individual behavior and personal conduct," according to "For Goodness Sake: Why So Many Want Religion to Play a Greater Role in American Life," a 2001 study prepared by Public Agenda and funded by the Pew Charitable Trusts. "If more Americans were more religious, people believe crime would go down, families would do a better job raising children, and people would be more likely to help each other." So when Bart is caught shoplifting a violent video game, Homer asks him, "Haven't you learned anything from that guy who gives those sermons at church? Captain Whatshisname?"

Most often in the series the debate about whether church is necessary takes place in the Simpsons' family car on Sundays, including one morning when Bart and Lisa announce they are contemplating converting to paganism. Bart's use of bad language in raising the question of why he has to go to church causes Marge to snap. "You just answered your own question with that commode mouth," she says. "Besides, you kids have to learn morals and decency and how to love your fellow man." How many parents, unsure of their own beliefs and their own moral leadership at home, drag their children to church with the same goal in mind, to "get a little goodness in them," in Marge's words?

The First Church of Springfield occupies an open city block near the center of town, on the edge of a run-down industrial and commercial area. It is a low-slung, weather-beaten, brick and stucco building, dominated by a sloped, two-story sanctuary lined with faux stained glass windows. There is a paved parking lot next to the building, surrounded by a chain link fence, where a yellow church bus is parked. The preferred parking spot reserved for the "parishioner of the month" is usually occupied by Ned Flanders's car. In front of the main entrance of the contemporary structure, which is flanked by boxes of foliage, is a marquee that changes weekly, with black letters on a white background. The sign features a variety of messages, ranging from halfhearted and self-conscious efforts to be hip—"God, the Original Love Connection"—to those more in keeping with the pastor's view of theology and the role of the church. The more illustrative include: "Sunday, the

Miracle of Shame," "No Shirt, No Shoes, No Salvation," and "Private Wedding: Please Worship Elsewhere." Ecumenism? "We Welcome Other Faiths (Just Kidding)."

Frequently, the signs serve to undermine what Lovejoy is saying in the pulpit, in the process highlighting the hypocrisy of the church, the preacher, or organized religion. Take gambling, for example. Lovejoy has gone back and forth on this moral dilemma, which has divided congregations across the country and brought churches into conflict with political leaders. He occasionally denounces gambling from the pulpit, but during one of these sermons the marquee outside the church advertises that the church offers the "Loosest Bingo Cards in Town." In fact, according to a *Simpsons* comic book, the bingo committee of the First Church of Springfield has exclusive rights to any gambling activities in the community, except for those operated by Native Americans. Other church signs in the show have promoted the congregation's Monte Carlo night and a "retreat" to Reno, Nevada. As the pastor explains it, "Once something's been approved by the government, it's no longer immoral."

Inside the church, which is too financially strapped to afford (or too far north to need) air-conditioning, the red-carpeted sanctuary appears to seat 100 to 150 worshipers—typical in size among American churches, according to a 2001 study by the Hartford Institute for Religious Research and Hartford Seminary—with a center aisle dividing the rows of wooden pews. Lovejoy preaches from a lectern in the middle of a wide, otherwise unadorned stage about four steps above the floor. A blue banner with a white dove of peace hangs from the lectern, which is flanked by simple floral arrangements. To the far left of the stage is a pipe organ. The liturgical music is normally traditional, and the organist, Mrs. Feesh, seems to play on automatic pilot. But Springfield Community is not immune to the "music wars" that have swept the nation's churches, dividing congregations over traditional and contemporary styles of worship.

Bart has strong feelings on the music issue, once burning pages from a hymnal to build a "holy fire" for a Hindu wedding. One Sunday, hoping to enliven the repertoire, he and his friend Milhouse print up a sheet with a new "hymn," which they distribute to worshipers. "From God's brain to your mouth," Bart promises gleefully. "Get them while they're holy!" The boys title the hymn "In the Garden of Eden" and credit it to "I. Ron Butterfly"—the latter probably a dig at L. Ron Hubbard, the founder of Scientology. The congregation dutifully begins to sing the 1968 rock classic "In A-Gadda-Da-Vida" by Iron Butterfly, and the church begins to rock with sweaty enthusiasm. Homer nudges Marge, reminding her of how they used to make out to this "hymn." A beach ball bounces across the pews and, as the soaring, seventeen-minute song ends, tiny flames flicker, and the exhausted Mrs. Feesh collapses onto her keyboard. Lovejoy suddenly realizes that the music sounds a lot like rock and roll. After the service he punishes Bart by making him clean the organ pipes "that you have befouled by your popular music." Yet even the minister succumbs to the power of contemporary music, inviting both a Christian rock group and a barbershop quartet (which included Homer) to perform during services.

Springfield Community is a full-service church, like many in America. There is a Sunday school for children, where young people ask questions like why God causes train wrecks and where an exasperated teacher can ask, in response, "Is a little blind faith too much to ask?" Bart has been expelled and, before he is readmitted, he is frisked for weapons. His teacher admits that the Bible teaches forgiveness, but she asks why he wants to return. While he was gone, she reminds him, "You were happy, we were happy, everybody was happy—particularly the hamster."

The church offers everything from groups dealing with alcohol abuse, Alzheimer's, and marriage counseling, to picnics and a weekly waffle breakfast. There is a thrift shop whose motto is "Nobody Beats the Rev," where the volunteer clerk, Principal Skinner's cranky mother Agnes, is quick to tell Bart, "Buy something or get out." In some of these settings, Lovejoy is portrayed as callous and judgmental in ways ministers are not supposed to be. After being tossed out of the house for a typical act of boorishness, Homer figures he has a natural ally in the minister. "Reverend Lovejoy will make Marge take me back," he confides to Bart. "He *has* to push the sanctity of marriage or his God will punish him." Not necessarily. On this occasion and again at a marriage retreat, Lovejoy suggests Marge divorce Homer rather than attempting to salvage their union. When Homer confesses at a church-sponsored alcohol abuse meeting that he was so desperate for beer that he "ate the dirt under the bleachers" at a football stadium, Lovejoy replies, "I cast thee out!" Lovejoy visits area prisons to minister to inmates, albeit in his own misanthropic way. Attempting to comfort a death-row inmate about to be executed, who complains that his last meal was filched, the preacher says, "Well, if that's the worst thing to happen to you today, consider yourself lucky."

Like other major characters, Lovejoy has had crises of faith, large and small. Some he overcomes and some he does not. Approaching a pricey new toll booth, the minister's wife worries that they might not have enough money. Lovejoy reaches into the collection basket and tells her, "This one's on Jesus." Suddenly the dashboard Jesus looks sad, so the preacher turns him to face away, saying, "Be cool for once." He reacts differently in the face of incipient disaster. A hoax involving a fake angel convinces the pastor and all of Springfield that the Day of Reckoning has come, prompting him to don his robe and urge people to be calm but also to be afraid. When Homer forgets to reprogram the computer at his nuclear power plant for Y2K turnover, he causes a universal meltdown that seems to end the world: People go to church, where Lovejoy tells them that judgment day has arrived but that it is not too late to repent of their sins, in particular the wearing of "miniskirts and Beatle boots." In another episode, as a comet approaches Springfield, Homer admits that "it's times like this I wish I were a religious man." The next shot is of Lovejoy, ostensibly the man of God, running down the street in a frenzy, shouting, "It's over, people! We don't have a prayer!" Yet when a caller to his radio show asks whether, with all the suffering and injustice in the world, he ever wonders if God really exists, the minister answers with a simple "No."

The church, in the minister's eyes, is synonymous with sacrament, and he is threatened when the two are separated. In a vision of her future, Lisa's wedding is suddenly called off, and Lovejoy tells her that "it never would have happened if the wedding had been inside the church with God instead of out here in the showiness of nature."

There have been at least three more serious challenges to his role in the community, and, significantly, each represents a major challenge facing mainline denominations: cults, New Age beliefs, and Pentecostalism.

1. The cult. Passing through the Springfield Airport one day, Homer falls into the clutches of a cult called the "Movementarians," who invite him to a free weekend at a local resort. The group believes a great spaceship will transport them to a cosmic paradise called "Blisstonia," which is reminiscent of the "Heaven's Gate" cult, whose Southern California members committed mass suicide as they waited to be transported to outer space. With their veneration of a great, all-knowing leader, the Movementarians also bear some resemblance to Scientology, the fashionable cult in Hollywood founded by science fiction writer L. Ron Hubbard. Like them, the Springfield cult's sacred writings include texts such as "Arithmetic the Leader's Way" and "Science for Leader Lovers," and, like the Scientologists, their deadliest weapons against critics are their lawyers.

Other members of the Springfield community are caught up in the cult, including the entire Simpson family. "When I join an underground cult, I expect some support from my family," Homer tells them. Marge, one of the show's strongest Christian believers, resists joining, but Bart volunteers that the cult and church are pretty much the same thing; the cult simply offers a different place to be bored on Sundays and does nothing to change their daily lives. This is yet another attack on the mainline worship experience, except that the seductive nature of many cults is that they offer much more of an emotional connection than traditional Judeo-Christian denominations—even if it is counterfeit and manipulative.

At the cult's wooded compound, Springfield's gullible residents are subjected to real cult practices, including hypnotic repetitions of chants, six-hour meetings glorifying the leader, and attack therapy sessions. Marge is not taken in and makes a daring escape.

Naturally, she goes to the church and the minister for help. She finds Lovejoy, his congregation shrunk to a handful who have resisted the cult, denouncing the Movementarians from the pulpit. Typically and inadvertently, he undercuts the denunciation by highlighting the similarities between "legitimate religion" and cults. "This so-called new religion is nothing but a pack of weird rituals and chants designed to take away the money of fools," Lovejoy says. "Let us say the Lord's Prayer forty times, but first, let's pass the collection plate." The collection is so meager that the minister considers setting fire to the church ("again") to collect the insurance money.

Lovejoy agrees to join Ned Flanders and Willie, the elementary school's strong-willed janitor, to kidnap and deprogram Simpson family members from the cult's compound. After the minister's attempts to subdue Homer with a baseball bat lead to no discernible effect, Lovejoy becomes convinced that the devil has given Homer superhuman strength. The janitor seizes the bat from the minister, dismissing him as a "noodle-armed choirboy." In the Flanderses' basement, where the family is taken, Homer is so resistant to traditional forms of deprogramming that the minister resorts to a more basic approach. He tells Homer that "our commandments" require him to accept a glass of beer, which has been forbidden by the cult. Freed by the taste of forbidden beer, Homer returns to the compound to denounce the cult, causing Lovejoy to shout, "Hallelujah!"

The sudden appearance of the cult's leader, hovering in what appears to be a giant spaceship, shakes the minister's faith. Lovejoy panics at the sight, believing that the cult is "the real deal." He rips off his clerical collar, throws it on the ground, and stamps on it. Just as suddenly, the spaceship comes apart and is exposed as a fake, leaving the leader to flee in what turns out to be an ultralight helicopter that uses his followers' bulging moneybags for ballast. Lovejoy realizes he has abandoned his religion too soon, muttering that he should have stuck with the Promise Keepers, the evangelical men's movement famous for stadium and coliseum rallies. Flanders notices the minister's collar on the ground and asks Lovejoy if it is his. Embarrassed, the minister retrieves it lovingly, wondering aloud how it got there.

2. New Age. Brad Goodman, a self-help guru and infomercial star whose psychobabble videotape has helped ease communication in the Simpson household, comes to Springfield to host one of his "Inner Child" seminars. Most of the community turns out, including the Simpsons. Bart's wisecracks get him called to the stage, where Goodman lauds the boy as an example of healthy, unrepressed behavior. He hails Bart's dictum, "I do what I feel like," as a perfect expression of the permissive, situational ethic. The town's residents are urged to act the same way, leading Bart to believe that this advice has turned him into a god. Even Christians like the Flanders family and Lovejoy are caught up in Goodman's feel-good hysteria. The minister preaches a sermon entitled "Be Like Unto the Boy," complete with readings from the "Book of Bart." (How familiar must this seem to church members who have seen their pastors embrace one fashionable therapy or another?) A "Do What You Feel" festival dissolves into anarchy, however, with two women dressed in togas holding aloft a gold statue of Goodman. "God is angry," Lovejoy decides. "We've made a false idol of this Brad Goodman."

3. Pentecostalism and charismatic worship. A college reunion prank gone awry leaves Homer with a bucket filled with superglue stuck on the top half of his head. Bart drills holes through the metal so his father can still drive, but the car skids off a rural road and through a cornfield, ending up at the "Brother Faith Revival." The service is exhilarating, an old-fashioned tent revival complete with folding chairs, sawdust on the floor, and a cross illuminated by an outline of light bulbs. Dressed in dazzling white, Brother Faith and his evangelical ministry are African Americans who take exuberant joy in worship. They sing and they dance and they exalt the Holy Spirit, urging worshipers to check out John 2:11, where Jesus turns water into wine at the wedding feast in Cana. Brother Faith is not a fake and, as Bart observes, "he dances better than Jesus himself!"

Once, in the rural South, faith healers were said to put a sign outside their tents reading "no broken bones"—for obvious reasons. Brother Faith is not so intimidated, and he successfully lays hands on the dislocated elbow of Cletus, the hillbilly, and shouts, "the power of faith compels you—heal! Take that, Satan!" Next up is the bucket on Homer's head, but this time Brother Faith cannot perform the miracle by himself, so he asks for a "holy helper." Bart, of all people, is chosen. Sure enough, with Brother Faith's help, they remove the bucket from Homer's head. After the revival, as Brother Faith is packing up his snakes, Bart asks how he *really* got the bucket off Homer's head. The evangelist explains that the power came from God, who gave some of the power to Bart. "Really," the boy says, "I would think he would want to *limit* my power." Brother Faith assures him that he too was a hell-raiser as a child until he saw the light and changed his wicked ways. He recommends the same choice for Bart. At first, the boy declines what is clearly a profound invitation, using the logic of many other pragmatic nonbelievers: "I think I'll go for the life of sin, followed by a presto change-o deathbed repentance." That is not "God's angle," Brother Faith says, suggesting, typically for the show, salvation through good works, rather than through grace. "Why not spend your life helping people instead? Then you're also covered in case of sudden death."

Back at Springfield Community Church that Sunday morning, Bart is exposed to his usual brand of Christian worship. Lovejoy drones on with a typical sermon, "Life in Hell"—which is also the title of *Simpsons*' creator Matt Groening's counterculture comic strip. The minister takes as his text Paul's letter to the Corinthians, which he manages to convey as a chain letter gone wrong, until he notices that Bart is squirming in his seat. Foolishly, he asks the boy if he is bored, and Bart answers honestly that he is. "I'm doing the best with the material I have," the minister says, referring to the Bible, although he might just as well be referring to traditional theology and worship. Thinking back on his recent experience in Brother Faith's tent, Bart says that church can be fun, a notion that seems so patently absurd to the rest of the congregation—including the faithful Flanders family—that they burst out laughing. "No, really," he says. "It can be a party, with clowns and lasers and miracles. A real preacher knows how to bring the Bible alive, through music and dancing." Bart's monologue is about as trenchant a critique of mainline Protestantism as one is likely to hear in the mass media. Is worship about substance or simply style? Perhaps he's just talking about "seeker-friendly" congregations like Willow Creek Community Church near Chicago.

Thinking over Brother Faith's advice, Bart decides to give religious revival a try—in a big way—by becoming a backyard evangelist, complete with a cape, a plan to work miracles, and a distinctive exhortation: "Satan, eat my shorts!" Using an exterminator's tent, he starts drawing big crowds, most from Springfield Community. Back at the church, only the faithful Flanderses are in the pew. Lovejoy wonders whether it might be time to "fight razzle with dazzle," but the best he can do is a fractured electric guitar version of "Michael, Row the Boat Ashore." It is, alas, hopeless.

For Lovejoy, the most poignant crises come from within his home—where a copy of *The Last Supper* hangs prominently—and from within his congregation. His family life is a trial. Helen, his sharp-faced wife, is portrayed as a judgmental, antisexual shrew, much like Dana Carvey's Church Lady on *Saturday Night Live*. She describes Michelangelo's statue of David as "filth" because "it graphically portrays parts of the human body, which, practical as they may be, are evil." (Far-fetched? In 2001, people in the small, central Florida town of Lake Alfred demanded that a replica of the masterpiece displayed outside a shop in the business district be draped.) Bart's use of the term "butt" causes her to cover her ears. She is also, as her husband acknowledges, an incurable gossip. After falsely maligning Marge, she pledges, "From now on, I'll use my gossip for good instead of evil." Every Sunday she can be found outside the church with her husband, dutifully greeting parishioners.

The couple's fifth-grade daughter, Jessica, is a classic PK (preacher's kid). While characteristically overdrawn, her story is likely to strike familiar chords among other clergy parents and children. Bart hears the girl, who has just arrived from boarding school, read the scripture one Sunday morning and is instantly smitten. Thinking it is the best way to come on to a minister's daughter, he tries a new persona, a good boy, although it is an awkward fit. "I don't think God's words have ever sounded so plausible," he says after the service. Lisa tells her brother that his chances with Jessica are slight, since "she's a sweet, kind reverend's daughter, and you're the devil's cabana boy."

Things are not always what they seem. Jessica, who now attends Springfield Elementary, takes pity on Bart when he earns three months' detention and invites him to the Lovejoy house for dinner. The meal is not a success. Bart's efforts to come across as a model of good behavior unravel and, in the midst of an off-color joke, the minister tosses him out the door by his ear. Outside, however, a surprise awaits. Telling her father she is going to her room to pray, Jessica slips out and catches up to her suitor. She tells him that he's bad, and she likes him for it. Bart says that she is his ideal first girlfriend—smart, beautiful, and a liar. They share a kiss—and a minor crime spree of vandalism and antisocial behavior.

Yet Bart is soon shocked and unsettled to learn that he is outclassed by the amoral Jessica, and with Lisa's encouragement he determines to break off the relationship at the next opportunity. That comes at church on Sunday, where the sermon topic is "Evil Women in History, from Jezebel to Janet Reno." Bart sits next to Jessica and tells her he wants to stop seeing her because "you're turning me into a criminal when all I want to be is a petty thug." The minister's daughter agrees to change her ways—as she is slipping the collection money into her purse. She allows Bart to be blamed for the theft, telling him later that no one will believe that "the sweet, perfect minister's daughter" would do such a thing. Lisa comes to her brother's rescue the next Sunday at church and exposes Jessica as the thief.

Despite the discovery of the collection money under his daughter's bed, Lovejoy cannot accept the truth, and claims that Bart framed his daughter. This is too much, even for Jessica. The theft, she tells her father, was a classic cry for attention. She reminds the disbelieving pastor that she was expelled from boarding school for stealing from the school chapel's collection, for fighting, and for building a pipe bomb and exploding the toilets. Lovejoy will not hear this—literally—and sings "Bringing in the Sheaves" to drown out his daughter's confession. "Come on, Dad!" she pleads. "Pay attention to me!" Sometimes comedy isn't pretty. The only response the minister can muster to punish the wayward girl, who is no demon seed, is by making her scrub the church steps, which she cons the ever-gullible Bart into doing for her. Still, in a later episode, Lovejoy is seen building a battlebot with his daughter, one with a cross on top.

Theft apart, finances are an ongoing problem at Springfield Community Church. The minister preaches tithing on the gross —not the net—and when the offering is insufficient, he is not shy about sending the long-handled pole and woven wooden basket around again. He urges members to give as if the person next to them is watching, and threatens them with an audit. Lovejoy claims his salary is so low (perhaps taxed by his daughter's private school tuition) that he has to borrow his Bible from the library. He implies that his meager collections inspired him to set a fire in the sanctuary in order to collect the insurance and that, unless things improve, he is contemplating doing it again. On the plus side, he does take care to tally the offering with the door to his office open, using a change counter (rather than a bill counter). The congregation is so desperate for funds it accepts ads for the church bulletin from Fat Tony, the local crime boss.

A deeper problem for the church is Lovejoy's sense of mission. The newly minted minister arrived in Springfield in the 1970s, driving a Volkswagen Karmann Ghia and listening to the Doobie Brothers' "Jesus Is Just All Right" on the radio. With the 1960s over, Lovejoy felt he was in his element, living in a time when "people were once again ready to feel bad about themselves." He called parishioners like Ned Flanders "brother" and invited them to "rap" with him. But by the 1980s he stopped caring and found that, given the atmosphere of the time, no one noticed.

A mere ten years later, Marge notices. Concerned about her family's dogged resistance to attend church and the pastor's failure to meet the spiritual needs of the congregation—mostly in the form of widespread sleeping during service—she goes to visit the pastor. "Sermons about 'constancy' and 'prudissitude' are all well and good," she says, "but the church could be doing so much more to reach out to people." Church, she says, "shouldn't be a chore. It should help you in your daily life." Lovejoy replies that Marge is naïve and idealistic, just as he was when he began his ministry, and that his failures have worn him down. She tells him he shouldn't let a few bad experiences sour him on helping people; he insists he should. But, stung by the criticism of his service to the congregation, he challenges Marge to volunteer and—admitting she is motivated in part by guilt—she agrees.

Marge starts her church work by cleaning up, sweeping the aisles and putting the collection plates in the dishwasher. At first, Lovejoy is grateful for the help, thanking Marge for giving him more time to study and enabling him to discover "a form of shame that has gone unused for seven hundred years." He asks her to answer the church's advice line, which brings her more unsettling news about the pastor. As the "Listen Lady," she learns from Moe, the bartender, that Lovejoy was not encouraging when he called earlier with a problem. With her compassion, common sense, and often-demonstrated commitment to Christian charity, she soon becomes a more and more popular counselor than the preacher. People praise her during Lovejoy's sermons and brush past the minister to speak with her after services. Marge starts to call the pastor "Tim," and treats him like a secretary. Lovejoy sinks deeper into despair. "I am a shepherd without a flock," he prays. "What have I done to lose them?"

The minister preaches that "the Lord will hear your lamentations and give solace to your spirit," and God soon gives evidence that he has heard Lovejoy's own lamentations. Help comes in the form of the saints pictured in the church's stained glass windows (who are imaginatively if improbably named), who come alive and suggest some answers. Thinking the voices are those of disrespectful parishioners, Lovejoy asks, "Could we please not yell out things in church?" The saints respond in kind. They ask what the minister has done to keep his flock, telling him he must inspire their hearts with his bravery. He interrupts and says he has recarpeted the vestibule, which one of the saints calls "the lamest reply I've ever heard. . . . You're just lucky God isn't here." Hmm. The pastor's devastation is nearly complete.

Marge receives a call on the advice line from Helen Lovejoy, herself despondent, asking for advice to perk up her husband, who has sadly retreated to his basement where he runs his electric train set. Marge suggests that he will bounce back after a few days off. When he returns to church, he finds that the Listen Lady is over her head with a problem. Ned Flanders has been abducted from work by a group of thugs and abandoned in a pit of carnivorous baboons at the Springfield Zoo. Lovejoy races to the scene and, making use of his model railroading expertise on the zoo's kiddie train, engineers a heroic, acrobatic rescue of his most faithful parishioner. "Say your prayers, you heathen baboons!" he says, fighting off a counterattack. Flanders thanks his pastor effusively, but Lovejoy passes the credit to Marge, who "taught me there's more to being a minister than not caring about people." The congregation is enthralled as their pastor recounts the rescue in his Sunday sermon, cribbing liberally from "The Charge of the Light Brigade." As he reaches the climax of his story, Homer exclaims, "*That's* religion!"

Absent such dramatic tales, Lovejoy's sermons are a major, ongoing issue, for him and the congregation. Typically, his message is along the lines of, "May we burn in foul smelling fire forever and ever," seasoned with a regular plug for his radio show. Jarred awake during one of the minister's eulogies, Homer shouts, "Change the channel, Marge!" Lovejoy's main complaint from the pulpit, one not unfamiliar in some mainline denominations, is that his parishioners are smug. "Today's Christian thinks he doesn't need God. He thinks he's got it made. He's got his hi-fi, his boob tube, and his instant pizza pie." The scripture passages he uses, when not mangled for comic effect, tend to be obscure, arcane, bloody, or simply meaningless selections from the Old Testament, or depressing readings from Lamentations. To wake people, he sometimes resorts to desperate measures, including sound effects like ambulance sirens and bird calls, and even his own rendition of the song "The Entertainer." Once he offers a baby-sitting discount for anyone who can recall the theme of the sermon he had just finished preaching, but the congregation stares blankly and no one responds with the correct answer: "Love." A sermon about the Samaritan woman at the well, inexplicably advertised out front as "Something about the Virgin Mary," is disrupted when Homer revs a newly won Harley outside the church. Lovejoy gives up, saying "What the heck," and dismisses the congregation, who cheer and stream out of the sanctuary. Homer's excited reaction to another sermon turns out to be a response to the football game he has been listening to with earphones. He admits to the pastor that when he is not sleeping during the sermon he is mentally undressing the female parishioners. Sometimes he even eats. "If God didn't want us to eat in church," he says, "he would've made gluttony a sin."

Kenneth Briggs, former religion reporter for the *New York Times* and a longtime *Simpsons* fan, sympathizes with the pastor: "When you look out at that congregation you get some sense of how difficult it would be to focus that lot on anything." Lovejoy, he said, personifies "the wounded servant. He's not a buffoon." Yet, with a straight face, Lovejoy can tell Bart and Lisa, whom he mistakenly believes are thinking about converting to Judaism, not to make a rash decision, since "the church is changing to meet the needs of today's young Christians." Not this church, however.

Beyond Springfield's congregation and its minister, organized religion in general is a target of many of *The Simpsons'* heartiest satiric wallops. "*The Simpsons* implicitly affirms an America in which institutional religion has lost its position of authority," according to the book *God in the Details*, "and where personal expressions have come to dominate popular religious culture."[3] Mr. Burns, the town's richest man and its most sinister character, warns children at the elementary school in a motivational talk that religion is one of the "demons you must slay if you wish to succeed in business. When opportunity knocks . . . you don't want to be sitting in some phoney-baloney church or synagogue." Bart, taken by his parents to a military school, desperately pleads to be taken home. "I'll do anything!" he says, echoing many recently indicted felons. "I'll find religion!" Before one of the annual Halloween specials, Homer cautions "some crybabies out there—religious types mostly—who might be offended" by the segments to come. The best thing about watching Sunday football on television, he says in another episode, is that it "gets rid of the unpleasant aftertaste of church." Marge tells her husband that "Church shouldn't be a chore. It should help you in your daily life." Well, Homer replies, "It should, but it doesn't." Lisa likes the time right after Sunday service because it represents the longest period before she has to return to church.

The targets are not confined to residents of Springfield or to the series' main narrative. Norman Vincent Peale's birthplace is destroyed in one throwaway sequence. In another, while Homer is dangling naked from a hot air balloon, he drags his rear end along the soaring glass steeple of a church in plain view of the congregation. The building is very reminiscent of the Reverend Robert Schuller's megachurch in Orange County, California. "Now, let us thank the Lord for this magnificent Crystal Cathedral, which allows us to look upon his wondrous creation," the minister prays, as Homer slowly slides by. "Now quickly!" the pastor says, suddenly changing course. "Gaze down at God's fabulous parquet floor. Eyes on the floor . . . still on the floor . . . always on God's floor."

Bart and his friend Milhouse find a copy of *Mad* magazine (in many ways a forerunner of *The Simpsons*' brand of humor) with a folding page designed as a riddle. The puzzle asks, "What do televangelists worship most?" Bart—for once the innocent, or at least the straight, man—says God, and his friend guesses Jesus; when folded properly, the answer is money. The boy's grandfather, Abe Simpson, justifies their attempt to defraud residents of the local retirement home by telling Bart that if they don't take the old folks' money, "they'll just send it to some televangelist."

The Western missionary experience is the subject of an episode in which Homer, trying to avoid paying a prank pledge to public television, flees aboard a Christian relief flight to a small island in the South Pacific. Ill-prepared to be a missionary, he is assured by his bright-eyed and clean-cut predecessors as they depart that they have already made a good start by ridiculing the islanders' beliefs, teaching them some English, and giving them the "gift of shame." After distributing Bibles, Homer's next contributions to their cultural devastation are alcohol and casino gambling, to predictable effect. As "God's messenger," he also provides his own admittedly distorted view of Judeo-Christian faith, although he is stumped when a question that recurs in *The Simpsons* is asked by one of the islanders: If God is all-powerful, why does he care if he is worshiped? When the islanders balk at Homer's suggestion that they build a chapel, he snaps, "Either grab a stone or go to hell." Pleased with their work, Homer says, "Now I may not know that much about God, but I have to say we built an awfully nice cage for him." With the church built, the islanders discuss how often they must attend services to avoid going to hell. Every Sunday for the rest of their lives, one says, while another laughs and asks for a serious answer. Clearly, this is an overdrawn portrait of the Christian missionary experience. Yet for anyone who has studied the experience of, say, eighteenth-century Franciscans in California or American Protestants in Hawaii in the nineteenth century, this episode includes painfully recognizable elements.

Reverend Lovejoy and the First Church of Springfield must be doing something right. Knowing the failures and weaknesses of the man and the institution does not keep people from returning week after week for solace and inspiration and calling when they are in trouble. Like Woody Allen's definition of a second marriage, it is the triumph of hope over experience. Kenneth Briggs, who teaches at Lafayette University, defends *The Simpsons'* overall treatment of Christianity. "I don't see anybody taking any cheap shots. It gives mainline Protestants a fair shake," he told me. "That group is almost constantly maligned or ignored. It's easy to ignore them. This one does give them a fair shake."

Five

Heaven, Hell, and the Devil: "I'd Sell My Soul for a Donut!"

In his version of *Doctor Faustus*, the famous tale about a man who makes a pact with the devil, German writer Thomas Mann described hell as a "soundless cellar, far down beneath God's hearing." Pope John Paul II declared in 1999 that hell is not a physical entity. "Rather than a place, hell indicates the state of those who freely and definitely separate themselves from God," he told a Vatican audience. It is not "a punishment imposed externally by God" but the natural result of an unrepentant sinner's decision to be apart from the divine.[1] Jews do not dwell on the specific nature of hell, called *Sheol* or *Gehenna* in the Old Testament, but view the underworld in a general sense as a dreary, dark, and noiseless place.

In recent years, a vigorous debate has emerged within the evangelical community on the nature of hell. Since the late 1980s, a dozen books have appeared on the subject, debating a provocative and, thus far, minority position that at judgment day, nonbelievers will be obliterated rather than forced to suffer eternal torment in hell. Philip E. Hughes resigned as president of Westminster Seminary to write a book supporting this view, called the "annihilationist" view. Even Billy Graham, one of the world's greatest Protestant evangelists, has questioned the existence of the fires of hell. Most evangelicals, however, hold the traditional view of hell that is embraced by *The Simpsons*. Heaven, for some reason, does not provoke the same intense speculation and drama as its alternative, although Homer attempts to capitalize on an end-of-the-world scare in Springfield with a commercial enterprise by warning that "No one gets into heaven without a glow stick."

Characters on *The Simpsons* have their own expectations and opinions when it comes to the hereafter. Although comic on the surface, they often mask serious theological concerns and controversies. Maude Flanders says she hopes that there will be *Us* magazine in heaven. Grampa Abe Simpson wants to go to "rich man's heaven." Another portrayal of heaven shows founding father Ben Franklin playing air hockey with rocker Jimi Hendrix. Bart's teacher, Edna Krabappel, upon finding herself in hell in a *Simpsons* comic book, observes that at least eternal torment in the underworld "beats teaching." In a Halloween fantasy episode of the show, Homer chokes to death on a piece of broccoli and is surprised to find himself before Saint Peter, who is playing solitaire at the pearly gates. His first reaction is to shout down to earth exultantly to his pious neighbor, Ned Flanders, that he got there first. However, in order to pass through the gates, Homer is required to do one good deed in the next twenty-four hours, which he does. Saint Peter, however, doesn't notice the accomplishment, so Homer lands in hell. Near death after a heart attack in another episode, Homer regains consciousness and tells the doctor he had a vision of "a wonderful place filled with fire and brimstone, and there were all these guys in red pajamas sticking pitchforks in my butt." In another episode, Homer, nearing death, acknowledges, "Now I prepare myself for an eternity of fire and poking."

Getting to heaven offers another possibility for exploring theology, especially in biblical subjects related to the end of the world: the rapture, the apocalypse, Armageddon, and the second coming. Generally grouped under the heading of "end times" and centered around the New Testament's book of Revelation, these issues form the basis of the fabulously successful Left Behind series of potboiler novels, which have sold well over fifty million copies. None of the readers of these books would have agreed with Thomas Jefferson, who had no affection for the book of Revelation. In an 1825 letter to his friend Alexander Smyth, the former president wrote that the last book of the New Testament, with its violent battle scenes and fantastical imagery, was "merely the ravings of a maniac, no more worthy, nor capable of explanation than the incoherences of our own nightly dreams."

The Simpsons' experience of the end times comes through a big screen version of the Left Behind series, here called *Left Below*—despite the fact that the original series was never a hit in theaters. Homer, Bart, and Lisa stumble into a cineplex in time to see the screen family having a discussion not unlike one that took place in their own home. It's Sunday morning and, while the mother and children in the movie are getting ready to leave for church, the father says he'd "rather play golf on the holiest day of the week." Homer instantly recognizes a kindred spirit and says he hopes good things happen to this character. The prospects are not likely, as the mother worries that world problems indicate that the rapture may be approaching. The father scoffs that "religion is just an old wives' tale." Sure enough, while the cynic is making out in a limousine with a woman who is not his wife, the rapture takes place, amid dark clouds and lightning. "The virtuous have gone to heaven—and the rest of us have been *left below*," the movie father says. "We were fools, and because we rejected God and tacitly accepted Satan, we must suffer through the apocalypse." Again, this is at least a partial misstatement of Christian theology: It is not virtue that provides a ticket to heaven; it is the acceptance of Jesus as savior. Although there is nothing in Revelation suggesting that a flood will immediately follow the rapture, the screen image does provide the opportunity for a good joke. A woman floating by on the rising floodwaters wails, "Why did I put my faith in science and technology?" She is hanging on to a TV set, answering her own question.

The movie has a mesmerizing effect on Homer, who takes the story as both fact and gospel. That night, he cannot sleep. "What if the rapture is coming and I haven't led a good enough life? I could be left below." Marge tries to comfort him, saying that God wouldn't spring the rapture on them without warning. But instead of the more traditional signs, "wars and rumors of wars," she suspects it will be something more dramatic, like all the dogs boarding spaceships and leaving Earth. Events—all obviously (to us) coincidental—conspire to play on Homer's foreboding. While

Homer is stopped at a light the next morning, a character dressed as the devil for a fast-food promotion approaches his car. A few seconds later, blood rains from the sky—from an injured whale being transported by helicopter. Homer needs no more proof that the day of judgment is at hand. He heads directly to a Christian bookstore, an outlet called "Gospel for Less," and, yes, Christian discounters do exist. There Homer loads up on books about the apocalypse, including one titled *1987: Year of Armageddon*. (This may be a dig at Hal Lindsey's apocalyptic book, *The Late Great Planet Earth*, which in 1970 predicted that the end of the world was approaching in the near future. More than fifteen million copies of the nonfiction book have been sold.) However, Homer is not entirely swept away by his religious fervor: he rejects the clerk's offer of the "Friends of Flanders" discount.

At the kitchen table, Homer immerses himself in his books about the rapture, and, using a chalkboard, calculates that the event is nigh—within the week, in fact. The date is 3:15 p.m. on May 18. Although he has not lived a virtuous life (much less professed faith in Jesus), Homer reasons that he can earn his way to the rapture by proclaiming its imminent arrival. "There's no way in God's heaven that I can get into God's heaven. But maybe he'll let me in if I warn others the apocalypse is coming." So he dons a sandwich board and carries a bell and a Bible, proclaiming in the streets of downtown Springfield that the end is near. "God loves you," he says. "He's gonna kill you!" Reading from Revelation 6:13 on TV, Homer warns that the stars will fall from the sky before the rapture. Kent Brockman headlines his story, "Sad drunk to mad monk?" Watching the report at home that evening, Lisa—ever the rationalist—tells her father she doesn't think the world will be coming to an end anytime soon; she figures it will end in about a hundred years, but that it will be caused by global warming. Marge and Bart agree that Homer should lighten up, and he acknowledges that it all seems a little silly. However, the next story on the news—a live broadcast—shows the Air Force's Blue Angels colliding with a Duff Beer blimp, dumping the celebrities on board to the ground. The stars are falling, just like it says in the Bible, as Homer nods knowingly.

The rest of Springfield interprets the event the same way, streaming to the front lawn of their prophet and asking for advice on how to save themselves. Taking them inside, Homer tells them that at the appointed time they should gather at Springfield Mesa, just outside town, a location that has come to him in either a vision or a drunken haze. (Here the allusion is to Steven Spielberg's 1977 film *Close Encounters of the Third Kind*, which ended atop Devils Tower in Wyoming.) Flanders wanders over, asking if this is a pre-rapture party to which he has not been invited. It is, but Homer runs him off by explaining that it is a meeting of "Gay Witches for Abortion." On the day of the rapture, a yellow school bus pulls up in front of the Simpsons' home with a banner reading, "Heaven or Bust." As usual, Lisa is skeptical. "All through history, self-appointed seers have predicted the end of the world," she reminds them, "and they've always been wrong." Homer insists he has a good feeling this time, and Marge says they are taking no chances. "No one in this family is going to be left below," she says. En route—with the Flanders family on board this time—they all sing a version of "Ninety-nine Bottles of Beer on the Wall" that goes, "Ninety-nine minutes until we're all saved, ninety-nine minutes to go. Unless it turns out, that we're not devout, then you're gonna be left down below." But when the appointed time comes, nothing happens except for rain. Homer beseeches them and then commands them to stay, to no avail. Everyone leaves except Homer himself, who finally gives up and returns to Springfield in disgrace.

Like any prophet who comes up short, or who delivers an unpopular message, Homer is reviled. "Nostradamus," the Comic Book Guy hisses. Neighborhood toughs beat him up. He can find no solace at Moe's Bar—it's no longer there. Believing his friend's prophecy, Moe sold to Japanese restauranteurs and donated the proceeds to charity. At home, Homer throws away his rapture books. But taking a second look at Da Vinci's *The Last Supper* painting, he suddenly realizes that he miscounted the number of people in the painting, which threw off his calculation for the rapture. Redoing the figures, he sees that the event is due in just thirty minutes. This time, even his family won't join him. Undeterred, he races to the mesa just in time to be raptured to heaven. He rings the bell at the pearly gates impatiently and is greeted by a vaguely effete guide, who takes him on an airborne tour of paradise. The place looks like an upscale destination resort—elegant rooms, pools, theater, water slide (under construction), nature walk—and offers anything he desires. Homer asks to see his family and, on a large, flat-panel TV screen he sees them on earth, swimming in a fiery lake and suffering various torments. The worst of these, he hears Marge say, is not seeing him again.

This is too much for Homer. He takes his case to God, riding the escalator to heaven's upper level. "I can't enjoy myself knowing my family suffers," he tells the Almighty. But he doesn't get much headway. "Oh, don't tell me about suffering. My son went to earth once," God says. "I don't know what you people did to him, but he hasn't been the same since." Jesus is seen, looking dazed and hurt, on a tangled swing. Homer says he'll be fine and asks again that his family be spared. "Pass," God says. Never one to understand his stature in the cosmos, Homer storms off, saying, "You made yourself a powerful enemy!" Still, he is no Lucifer. The worst he can do is go on a rampage, dumping trashcans, smashing storefronts, and annoying the other inhabitants. This brings God back, arms folded and tapping his Birkenstock, trying to decide what to do with Homer. "I'm sorry," Homer says, "but heaven isn't heaven without my family in it." God sighs and asks Homer what he wants. To put off the rapture, he replies, which would require turning back time. When the Almighty protests, Homer reminds him that Superman did just that in a movie. God agrees, and Homer asks for one more favor, which he whispers in his ear. Saying the magic—if ironic—words "Deus ex machina," God turns back the clock. Homer awakens on the mesa, returns to Springfield, and finds that his other request has been granted: Moe's is back the way it was. "Thank you, Lord," Homer says, taking his place at the bar. "This is heaven." As the camera pulls back, the lineup along the bar replicates *The Last Supper.*

This episode is the second treatment of the rapture and the apocalypse in *The Simpsons*, repetition being an occupational hazard for a long-running series with an interest in faith and religion. In an earlier episode, the family sleeps through an Easter service, only to see that the apocalypse has begun. Despite her religious skepticism, Lisa's pure heart allows her to drift toward heaven with the Flanders family and other Christians—until Homer grabs her by the foot and brings her back to earth. The ground opens up and Homer descends to hell, first happy to smell barbecue but then screaming in agony as he learns that they are out of hot dogs and there is only German potato salad and coleslaw with pineapple.

The nature of heaven and hell is a topic that comes up often at Sunday school at Springfield Community Church. Unlike many mainline Protestants—and the pope—characters in *The Simpsons* believe unquestionably in a very literal interpretation of both concepts. If a person has been good, says the teacher, Ms. Albright, he or she will go to heaven, where "you get to do whatever you like best." This, of course, runs counter to Protestant theology, in which salvation comes through grace and not works. Still, the hair-splitting children want to know where God draws the line for admission. The teacher's call is "yes" for righteous ventriloquists but "no" for their dummies, "no" for cavemen, and a toss-up for robots with a human brain. Bart raises the question, in deceptively simple fashion, about bodily resurrection, which echoes some of Christianity's early theological debates. He wants to know if a good person who loses a leg in a fight will be reconnected with the limb in heaven. Ms. Albright replies yes, the body will be made whole. For the children, the teacher's most disturbing ruling, concerning the nature of the soul, is that animals won't be going to heaven. This thought literally dumbfounds Homer when Bart passes along the news on the way home from church. "I can understand how they wouldn't want to let in those wild jungle apes," he says, "but what about those really smart ones who live among us, who roller skate and smoke cigars?"

Hell exerts an equal, if not greater, fascination for the children in Sunday school. It is, Ms. Albright explains, a terrible place: "Maggots are your sheet, worms your blanket. There's a lake of fire, burning with sulfur. You'll be tormented day and night, forever and ever. As a matter of fact, if you actually saw hell, you'd be so frightened you would die." Martin, one of Springfield's brighter children, takes the obvious message from his teacher's description. "So what you're saying is that there's a downside to afterlife," he says, and asks how to "steer clear of the abode of the damned." Again, the teacher's answer is "do good works and avoid sin" rather than "accept Jesus." Bart wonders if hell might not be something you would get used to, like water in a hot tub, and is assured it is not.

Reverend Lovejoy's visions of the torments of hell are at least as vivid as the Sunday school teacher's and would be familiar to worshipers in the most primitive of backwoods churches. Trying to get the children to confess to a prank, the preacher has them repeat what is obviously a familiar litany of what will happen to them if they fail to come clean. The consequences, they acknowledge, include going straight to hell, where they will "eat naught but burning hot coals and drink naught but burning hot cola. . . . Where demons will punch me in the back. . . . Where my soul will be chopped up into confetti and strewn upon a parade of murderers and single mothers. . . . Where my tongue will be torn out by ravenous birds." The exercise has the desired effect. Bart's friend Milhouse gets the minister's message, is appropriately terrified, and turns Bart in.

There is some speculation about whether Bart is himself demonic. His teacher at Springfield Christian School, where the boy goes after being expelled (again) from public school, warns the other students to avert their eyes from him because the trouble-making boy might take on other manifestations. Bart gets a closer look at hell in another episode when, while recklessly skateboarding, he is hit by a Rolls-Royce carrying his father's boss, Montgomery Burns. The boy seems to be dead, and his spirit rises skyward from his body, riding a celestial escalator. A heavenly voice warns Bart to hold on to the handrail and not to spit over the side—which he immediately does, sending him straight to hell. The underworld tableau he finds is a variation of Hieronymous Bosch's *Garden of Earthly Delights*. Bart introduces himself to the devil in typical fashion, asking, "Who the hell are you?" The devil replies that the boy has earned eternal damnation for a lifetime of evil deeds and that spitting over the handrail just clinched it. But Satan checks his computer and finds that a mistake has been made, that Bart is not expected for almost a hundred years. "Boy, is my face red," the devil says. Departing for the world above, Bart asks if there is anything he can do to avoid returning to hell. Yes, the devil says, but it would mean changing his life in a way he wouldn't like. Instead, the devil instructs him to "lie, cheat, steal, and listen to heavy metal music," which Bart enthusiastically agrees to do.

In a Halloween fantasy segment, Bart cheerfully volunteers that he would be willing to sell his soul for a Formula One racing car, which the devil tells him can be arranged. The boy changes his mind in time to avert disaster, and his mother tells him to stop pestering Satan. But on another occasion, Bart takes the prospect of a soulless existence much more seriously. His revelation follows a debate among three children on the nature of the soul. Bart says he does not believe the soul exists, that it is just something people have made up to scare children, "like the boogie man or Michael Jackson." His friend Milhouse disagrees, explaining that every religion believes in the soul, that it is strong enough to swim away if you die in a submarine or roll on wheels if you die in the desert. He also tells Bart, correctly, that people once believed the soul could escape the body during a sneeze. That is the reason we say "God bless you," Milhouse continues, to squish it back in the body. Sister Lisa, ever the voice of enlightenment, argues that the soul is "the most valuable part of you," the only one that lasts forever. Whether or not it is physically real, she says, "it's the symbol of everything fine inside us." (The humor in the scene notwithstanding, bear in mind that this discussion is taking place in an animated sitcom, not on a Bill Moyers special on PBS.)

Bart determines to test his thesis of the soul's nonexistence by selling his to Milhouse for five dollars, writing out the deed on church stationery and immediately spending the money on a set of colorful dinosaur sponges. Suddenly, his life begins to change dramatically: Automatic doors don't open when he approaches, his breath does not produce condensation on the door of a frozen food compartment, he sees no humor in his favorite television cartoon show, and he takes no joy from pranks. He realizes that his essence has departed. Lisa reminds him of his error by saying grace before dinner that pointedly asks blessings for "every soul in Christendom." Bart gets the message. He tries to buy his soul back from Milhouse, only to learn that the price has gone up to fifty dollars, which he does not have. That night, he dreams of his friends cavorting with their beloved souls while he has none, and he awakes screaming. Returning to his friend to plead for his soul in the middle of the night, Bart is told that Milhouse has sold it to the creepy guy who owns the comic book store. At dawn, the owner tells the boy that it has been sold again to a buyer he will not identify.

In crisis, Bart turns to prayer again, and again on his knees. "Are you there, God?" he asks plaintively. "It's me, Bart Simpson. I know I never paid too much attention in church, but I could really use some of that good stuff now. I'm . . . afraid. I'm afraid some weirdo's got my soul and I don't know what they're going to do with it! I just want it back. Please?" he says, weeping. With that, his soul miraculously floats down from above. But the intervention is not entirely divine, and the explanation for it is not directly from the Judeo-Christian tradition. Lisa tells him she went into her piggy bank to buy back her brother's soul. You know, she tells him, "some philosophers believe that nobody is born with a soul—that you have to earn one through suffering and thought and prayer, like you did last night."

In the DVD commentary that accompanies this episode, Matt Groening points out that this is a typical example of how religion is treated throughout the series. "We have it every which way," he says. "There is a heaven. There is a hell. We show God. He had a white beard." The episode's writer, Greg Daniels (who would go on to create *King of the Hill*), chimes in that he went to church as a child and even attended a Baptist retreat, where he pulled a similar stunt. He paid fifty cents for the soul of a gullible camper, later extorting much more to give it back. "I love these religious shows, these spiritual shows," says Groening, "because they please both the Christians and the atheists. Each has their own belief or nonbelief system." Another voice on the commentary says, "This episode actually is religious, but it's sort of in a secular way. It does advocate the concept of a soul, but no particular religion is really specified." Plus, it gets in the requisite jabs at organized religion. Matt signs off the commentary by saying, "See you in hell."

Homer has an even closer call with eternal damnation in another Halloween fantasy episode. Daydreaming—as usual—at his workstation at the nuclear power plant, he wakes to find that his coworkers have made off with all his precious donuts. "I'd sell my soul for a donut," he exclaims, and the devil suddenly appears to offer the deal, in the person of Ned Flanders ("It's always the one you least suspect," he says). Taking a stab at fairness, Satan wants to explain the ramifications of the deal, but Homer cuts him off, asking if he has the donut or not. He takes the devil's fiery pen, signs the agreement, and begins to gobble the cruller. According to the deal, the instant the donut is consumed, Homer's soul will belong to the devil. In an unexpected and uncharacteristic display of wit, he saves a tiny piece of the donut and, in so doing, all his soul. "I'm smarter than the devil," Homer concludes from the experience, still facing an eternity of hard time. Infuriated at being outwitted, the devil turns into a fearsome beast—to the strains of Mussorgsky's *A Night on Bald Mountain*—and hurtles back to Hades in a ball of fire.

There are limits to Homer's self-control, as there are to his intelligence. That same night he wanders sleepily into the kitchen, reaches into the refrigerator, and finishes off the last morsel of the donut. Instantly, the devil is back to collect his prize. Homer's noisy resistance to being dragged to hell attracts the rest of the family, and quick-thinking Lisa demands a fair trial. The devil agrees to a midnight hearing the next day, insisting on taking her father to hell until then. Life in hell is not a pleasant one, as Matt Groening has made clear for years in his comic strip. First, Homer is hacked to pieces and fed into a sausage machine. Then his head is used as a bowling ball by a demon, striking spiked pins. There is a room called "Hell Labs: Ironic Punishments Division" (a crib from Dante's *Inferno*) in which Homer is strapped to a chair and force-fed donuts. Alas, the irony is lost on the gluttonous prisoner, who exhausts his robotic metal tormentor before the device exhausts his appetite.

Homer's trial that night in the Simpson family living room is an adaptation of Stephen Vincent Benet's "The Devil and Daniel Webster." Locked in a flaming cell, Homer has little to say in the proceeding. As in the famous story, the devil here stacks the jury with infamous malefactors, including several of Benet's originals such as Benedict Arnold and the pirate Blackbeard. Among *The Simpsons'* additions to the panel is Richard Nixon, who addresses Satan as "Master." The devil presents what seems to be an open-and-shut case, and the Grim Reaper is about to flip the switch on Homer. He is saved only when Marge offers as last-minute evidence their wedding picture, on the back of which the groom has written a pledge to give his soul to her forever. The unambiguous message? Traditional family values: true love and marriage will save your soul.

But what happens when the Simpsons' marriage itself comes under siege, as it has from time to time in the show's run, or when Homer and Marge are divided over a moral issue? Is there enough individual religious faith to sustain them and help them make the right decisions?

Six

Moral Dilemmas: "Dad, We May Have Saved Your Soul."

C haracters in *The Simpsons* face moral dilemmas, large and small, on a regular basis. They often fall short when confronted by these challenges: Bart lies and steals, almost reflexively; Lisa sometimes does not honor her father; Homer covets Ned Flanders's wife and those of his neighbors' possessions he has not already borrowed; even saintly Marge becomes addicted to gambling. On the big issues, at least when cornered, they do better. Four episodes in particular place major moral dilemmas center stage, one dealing with theft and three dealing with adultery. In each case, the characters grapple with temptation in a serious way and, in the end, do the right thing. But what is as instructive as the resolution of these dilemmas is the process the characters go through to make their decisions, and the lessons they take from them.

The episode "Homer vs. Lisa and the Eighth Commandment" has the structure of an exquisitely crafted, twenty-two-minute sermon. It could easily have been composed in the finest of seminaries—evangelical or mainline, Christian, Jewish, or Islamic. Good sermons begin with scripture, and this one is no exception. Homer dreams that he is with the children of Israel at the foot of Mount Sinai as Moses returns with the law. He is identified as "Homer the thief," and his friends are a carver of graven images and an adulterer. (The carver of graven images bears a resemblance to Reverend Lovejoy; the adulterer to Jacques, a bowling alley gigolo we will soon meet.) The lives of all three are about to be fundamentally changed as Moses reads the Ten Commandments: Now they are all out of work.

Homer is brought back to the present by the sound of neighbor Ned chasing off a cable television installer who has offered an illegal hookup for fifty dollars, with no monthly payments to follow. The deal sounds so good to Homer that he tracks the man down and is soon plugged in, making the announcement to his family when they return home. Marge is concerned about the arrangement's illegality, but she is distracted when a women's network comes on the screen. As the days wear on, the family becomes increasingly fascinated by the diversity—and triviality—of the world of cable.

At church the next Sunday, Reverend Lovejoy preaches a sermon about the love of possessions and self-satisfaction, making no impression whatever on Homer. In Sunday school, however, the lesson is about the Ten Commandments, and when the teacher gets to "Thou shalt not steal," Lisa makes the connection. She envisions her house falling away, replaced by the fires of hell, where the devil has joined her family on the couch to watch cable programming. Satan invites her to join them, saying there would be no cost—"except your soul!" Returning to reality, she runs screaming from the living room. Later, she confronts her father, who is increasingly fixated on the new television programming. With typical overstatement, Lisa tells him that one reason that the world is a cesspool of corruption is widespread theft, which is a sin. Homer agrees, until his daughter points out that watching television on the illegal hookup is a good example of theft. He is impervious to her arguments and tries to compromise her with programming about her beloved horses. She resists, saying she'd rather go to heaven than watch.

In creating this episode, said writer Jeff Martin, the staff decided from the outset to use "a very strict construction of the Eighth Commandment," despite the fact that cable theft is "essentially a victimless crime, the kind of thing that many, many good people do." Thus, this apparently benign occasion of sin begins to have wider implications for the family, as it often does in real life. While his parents were out of the house, Bart discovered an adult cable channel that features naked women and is now charging admission for his classmates to watch. Homer discovers them and tells Bart not to watch because the channel is only for "mommies and daddies who love each other very much," an interesting rationale for his libertarian view of soft-core pornography. The rot has clearly set in, and it is spreading.

The next day the cable installer lets himself into the Simpson house and offers to sell Homer some stolen stereo equipment, figuring that someone open to pirated cable would be open to other stolen goods. Homer refuses, but because the cable installer had so easily gained entry into his house, he becomes obsessed with security and installs bars on his windows and a sign saying "No Thieves" on his lawn. "There are thieves everywhere," he explains to Marge, "and I'm not talking about the small forgivable stuff." That would be forgivable stuff like illegal cable television. The message is clear: For every thief there is a victim of theft, buying stolen goods makes you complicit in the theft, and often the perpetrator becomes a victim-in-kind; or to return to the Bible, "A man reaps what he sows" (Gal. 6:7).

Stymied in her efforts to save her father from sin, Lisa goes to Reverend Lovejoy for advice on how to handle the situation at home. She asks if it is stealing for a person to take bread for a starving family. The pastor replies that it would be stealing only if the thief put jelly on the bread, that is, if he or she took more than what was needed for survival. After this bit of sophistry, the pastor gives the girl some good advice, applicable for other children who find themselves in similar straits where their values are out of sync with those of their parents. Lovejoy suggests that she set an example by not watching cable television and that she explain to her family why she has made that decision. There is theological precedent for this approach, a principle in Jewish law called *shalom bayit*, translated as "peace in the home." What this means is that family harmony should prevail whenever possible, with an emphasis on flexibility, without compromising personal integrity. Lisa takes the minister's advice, announces her decision to her father, and pledges to say no more on the subject.

Her campaign has an effect, and Marge begins to waver. She suggests to her husband that they unhook the cable, but he is adamant. A highly promoted heavyweight title fight is coming up

and is available only on cable. Homer invites friends and coworkers to the house, which raises even more discomfort. Frantically,
he asks Bart to help him hide items that he admits he has stolen
before their owners arrive at the house: mugs from Moe's Tavern
and a computer from the nuclear power plant. The web of deceit
widens. Two police officers come to the door and announce that
they have heard Homer has an illegal cable hookup. Homer, fearing he is about to be arrested, blames it all on Marge. Instead, the
lawmen say they simply want to watch the fight—more corruption. In a prefight interview, one of the boxers talks about his time
in prison, and Homer imagines himself in the same situation, cut
off from his family. He gives up.

On the lawn, where Lisa and Marge are camped out in protest,
Homer apologizes for interrupting their judging of him. He
makes two announcements: He will cut the cable when the prize
fight is over, and he is not too fond of his wife and daughter for
having driven him to this decision. Unfazed, Lisa says, "Dad, we
may have saved your soul." Despite Bart's pleas to reconsider—
"tractor pulls, Atlanta Braves baseball, Joe Franklin"—Homer
cuts the cable.

Marge has both thrown her husband out of the house and left
him a number of times over the course of the series. Yet after ten
years of marriage, they appear to have a healthy and loving union,
which includes a realistic sexual relationship that ranges from arid
to exuberant. It is also apparent that when it comes to thinking
about other women, Homer is no angel. He likes skin magazines
and he makes lascivious remarks about Maude Flanders—although
with no intention of pursuing her. On a wild, drunken binge in
Las Vegas with Ned Flanders, the two men may have married
cocktail waitresses, matches apparently not consummated. Homer
goes to a bachelor party at a local restaurant where Bart uses a
mail-order spy camera to photograph him cavorting with a belly
dancer. The picture circulates around town, mortifying Marge
and getting Homer kicked out of the house. He finishes the
episode on the stage of a burlesque show, telling the audience
(including Marge) that, "as ridiculous as this sounds, I would

rather feel the sweet breath of my beautiful wife on the back of my neck as I sleep than stuff dollar bills into some stranger's G-string."

In each of the episodes that focus on the serious temptation of adultery, neither Homer nor Marge seeks to stray from marital vows. They are, in that sense, typical innocents who run into danger by happenstance, good intentions and, in Marge's case, emotional need.

Homer embarrasses Marge yet again, in this case at the movies, by loudly giving away the ending of a suspense film. His wife shuts him up, to the applause of audience members and to Homer's shame. On the drive home with the kids, Marge fails in her efforts to apologize to her husband, and Homer is still hurt and angry as a result of the public humiliation. He drops the family off and says, angrily, that he's going and "I don't know when you'll see me again." Driving out into the boondocks, he finds a rowdy country-and-western bar. A waitress named Lurleen Lumpkin sings a song she has written, "Your Wife Don't Understand You, But I Do," which Homer later tells her, "touched me in a way I've never felt before." He returns home the next morning, singing the song and affecting a Southern accent. When he goes to his regular tavern he reveals that he has been to another bar, an act of unfaithfulness that shocks Moe, the proprietor. Unable to get Lurleen's tune out of his head, Homer goes to visit the waitress in her mobile home and tells her he wants others to hear it as well. He takes her to a nearby mall, where she records the song on a CD at Lucky Records, for twenty-five cents. The clerk at the recording booth likes it and asks Homer if he can pass it along to his brother, who owns a local radio station.

The plaintive song is an instant hit, captivating listeners in all walks of life. Although Bart is immune, even level-headed Lisa is taken with it: "I can feel her sweet country soul in every digitally encoded bit." Marge recognizes that the situation is getting out of hand and she demands to know from Homer what is going on. He tells her, truthfully, that nothing untoward has taken place. "Nothing," however, includes watching Lurleen try on outfits in her trailer, which he insists is not seamy. When Lurleen calls the house and asks Homer to come over, he asks Marge's permission before agreeing. At her trailer, the singer says that one of the reasons she trusts him so much is that no other man in her life has been nice to her without wanting something in return. Homer does not understand what she is saying, but he agrees to become her manager. She takes him to a store called the "Corpulent Cowboy," where she outfits him in a white-fringed jacket, bolo tie, and Stetson.

Homer, who now calls himself Colonel Homer, returns home after midnight to find a furious Marge, who again wants to know if he is having an affair with Lurleen. Her husband denies it, but admits that he let the singer kiss him several times. Marge says she doesn't want Homer to be Lurleen's manager, something he says is his boyhood dream. He is determined to make her a star. Marge fumes and Homer leaves. But the entire Simpson family now becomes involved in the star-making machinery and, to his wife's chagrin, Homer invests their life savings in the effort. At the recording studio, Marge meets Lurleen for the first time and doesn't like what she sees, starting with the kiss the singer gives her husband and the fact that she is not, as Homer told her, overweight. Lisa accompanies Lurleen on the recording of another love song, "Bagged Me a Homer," but the session is disrupted by the sound of Marge grinding her teeth. The new song is a hit, and the Simpson children become totally involved in Lurleen's burgeoning career by packaging the CDs. At the same time, they are not oblivious to the darker side of success. Lisa says that she never thought she'd see another woman in her dad's life; Bart disagrees, citing Betty Crocker, Sara Lee, and Aunt Jemima.

When Homer arranges a television appearance for Lurleen, she suggests a new song she has written that might "heat things up," called "Bunk with Me Tonight." The lyrics constitute a direct, almost explicit invitation to Homer. Nonetheless, it takes a second run-through before Homer understands what is being offered. He declines the offer and returns home, where the crisis has not passed. Marge tells her sister that she is in a no-win situation and doesn't know whom to root for. If Lurleen's career fails, the family is broke; if the singer succeeds, Marge loses her husband. The climactic event is Lurleen's television appearance. As the Simpsons prepare, Marge says, "You've got a wonderful family, Homer. Please don't forget it when you walk out that door tonight."

In the singer's dressing room, Lurleen makes one more attempt. She locks and bolts the door and kisses Homer, asking if there is anything he needs. At this moment, he tells her, he sees his entire sex life flashing before his eyes—a series of slaps and rebuffs until he meets Marge. He tells Lurleen that all he wanted to do was to share her voice with others and that he has accomplished that. Homer knows what his priorities are: "I'd better get out of here before I lose my family." Just to make sure he knows what he is giving up, he sticks his head back in the room and asks the singer if she was offering to go "all the way" with him, and she nods. Homer sells Lurleen's management contract to a Japanese company for fifty dollars and heads home. Marge is in the bedroom, naked beneath the covers, watching Lurleen's show on television. Homer, abashed, asks his wife if there is room in their bed for a "gad-durned fool." There always has been, she replies as he undresses. Lurleen sings another song for Homer, "Stand by Your Manager," with the last line, "I hope Marge knows how lucky she is." Marge says that she does, and Homer throws his hat onto the camera, turning the screen black. The marriage is preserved and Homer's fragile self-image is restored. If only life were always that simple.

Many adulterous affairs begin at the workplace, experts say. Factors such as the familiarity of day-to-day contact, a sense of common purpose, and business trips can offer a multitude of opportunities for a partner to stray. All of these factors are present in "The Last Temptation of Homer." There is a vacancy in the safety section of the Springfield Nuclear Power Plant, and the Labor Department tells Mr. Burns that it is time to hire the plant's first female employee. This sets up a situation that has been of great concern to stay-at-home wives like Marge Simpson who believe that women in the work place—especially in high-stress, blue-collar jobs like police work, firefighting, and the military—can pose a threat to marriage. Can men and women be coworkers and avoid romantic entanglements?

In typical fashion, the candidate selected for the job at the nuclear power plant is overqualified: Mindy Simmons has an engineering degree and is assigned to work with Homer, who barely finished high school. She is also attractive, and the moment the introduction is made, Homer has a vision of Mindy naked on a clamshell, à la Botticelli's *The Birth of Venus*, a hallucination accompanied by swelling violin music and hovering cupids. Wisely recognizing trouble in the making, he flees his new colleague. After work, Homer notices Mindy leaving on her motorcycle and he is pleased to note that he is not reacting the same way he did when he met her—no visions or goose bumps. After driving off, Homer assumes that his earlier reaction was just a fluke, but his relief is short-lived. He is actually driving in reverse and crashes into a trout hatchery. In the vision that follows, the fish are dancing in a chorus line, singing "Homer loves Mindy! Homer loves Mindy!"

Troubled by his feelings, Homer turns to his favorite source for advice and counseling: Moe's Tavern. He confesses his attraction to Mindy to his friends. They suggest it is infatuation based on physical attraction and that the best way to deflate it is to speak with Mindy and find that they have nothing in common. This strategy backfires. At work the next day, Homer learns that he and Mindy have a lot in common, including an appetite for donuts, watching television, and napping on the job before lunch. "Foul temptress," he thinks, implying that she has cultivated these interests knowing they are identical to his own. Yet he continues to resist, avoiding her for the rest of the day. As he congratulates himself for this victory, he steps into an elevator where he is crammed in with the woman. He does his best to overcome the situation, commanding himself to think unsexy thoughts: Marge's unattractive sisters shaving their legs and his friend Barney, an overweight barfly, in a thong bikini. Failing again, Homer pushes the emergency stop button, forces the door open, and steps out into thin air.

Back at home, he tries to fortify himself by reminding himself of the benefits of a loving family. Alas, the realities of domestic life conspire against him as well. Marge has a cold and the household is in chaos. She gives him a present she has picked up for him at the mall: a tee-shirt of her face, which has come out wrong and makes her look like a grotesque harridan. While watching television together, the couple is bombarded by news and entertainment programming that is a constant stream of debased sexuality and double entendres, sending Homer screaming from the room.

Homer's desperation is deepening. He wants to do the right thing or, more properly, not do the wrong thing. As a last resort, he goes to a phone booth and calls the church's marriage counseling hotline. Confessing his attraction for another woman, he finds the voice at the other end of the "anonymous" line is his neighbor Ned, who immediately recognizes him and suggests a conference call with Marge. (He might have been better off calling Dr. Laura or Dr. Phil.) In a panic to escape the call and confrontation, he tips over the phone booth and knocks himself out. Unconscious, he has a vision of a guardian angel who, in a play on the movie classic *It's a Wonderful Life*, shows him how his life would be if he was married to Mindy instead of Marge. Homer sees that he would be living in a mansion with a butler, happily playing tennis with his coworkers, while Marge—shorn of her inept spouse—would be in the White House. The guardian angel admits the dream is not having the desired effect and drops Homer back to consciousness on the sidewalk.

Clearly, Homer is losing the battle. He is uncharacteristically chipper as he prepares for work, using deodorant all over his body and singing Barry Manilow's song "Mandy" as "Mindy." Lisa is curious and doesn't take too long to analyze the situation. "Judging from your song, you're infatuated with a woman named Mindy," she says, despite his denial. The encounter with his daughter has an effect, though. Again Homer resolves to distance himself from Mindy because of their "uncontrollable attraction." The breakup speech he had prepared, written on his hand, dissolves into sweat and gibberish. As Homer tries to make himself understood, the exchange is observed by Mr. Burns on a security camera. The plant owner assumes that what he is watching is an example of friendship and teamwork on the job, so he decides to send the pair to an energy convention in Capital City to represent the company. "This is the worst crisis my marriage has ever faced!" Homer exclaims after being told of the honor.

He is not exaggerating. Homer and Mindy are put up in adjoining rooms at the convention. A lascivious bellboy points out the king-sized bed and its possibilities to Homer. "Stop that!" he cries. "I love my wife and family." Mindy is no help. "If it weren't for this wall," she says, "we'd be sleeping in the same bed." When Mindy says she has "a really wicked idea," Homer assumes the obvious and tells her "we have to fight our temptation." She assures him that her idea is to call room service for dinner, which they do. Sitting on Homer's bed, they work on a chili dog from opposite ends and meet in a kiss. Homer recoils and pops his shirt buttons, revealing the tee-shirt with Marge's fearsome visage. He thinks he hears Marge growling and flees the room, only to find the noise is coming from a floor waxer in the hall.

The next day Homer and Mindy are at the nuclear plant's booth, trading insults with outraged convention delegates who accuse them of poisoning the planet and creating another Chernobyl. Tension between the two has dissipated and Homer begins to congratulate himself, which sets up the announcement that they have been crowned King and Queen of Energy, winning a romantic dinner for two at "the sexiest Chinese restaurant in Capital City." The fortune cookie after their cheeseburgers seems to tip the balance. "You will find happiness with a new love," it reads, which Homer interprets as a prediction he will have sex with Mindy. "What's the point?" he asks. "You can't fight fate." (A scene in the back of the restaurant reveals that the fortune was just bad luck. The barrel with the "Stick with your wife" fortune cookies was not used.)

At the hotel, Mindy invites herself into Homer's room, where they sit on the bed again. Homer is overcome and begins to sob, but Mindy reassures him that he doesn't have to do anything he doesn't want to. That, of course, is the moral dilemma. Homer says that he may want to, but then he thinks about his wife and his family. Mindy tells him she understands and urges him to "look into your heart. I think you'll see what you want." They kiss, but only briefly. The next scene shows Homer in the hotel bedroom, Barry White's "Can't Get Enough of Your Love" playing in the background, with the outline of a naked woman who is revealed to be—Marge. He called her to join him, which she has done with enthusiasm.

Marge, the Simpson family's strongest believer, is "my candidate for sainthood," says Kenneth Briggs. "She is the model saint. She lives in the real world, she lives with crises, with flawed people. She forgives and she makes her own mistakes. She's a forgiving, loving person. She is absolutely saintly." Her idea of cursing is that a local prison is a "gosh-darned heck hole." Yet even saints are not immune from the temptation to fall into sin. In the same episode, Marge lies to help a prison inmate, only to have the sociopath reproach her for it. "The Lord will forgive me if it means giving you a second chance," she says, ensuring that her misguided effort at rehabilitation will end in disaster, which it does.

In another episode, Homer forgets Marge's birthday and then compounds the oversight by rushing out to buy her a belated and particularly inappropriate present: a bowling ball drilled to fit *his* fingers, with *his* name inscribed—which he accidentally drops onto her birthday cake. Marge's sisters, Patty and Selma, who have joined the family celebration at a restaurant, suggest she dump her thoughtless oaf of a husband. They remind her that the age of thirty-four is "time enough to start over with a new man." Marge is as crushed by the birthday gift as her cake. When Homer asks how she likes his gift, she screams that it is hard for her to judge since she's never bowled in her life. Her husband says that if she doesn't like it she knows someone who would. That night in bed Marge dismisses Homer's feeble attempts to explain his choice, informing him that she accepts his gift and intends to use it.

At Barney's Bowl-a-rama, she makes an inept effort to get started, brushing aside an attendant's offer of help by explaining that she is just there out of spite. However, she attracts the attention of the bowling alley's sleazy pro, Jacques, who introduces himself and begins to explain the game. He also starts coming on to her, caressing her hands and proffering compliments. Her fingers, Jacques says, are too tender and feminine for the ball she is using. She requires something lighter, more delicate for her tapered fingers. He offers her the use of his own ball rather than the one with the name "Homer" inscribed on it, but she declines. "Many people have senseless attachments to heavy clumsy things such as this Homer of yours," he says. The gift bowling ball is about to become the engine of domestic destruction. Marge accepts Jacques' offer of bowling lessons at a reduced rate, and soon she is bowling strikes. She says he is a good teacher, and he replies, oozing charm, that he is indeed a very good teacher and that "I can teach you everything."

At the Simpson home, Homer is taking up the slack created by Marge's time at the bowling alley. Dinner is usually take-out, but he is still exhausted by the nighttime routine of child care and is shocked when his wife tells him she will be going back to the bowling alley for lessons. This was not part of Homer's plan. Jacques continues his practiced campaign for the affection of a neglected wife by giving Marge a bowling glove that is her size, with her name on it. In marked contrast to her husband's gift, it is meant for her and her alone, and she is thrilled. His lessons become increasingly personal, with much touching and many compliments. "Marge, do you know how beautiful you look in the moonlight?" he asks as he drops her off at home. But I am married, she says. "My mind says stop," Jacques says, "but my heart—and my hips—say proceed." He invites her to meet him away from the bowling alley for brunch, a concept he has to explain to the unsophisticated Marge. At first she says no, then agrees.

Moments later, inside the house, Homer senses that something is wrong, although he isn't certain what it is. They sleep apart from one another on the bed. Lisa, as always, is the first to zero in on the problem. Bart notices that their mom is preparing vastly improved lunches to take to school. This is not a good sign, his sister informs him. It is, she explains, "what the psychologists call overcompensation. Mom is wracked with guilt because her marriage is failing." This is something that happens in homes where the parents no longer love and cherish each other, says Lisa, and there are separate and distinct stages that children in such homes go through. She is in stage three: fear. Bart, lagging a bit, is in stage two: denial.

Jacques takes Marge to brunch at a Cajun restaurant and offers her a mimosa—the name of what is for her an exotic drink—which she mistakes for a pass until he explains what it is. As one might have predicted, Marge is spotted by Helen Lovejoy, the minister's wife. She explains that she noticed Marge having brunch "with a man who isn't her husband" and had to come over and say hello. Marge stammers, but Helen assures her that she doesn't have to squirm on her account and tells her she will see her at church on Sunday. Jacques launches more compliments, saying her laughter is like music to him, before making his play. He invites her to meet him at his apartment the next day, "away from prying eyes, away from the Helens of this world." The offer is unmistakable.

Marge, the faithful wife and believing Christian, faints. She dreams what the meeting might bring. It is a rosy vision: she in a ball gown and Jacques in a tuxedo. They dance through the lavishly furnished apartment at Fiesta Terrace. She notices a glass cabinet filled with trophies she takes to be for bowling; he informs her they are for lovemaking. They sip champagne at the bar and engage in witty and soulful repartee. At this point, Jacques revives her. If this is what adultery will be like, she decides, she is game. She asks if the following Thursday will be all right for the assignation.

The Simpson family is not unaware of what is going on. Homer discovers the bowling glove and is disconsolate, returning it to the dresser and sitting forlornly on the couple's bed. Asked by Bart to toss around a baseball, he says, "Son, I don't know if I can lift my head, let alone a ball." The boy is concerned enough to turn to Lisa, admitting she is right about their parents' marriage, but she says she cannot help because she is mired in stage five: self-pity. Thursday morning arrives and Homer cannot think of what to do to rescue his relationship. As Marge makes sandwiches, her husband tries to reach for her hand, only to grab his lunchbox. Instead, he compliments her on the way she makes peanut butter and jelly sandwiches—the best the inarticulate man can do. As he leaves the kitchen he says, "Good-bye, my wife." Later in the day, at the plant, he sits staring at his lunch, unable to eat, a sure sign of a major crisis.

While driving to Jacques' apartment, Marge sees the spectrum of married life: a wedding, a couple walking with a baby carriage, a family on a picnic, an old couple walking hand in hand, and, finally, two gravestones side by side. She comes to a fork in the road, one direction heading to the nuclear power plant, where her husband works; the other to Fiesta Terrace, where her would-be lover is waiting. Marge heads toward Jacques' apartment, then pulls over to the side and turns around. The closing scene is a take-off on the movie *An Officer and a Gentleman.* Marge walks into the plant and up to Homer, who is completely surprised. She dons a hard hat and he carries her out, to the applause of his coworkers, telling them proudly, "I'm going to the backseat of my car with the woman I love, and I won't be back for ten minutes!"

These three temptations of adultery, though exaggerated to be sure, nevertheless together embody familiar situations that provoke infidelity in the noncartoon world. In each case, the sanctity of the marriage vow is tested fundamentally—and preserved. Another victory for traditional family values.

Seven

The Bible: "I Think It May Be Somewhere towards the Back."

A survey released in late 2000—and supported by more recent polls—reported that 86 percent of respondents believed the Bible is relevant in today's world. A slightly smaller majority, 80 percent, said that the Bible could address most of today's problems, although the same percentage felt that the language of the Bible could be confusing. All of these findings are mirrored in *The Simpsons*. Like Ned Flanders, who owns multiple translations, over half the adults surveyed by Zondervan Publishing said they trusted the Bible to get facts correct more than a history book or the local newspaper.[1] Among committed evangelical Protestants like Flanders, this belief is even stronger. An August 2006 study conducted by the Pew Forum on Religion and Public Life found that "fully sixty-two percent of white evangelicals say the Bible is the actual word of God, to be taken literally." The same survey found that 60 percent of the same group believes that the Bible should have more influence on U.S. laws than the will of the American people.

As a child on a Boy Scout trip, *Simpsons'* creator Matt Groening stole a Gideon Bible from a motel and underlined the "dirty" parts, he told an interviewer for *My Generation* magazine in 2001. "Plus, there's lots of stuff that's just weird. For instance, there's a parable about Jesus driving demons into a herd of pigs, and the pigs jump off a cliff. I wanted to know what the pigs did to deserve that."

Characters in Groening's series bring their own widely divergent views of faith and religion to their readings of the Bible, and do not hesitate to use it for their own purposes. The "Rainbow Man," a zealot in a rainbow-colored wig who popped up at various televised sporting events during the 1990s carrying a sign reading "John 3:16," appears in various crowd scenes on the show. Trying to look innocent after doing mischief, Bart pretends to read the Bible—upside down. Homer is saved from serious injury in a car wreck by a Bible in his crotch, and in another episode the Scripture is used to smuggle alcohol to him in a rehab program. "No wonder they call it the Good Book," Homer says. The show's writers freely mix accurately quoted passages with those they make up, including plausible-sounding gibberish. "And so when Eliphaz came down from Mount Hebron bearing figs, he offered them to Mohem, who you will remember is the father of Sheckhom," Reverend Lovejoy reads, "and to Hazare on the occasion of their matrimony." In *The Simpsons Guide to Springfield*, the minister quotes from "somewhere in the Bible," possibly "First Thessaleezians," that "blessed is a man who perseveres until trial."[2]

At Sunday services, Lovejoy has a predilection for misinterpretation and choosing inappropriate selections, especially bloodthirsty passages that he claims are from the Old Testament ("With flaming swords the Aramites did pierce the eyes of their fellow men, and did feast on what flowed forth") and meaningless recitations of genealogy. He advises Seymour Skinner, the elementary school principal who has come to him for advice, to read the Bible, but when the preacher is asked what part to consult for guidance, he answers, "It's all pretty good."

However, the advice Lovejoy gives Ned—who is concerned that he has offended his neighbor Homer—from Proverbs 15:1 proves appropriate and effective: "A gentle answer turns away wrath." On a deeper level, though, the minister has an exceptionally dark view of the Bible's essence, favoring dire, Old Testament judgment to the love, charity, and forgiveness of the New Testament. "Have you read this thing lately?" he asks Marge, holding the Bible. "Everything's a sin. Technically, you can't go to the bathroom."

Lovejoy often relies on biblical citation to support his arguments. When Homer decides to stop going to church, he quotes Matthew 7:26 about the foolish man who built his house on sand. However, the minister can be a little shifty if someone quotes a verse that undermines his own views. After condemning Bart (prematurely and unjustly, as it turns out) for stealing from the collection plate, the minister is brought up short when Lisa repeats one of her favorites, Matthew 7:1: "Judge not, lest ye be judged." The verse might be in the Bible, Lovejoy acknowledges, but if so it is "somewhere towards the back," implying that is has less divine authority. On another occasion, Lisa challenges Springfield's annual "Whacking Day," when residents beat snakes to death. Lovejoy tells her the festival has biblical roots, pretending to read: "And the Lord said, Whack ye all the serpents which crawl on their bellies and thy town will be a beacon unto others," he says. "So you see, Lisa, even God himself endorses whacking." When the girl asks to see where in the Bible it says that, the preacher refuses to show her.

Homer is extremely hazy on many of the particulars of the Bible: He thinks Goliath defeated David and that the story of Hercules and the lion is from scripture. His inattention, leading to misunderstanding, is monumental: He believes God "teased" Moses in the desert, until Marge explains that God actually "tested" the leader. Pressed for a Bible verse to avert a spider's curse, Homer draws a blank, getting no further than "Thou shalt not. . . ." Like Lovejoy, he spouts garbled scripture. As an involuntary missionary in the South Pacific, he introduces Judeo-Christian faith to the natives by reading this selection from the book of Psalms: "God will shatter the heads of His enemies. The hairy crown of those who walk in their guilty ways that you may bathe your feet in their blood." The incomprehensible passage, he says solemnly to the bewildered congregation as he closes the Bible, is "as true today as it was when it was written." Also like Lovejoy, Homer uses the Bible when and how it suits him, justifying gambling on sports to Lisa by telling her that it is permitted in the Bible—"somewhere in the back." When Otto, the stoned school-bus driver, becomes homeless, he is invited by Bart to move into the garage, to his father's chagrin. "I know we didn't ask for this, Homer," says Marge, "but doesn't the Bible say, 'Whatsoever you do to the least of my brothers, that you do unto me'?" Yes, Homer replies, "but doesn't the Bible also say, 'Thou shalt not

take moochers into thy hut?'" Marge's verse is from Matthew
25:40; Homer's is from his imagination.

To Bart, Homer cites equally spurious biblical authority for
afflicting former president George H. W. Bush, who has moved
to Springfield, with a plague of locusts. "It's all in the Bible, son.
It's the Prankster's Bible." Introducing a segment of a Halloween
fantasy episode, he claims to be swearing on a Bible—until Marge
points out that it is actually a book of carpet samples. Homer tells
Lisa, who wants to play ice hockey on a boys' team, that she is
going against the Word: "If the Bible has taught us nothing else—
and it hasn't—it's that girls should stick to girls' sports, such as hot
oil wrestling, foxy boxing. . . ." With Bart, he uses the Good Book
as a prop in an attempt to convince Flanders that his wife ordered
a gold-embossed Bible before her death, a disgraceful but venerable American con. But Homer recognizes the importance of
scripture when it counts. The last thing he does when he thinks
he is going to die from eating a poisoned blowfish is to turn to the
Bible—in this case a recorded version read by Larry King.

The most detailed representation of the Bible in *The Simpsons*
came in the spring of 1999 in an episode titled "Simpson Bible
Stories." It is a sweltering Easter Sunday morning, and the Simpsons have gathered at the First Church of Springfield. In the pulpit, Reverend Lovejoy makes no reference to Jesus, crucifixion, or
resurrection. (The school chalkboard segment at the start of this
episode has Bart writing, "I cannot absolve sins," one of the few
clear references to Christianity's most important holiday.) Instead,
the minister announces that on this day his congregation is in need
of "a hefty dose of the Good Book."

When Ned Flanders calls out from the pew that the noise of
the fans is making it difficult to hear, the minister's solution is to
switch them off, plunging the congregation into dreamy somno-
lence. Lovejoy begins his sermon with the book of Genesis, and
as he does, the Simpsons nod off and begin to dream, each in turn.
In their biblical dreams, family members and their friends assume
roles in much the same way as characters do in the movie version
of *The Wizard of Oz*. Theologically, the Simpsons' visions are to

scripture what "Fractured Fairy Tales" on the *Rocky and Bullwinkle Show* were to the Brothers Grimm. Creator Matt Groening was especially proud of the episode, calling it "our *Prince of Egypt*," although it is anything but DreamWorks' elegant, reverent retelling of Moses and the exodus. Periods and characters from different books of the Bible appear out of chronological order, and events are turned upside down for comic effect. Groening joked before "Simpson Bible Stories" aired that the reason it was written was that executive producer Mike Scully told him the show hadn't been getting enough angry letters.

Genesis. Marge dreams first, of the Garden of Eden. She is Eve, Homer is Adam, and, naturally, Ned Flanders provides God's deep, booming voice, speaking from a cloud. Everything is idyllic: There is no pain or want, the lion lies down with the lamb, and a vivid rainbow hangs in the sky. Even pork, ripped from a willing pig, is kosher. It is "almost like paradise," Marge tells Homer. In addition to his voice, God makes his presence known with a strong right arm, wearing Flanders's signature sweater, and a hand with four fingers. Homer and Marge, wearing fig leaves, fall to their knees whenever they hear the voice from heaven. "You're too kind and wise and righteous," Homer says. Warned that all things are permitted to eat, except for the sparkling tree of knowledge, Homer naturally tries to work the angle to his advantage. He says that such temptation would be easier to resist if he could have a few extra wives.

The couple is then importuned by the serpent, tempting them to sample "God's private stash." In this version, however, it is Homer's Adam—not Marge's Eve—who is the first to succumb to temptation. "They said it was forbidden," Marge says. "Please stop eating that. God's going to be furious." Homer, his eyes newly opened by knowledge, replies that she is "pretty uptight for a naked chick." She reflects that "it *is* a sin to waste food" and joins him.

Thunder follows, as Marge predicted, and God wants to know if anyone has tasted the forbidden fruit. Homer implicates Marge, who admits that she has. She is expelled from the garden, pleading in vain for Homer to say something in her defense. The world outside Eden is a terrible place, she soon learns, now wearing a dress. Asked by Homer, who is still in the garden, what she is doing, she says, "Toiling—what does it look like?"

Guilt-stricken by his betrayal, Homer decides to sneak Marge back in, believing that "God can't be everywhere at once, right?" He enlists a unicorn to dig a tunnel and, just as Marge rejoins him, they are discovered. God appears again, and again the couple fall to their knees. Wrong again. "This is how you repay me?" the Lord asks, even more angry this time, seeing the last unicorn expire. Homer asks that God not do anything rash and makes a feeble attempt at proto-Christian theology in their defense. He asks, "God is love, right?" but he is in the wrong testament. The couple is expelled, this time for good, to a world of pain and want and misery. But it is also a world of hope and optimism. "I'm sure God will let us return soon," says Marge, with no grasp of the concept of original sin and its durability. "How long can he hold a grudge?"

Exodus. Lisa dreams of the Egyptian captivity, where she is the woman behind Moses, who appears in the person of Bart's friend Milhouse. The Israelite slaves are all children who, when not building the pyramids, jump rope while reciting the genealogy of the patriarchs. Bart, naturally, is a troublemaking slave who infuriates Pharaoh with irreverent graffiti. When Pharaoh, played by Principal Skinner, threatens to slay all the firstborn—again—until he finds out who is responsible, Bart is denounced by the burning bush. Making a rare appearance without her signature pearls, Lisa urges Milhouse to tell Pharaoh to let their people go. Pharaoh refuses and is afflicted with a series of plagues. But the frogs the children dump on the Egyptian leader are purchased at the market and do not come from God. Pharaoh finds the amphibians tasty, taking the plague as a message from the sun-god above: "Ra has rewarded my cruelty to the slaves." Lisa tries to explain the subtleties of the divine plan to dim-witted Pharaoh: "It's a plague, you moron!"

Milhouse finally rouses the slaves, telling them their time has come, and urges them to follow him to freedom. At last they are permitted to leave but are then pursued by Egyptian chariots to the shore of the Red Sea. Here, Moses wavers in his faith. "Screw this," he proclaims, falling to his knees and bowing to the sun. "I'm converting. Save us, O mighty Ra!" Lisa bucks him up and he parts the sea, enabling the Israelites to cross to safety. "It's a miracle!" he says, clearly astonished, and drawing the wrong conclusion. "I'm a genius!" he cries. On the other side, Moses asks Lisa what's ahead—a land of milk and honey? After consulting a Torah scroll, she tells him it's forty years of wandering in the desert.

Kings. Lovejoy announces that the next reading will be from the book of Kings, about King Solomon, whose wisdom was "like a drill, boring into the rock of injustice." On the word "boring," Homer dreams that he is King Solomon, judging disputes among the people in a *People's Court* setting. His coworkers from the nuclear power plant, Lenny and Carl, appear as ancient Israelites who dispute the ownership of a pie. The incident is a variation of 1 Kings 3, in which two women claim they are the mother of the same baby. King Solomon orders the infant cut in two and divided between the two claimants. The true mother is revealed when she pleads not to slay the child, and instead to turn it over to the other woman. This time, Homer orders the pie in dispute to be divided and the two disputing claimants slain. Then he eats both halves of the pie.

Samuel. Bart imagines himself as King David, living in Jerusalem in 970 BC (although the walled city's appearance seems more like the first century AD). It is an action movie sequel to 1 Samuel 17, when as a young man the future king kills Goliath, the Philistines' gigantic champion, with a sling. Years later, King Bart has become an arrogant, sybaritic monarch. He is challenged by Goliath's son, who is played by the bully Nelson Muntz. At first, Bart confuses the giant with Samson, cutting his hair to no effect. "I hope this doesn't get into the Bible," he says. This time around the giant bests Israel's greatest king, knocking him into the next country and seizing the crown. A shepherd recognizes the deposed warrior king and tells him, "I love you 'cause you kill people."

"Goliath II is gonna pay," Bart vows, "and this time, it's biblical." Improbably, the insurgent monarch learns that Goliath II is responsible for the deaths of Jonah and Methuselah, enraging him. Bart climbs the tower of Babel, where Nelson is hiding, and brings the giant down, only to learn that during his exile the

Philistine had become a wise king beloved by his Israelite subjects, was known as "Goliath the Consensus Builder," and had constructed roads, hospitals, and libraries. Bart is jailed.

Revelation. The family awakes in church after the service, only to find themselves alone in the pews. It's not the end of the world, Homer says, as they walk out the door. But it is. They appear to have walked into the end of the world. The heavens are raining brimstone and the world is ablaze. The four horsemen of the Apocalypse ride across the fiery sky. Marge realizes what is happening as pure Christian spirits, such as those of their neighbors the Flanderses, kneeling together in prayer, are ascending to the sky. The Simpsons remain firmly earthbound and Marge wonders why they aren't rising to heaven. "Oh right, the sins," she says. Lisa recognizes that the rapture is taking place, and regrets that she has never known true, earthly love. She begins to rise, only to be yanked back by Homer. "Where do you think you're going, young lady?" he asks. This family started together and it will finish together.

The ground near them opens with a ramp to a fiery pit, and the Simpsons descend. At first, Homer is unabashed, saying that he smells barbecue. Then he learns the horrible truth about hell: "They're out of hot dogs, the cole slaw has pineapple, and it's German potato salad!" The closing credits role as the heavy metal rock group AC/DC sings "Highway to Hell."

In one Christmas episode sequence, the nativity story is retold by *Simpsons* characters in a similar fantasy sequence, but in this case the script sticks close to scripture. Following the success of Mel Gibson's *The Passion of the Christ, The Simpsons* offered another cinematic take on the Good Book. Ned is watching television with his children when a commercial comes on for an erectile dysfunction treatment for old men. Like many parents in a similar situation, he is upset, declaring there is nothing but filth on TV. But unlike most, Ned decides to take direct action, creating a religious alternative. Using his video camera and a backyard set, he films *The Passion of Cain and Abel,* starring Rod and Todd, with himself in the supporting role of Adam. The film is screened in the church basement to a packed house. In one scene, Ned tells the boys that God "is vacuuming heaven for when dead people show up." As the gory, drawn-out sequence of fratricide appears on the screen, it is intercut with nightmarish newspaper headlines such as "Massachusetts Okays Gay Marriage" and "Stem Cells Cure Alzheimer's." Most of the crowd loves the movie, but Marge is uncomfortable, because of the violence and the negativity. Mr. Burns, the owner of the nuclear power plant, notes the reaction of the viewers and tells his aide, Smithers, that there is money to be made in Bible-based movies—as well as an opportunity to launder money.

Burns finances a big-screen sequel, based on the exodus and shot with a large cast and sets, but still in the Flanders backyard. This movie, even more violent and distorted than the first, premieres in a Springfield theater. Again, most in the audience love it, except for Marge, who protests that "there's more to the Bible than blood and gore." Ned, the auteur, is stung. "I guess you'd rather see a film about a liberal European wizard school or the latest sexcapade of Miss Ashley Judd," he says. Marge doesn't back down, telling him she doesn't like his movie and that she intends to urge a boycott. With that, Burns abandons his backing.

Because of his own success teaching professional athletes how to showboat, Homer has been asked to produce the halftime show at the Super Bowl. Bereft of an idea the night before, he wanders into church at 3 a.m., where he finds Ned, praying alone about his movie. "I'm just like Michael Moore," he tells Homer, "except I'm skinny, my jeans are washed, and God loves me. I wish I could find a way to spread my message." To Homer, this appears to be a miraculous opportunity. "You've got a message—and I've got a medium," he tells his neighbor. "Maybe God brought us together for a reason." Or maybe not. The coproduction, in which the football stadium is flooded to recreate the story of Noah, is a failure, producing a chorus of boos and bad news reports. Local TV anchorman Kent Brockman intones that fans were "outraged by the Super Bowl halftime show's blatant display of religion and decency," citing a local family of secular humanists interviewed on the street.

Much of the reporting I have done about the Bible has involved the issue of inerrancy—the literal, word-for-word truth of scripture. In a classic example of what political scientists call a "wedge issue," conservative Southern Baptists were able to use this theological debate more than two decades ago to help leverage control of the nation's largest Protestant denomination. My sense is that this debate over the biblical truth of the Good Book is largely beside the point to most believing Christians and Jews, who tend to agree that it is divinely inspired and, at the least, a source of practical wisdom and moral instruction. They are more concerned with what is in the book than the manner in which it was transmitted to the world. Like the characters on *The Simpsons*, they return to the Bible for support and sustenance, justification and inspiration. For, as Homer says, it is "as true today as when it was written."

Eight

Catholics: "That's Catholic, Marge . . . Voodoo."

From almost the outset of *The Simpsons*, former education secretary William Bennett, a Catholic, had a clear idea of what he was up against and how to deal with it. In the midst of his public flap with the show, he said that there was nothing wrong with Bart "that a Catholic school, a paper route and a couple of soap sandwiches wouldn't straighten out."[1] Is Bart's time at the chalkboard at the beginning of each episode a form of confession or penitence or both? Unlike Bennett, Mark Fischer, an instructor at St. John's Catholic Seminary in Camarillo, California, allowed his two sons to watch the show, although he too had concerns about Bart's behavior. Fischer said he paid closer attention to Homer. "Catholics would say his sins are venial, rather than mortal," he told the *Ventura County Star* in 1999. "He willfully does wrong, but never rejects God or the idea of divine justice. He's simply weak."[2]

Of all the controversies the series has ignited over religion and values, the most serious was with its portrayal of Catholics and the Church of Rome. It was also one of the few cases where Fox Television made the otherwise free-spirited show back down and censor itself—to loud complaints from the executive producer, Mike Scully. The way Catholicism is represented in *The Simpsons* is complicated and subtle, like much of the show's humor, but it has an undeniably hostile, sometimes gratuitous edge to it. At times, the tension between writers and producers and the denomination has assumed some aspects of an intimate, deep-seated family feud. Scully, for example, has described himself as a "lapsed Catholic." Another executive producer and writer, George Meyer, has had an enormous influence on shaping the series over the years, by all accounts second only to the show's three creators. Meyer has also had a problematic history with the Catholic Church. He told an interviewer in the *New Yorker* that as a child he struggled with his parents' strong religious beliefs.

Animus like this has popped up in different forms in the series. Moe the bartender is heard taking a bet over the phone from someone he addresses as "your eminence." Smithers, Mr. Burns's sycophantic assistant at the nuclear power plant, is seen in a confessional. Springfield's most prominent Catholic is Mayor Joe Quimby, a crook, a lush, and a womanizer whose build and accent remind many viewers of Teddy Kennedy. Holy water and its mystical power provide a running gag. Two violent, cartoon-in-a-cartoon characters, Itchy and Scratchy, appear to be reciting a prayer in Latin. At the beach, Ned Flanders is concerned that his son's sand castle looks too much like a Catholic cathedral. Disputes sometimes flare between Catholicism and Protestantism. One Springfield Community Church sign reads, "Welcome Pissed Off Catholics." Marge obliquely suggests the pope has been letting things slide lately, a reference to the unfolding clergy sex abuse scandal of the early 2000s. In another episode, she and Lovejoy nearly come to blows with a Catholic priest. Marge tells the cleric she is not Catholic, and he replies, "In that case I hope you'll enjoy your time in hell." Lovejoy compliments the priest on his "dress," whereupon the priest tells the minister to go home and sleep with his wife. A fistfight nearly follows.

Sometimes these shots come in the form of casual Protestant bigotry. Marge, fearful that Grampa Abe Simpson is about to die because of a failing kidney, asks Reverend Lovejoy to anoint her father-in-law, to administer what was once called the Last Rites or Extreme Unction, now simply referred to as Anointing. "That's Catholic, Marge," the minister replies dismissively. "You might as well ask me to do a voodoo dance." In an issue of *The Simpsons* comics, Lovejoy is hypnotized by a local thug, who orders him to take the collection money and gamble at an Indian reservation casino—while dressed in a nun's habit. Driving home from church one Sunday, Bart is ravenous with hunger. He asks his mother if the family can become Catholic, "so we can get Communion wafers and booze." Rather than correct her son's caricature of the denomination, Marge compounds it by equating the Vatican with its opposition to birth control. "No one is going Catholic," she says. "Three children is enough, thank you."

Marge's joke, which aired in November 1998, attracted the ire of a New York–based group called the Catholic League for Religious and Civil Rights, headed by William Donohue. Founded in 1973, the organization's goal is to defend the rights of Catholics "to participate in American public life without defamation or discrimination." Patterned after the NAACP and the Anti-Defamation League, the Catholic League is donor supported and nonpartisan, but its board is dominated by conservative activists and intellectuals such as Bennett and Dinesh D'Souza.

The Catholic League is best known for attacking the portrayal of Catholics in various media in recent years, in particular the television shows *Nothing Sacred* and *Ally McBeal*, the movie *Dogma*, and the "Sensations" art exhibit at the Brooklyn Museum of Art. Donohue has charged that these representations are part of a modern wave of Catholic bashing. It is unclear how many of the nation's sixty million Catholics the organization actually represents; it takes out large newspaper ads in major cities to voice its objections, but its individual demonstrations and letter-writing campaigns have never numbered more than five hundred supporters, according to critics. Nonetheless, these efforts were lauded by the late Cardinal John O'Connor of New York. He said the League played an "indispensable role in defending the rights of Catholics" when "they are unfairly attacked, or the Church is unfairly maligned."[3] There has been a backlash to the League's activities, however, which the organization acknowledges. "We are accused of advocating censorship when all we want to do is eliminate the censorious power of political correctness," according to its statement of purpose. "We are not trying to impose Catholic values on our society to promote Christian ends."[4]

Donohue wrote to Fox regarding the interchange between Marge and Bart, asking, "Can you possibly explain why this dialogue was included in the show?" At first, his complaint seemed to go nowhere with the network. He received a lengthy reply from Thomas Chavez, manager for broadcast standards and practices, which seemed like a polite brush-off. The letter, reprinted in the League's newsletter, *The Catalyst*, read in part:

> In your letter you questioned an exchange in dialogue between Bart and his mother, Marge. Because Bart is starving, he suggests they convert to Catholicism since he is aware communion wafers and wine are dispensed in the Catholic ceremony. Just like other children that are not knowledgeable, Bart sees the wafer merely as food and wine as a forbidden drink. Because many families wait to eat until after they have attended church, it is not atypical that a child would pose a question such as this unknowingly. The writers chose not to have Marge respond to Bart's ridiculous desire to satisfy his hunger with the Sacrament but rather, elected to have Marge respond by stating why she would not be comfortable converting to Catholicism. Her views regarding birth control are obviously contrary to the Catholic Church's belief. While Marge's response may be perceived as short and curt, it also conveys the impression that one's choice of religion is based on more than the religion's rituals.[5]

The League was not persuaded by this response, commenting sarcastically in its newsletter, "Now why didn't we think of that? Just goes to show how thoughtful the Hollywood gang really is."[6]

On January 31, 1999, *The Simpsons* aired an episode that coincided with the Super Bowl, which had been broadcast earlier that evening on Fox. A short segment in the show spoofed both the innovative—but sometimes obscure—commercials aired during the football game and the advertising campaigns by different groups within the Catholic Church to show that the denomination has changed with the times. The "commercial" was based on an old music video showcasing the raucous Texas rock band ZZ Top, a group known for its beards, dark glasses, and black attire. A car pulls into a windblown gas station in the middle of nowhere. The driver gets out and, seeing no one, honks the horn for service. Out of the station file three buxom, scantily clad young women to provide "service." One lifts the hood suggestively while another slides the gas pump nozzle into the tank in an image too obvious to ignore, but the driver's eyes are riveted to a shiny cross dangling from one woman's quivering cleavage as the rock music soars. What is this all about? The voice-over explains: "The Catholic Church: We've made a few . . . changes." Watching the commercial at home with her mother, Lisa pronounces it "weird."

The Catholic League preferred to call it offensive and complained again to Fox, saying it was the last straw. "We wrote to Mr. Chavez again," the League informed members in the next newsletter, which made the incident its cover story. "We also told him that he'd be hearing from you. So don't disappoint us."[7] The letters evidently poured in and provoked a response at *The Simpsons*. "The joke was an observation on crazy Super Bowl commercials, not a comment on the Catholic Church," Scully told Howard Rosenberg, television critic of the *Los Angeles Times*. "We had the idea for the content of the commercial first. Then we pitched several tag lines. One of the writers pitched the Catholic Church line, and it got the biggest laugh."[8] Obviously, the League didn't see it that way. "We got a couple of hundred letters, and it was very obvious from reading a majority of them that [the Catholic letter writers] had not seen the show. Some of them were from third-graders, all saying the same thing: 'Please don't make fun of my religion.' Which we all know third-graders are very adamant about."[9]

Ordinarily, that would have been the end of the matter for *The Simpsons*. After all, they've drawn protests before and simply ignored them. This time, however, the show was in for an unpleasant surprise. Several months later, the Catholic League contacted Fox again and specifically asked that the word "Catholic" be excised from the voice-over when the episode repeated in September 1999 on the network, as well as in its subsequent syndicated airings. The network agreed, and Roland McFarland, Fox's vice president of broadcast standards, ordered Scully to make the one-word cut or to eliminate all reference to religion. When Scully refused, McFarland offered another solution: replace the protesting denomination with a Protestant substitute—Methodists, Presbyterians, or

Baptists. Scully asked the executive, "What would be the difference changing it to another religion, and wouldn't that just be offending a different group of people?" McFarland explained that "Fox had already had trouble with the Catholics earlier this season," Scully told the *Times*. Given the previous decade's experience—and freedom of expression—Scully was perplexed. "People can say hurtful things to each other about their weight, their race, their intelligence, their sexual preference, and that all seems up for grabs," he said. "But when you get into religion, some people get very nervous."[10]

Rosenberg, no fan of the League's earlier efforts (he called the campaign against *Nothing Sacred* a "fanatical crusade" that "helped drive that achingly noble ABC series off the air"), asked if Fox's actions on *The Simpsons* did not imply that there are "different standards for different religions."[11]

Not surprisingly, the League saw it differently:

> Consider this: All along, we have been told by Fox that none of our complaints were valid because none of the material was truly offensive. But now we have a Fox executive producer disingenuously giving away his hand by protesting why it should be okay to offend another group of people with the same material he initially said wasn't offensive to Catholics! And isn't it striking that Rosenberg is upset with the fact that the double standard—which now, for the first time works positively for Catholics—is a real problem? Never do we remember Rosenberg protesting the double standard that allows "artists" to dump on Catholics while protecting most other segments of society from their assaults.[12]

(Scully and *The Simpsons* were more amenable to making a cut in 2001 when another group, the Media Action Network for Asian Americans, complained about an exchange in which Mr. Burns, the nuclear plant owner, calls Smithers a "Chinaman" while the assistant pulls him in a rickshaw. "There was no malicious intent behind the joke," Scully told the *Los Angeles Times*. "It was supposed to be one of Mr. Burns's typical antiquated expressions." The irony clearly escaped the group, and Scully agreed to delete the term in future airings. "For future runs, we will change the line to offend another ethnic group," he joked.)

The lesson of the controversy for the League was clear: "It just goes to prove what can be done when Catholics get actively involved." It also proved how many Americans feel about censorship, pressure politics, and *The Simpsons*, after Rosenberg's article was reprinted around the country. The League reported that it was itself deluged with critical and sometimes obscene e-mail and letters. And the series has not been hesitant to strike back, although less directly. A 2000 episode purporting to show a "behind the scenes" retrospective of *The Simpsons* has Bart including among the show's merchandise a tee-shirt with his face on it with the message, "Life Begins at Conception." In another, Bart crosses himself when he finds a dead gerbil in the couch. Although not a Catholic, Mr. Burns's assistant, Waylon Smithers, darts into the downtown Catholic church to confess his sins, only to find Police Chief Wiggum has been listening in. The League won, but *The Simpsons* fires the final shots, bloodied but unbowed.

Kenneth Briggs says that one reason for the success of the League's campaign may have been that "there is much more sensitivity toward Catholic references because there is still a feeling out in the world that there is a powerful anti-Catholic element in the media. I don't think that's true, but it is the perception." Another explanation for Fox's yielding to pressure from the League, he said, is that "the Catholic Church is perceived to be hierarchical, and hierarchical structures are perceived to be more powerful than egalitarian ones. . . . The Church's hierarchical structure probably gives it, whether intended or not, a degree of intimidation. I find this rather interesting."

The Catholic Church's representation in *The Simpsons* is not uniformly negative and, Scully's protests notwithstanding, the show's writers know when to tread carefully. Catholics are a part of the Springfield community, attending the downtown church, Our Lady of Perpetual Sorrow, whose sign advises would-be thieves and muggers that "Archbishop Carries Less Than $20"—perhaps a small nod to the denomination's commitment to impoverished urban centers. The congregation sponsors an annual Fun-and-Food Fest. Monsignor Kenneth Daly appears with Lovejoy on "Gabbin' about God," a weekly radio program. There is also a parochial school in Springfield, Saint Sebastian's School for Wicked Girls, which is run by nuns.

Pope John Paul II, a universally beloved figure, was often portrayed as a tiny figure, silent but benign. Wearing his miter and carrying his shepherd's staff, he popped up waving from an open car in a ticker tape parade and in unlikely crowd scenes, such as the unveiling of a new car designed by Homer. The closest thing to a dig came in one brief sequence where the Pope is at the Mayo Clinic, apparently being treated for flatulence. In an episode dealing with the apparent end of the world, based on a sign found in Springfield, the news is carried to the Vatican. From an exterior shot of St. Peter's Basilica the scene shifts inside, where the pope is seen sitting on a lawn chair, reading the newspaper *La Stampa*. This pope is not John Paul II, however, but another man wearing glasses. Asked by his aide what to do about the news from America, the pope says, "Keep an eye on it."

On a deeper level, the Catholic Church as portrayed in *The Simpsons* is a reflection of what George Weigel, author of *Witness to Hope: The Biography of Pope John Paul II* and a Catholic League board member, calls "the conventional story line" of the American media. Catholics, he said in a conversation sponsored by the Washington, DC-based Ethics and Public Policy Center, "are probably the most varied, multi-hued religious community in the nation. Yet for almost forty years, the Catholic story has been reported in starkly black-and-white terms."[13] In *The Simpsons*, the Catholic Church is the sum of its least popular stands, such as opposition to birth control. Still, the ubiquitous presence of the small, mute figure of the pontiff, moving through the scenery, acknowledged John Paul II's longevity and—by not attacking or satirizing an otherwise perfect target—his popularity.

Ironically, the Christian theology represented by *The Simpsons* —salvation by works as well as by grace—may come closer to that enunciated by Pope John Paul II in late 2000. Speaking to thirty thousand pilgrims gathered in St. Peter's Square, the pontiff proclaimed that all who live a just life will be saved, even if they do not believe in Jesus. That sounds a lot like Homer Simpson and other characters in the show. John L. Allen Jr., Vatican correspondent for the *National Catholic Reporter,* a liberal weekly, and a long-time *Simpsons* fan, is not troubled by his denomination's portrayal. He says his reading of the series is that "Catholicism as such is not a major target, perhaps reflecting a tad the Ivy League generic Protestantism of the show's writers. . . . I would say Catholicism gets off comparatively easy."

Briggs, who now serves on the board of the *National Catholic Reporter,* agrees. "It's a real big stretch to make *The Simpsons* anti-Catholic; it's anti-hypocrisy. My first impression is how little Catholic content there is in it—and I'm surprised. Everyone takes a shot on *The Simpsons,* so it's common sense that there are little comments here and there. Compared to the general foibles in Lovejoy's life and church, I can't think of how they would stack up to much."

In recent decades, evangelical and fundamentalist Protestants have been quite willing to make common political cause with the Catholic Church in a marriage of convenience over issues such as abortion, euthanasia, stem cell research, and gay marriage. But theologically, and behind closed doors, old prejudices die hard. This conflict is well illustrated in a 2005 episode, when *The Simpsons* revisited Catholicism. The genesis for the show was simple, writer-producer Mike Reiss told the Australian magazine *Encore* in April 2005: "Someone came in one day and said 'Homer should want to become a Catholic,' once he realizes Catholics can get absolution for what they do, and they get to drink wine at church. When I heard that idea I said 'This is going to be fantastic episode.'" By the time it was written (by Matt Warburton), edited, and produced, it was much more than the original premise, as is often the case with *The Simpsons,* and was nominated for a Writers Guild of America award.

Bart is accused of yet another disruptive school prank—in this rare instance, unjustly—and expelled yet again from Springfield Elementary. In part because of its relative affordability, his parents decide to send him to St. Jerome's Catholic School. Homer is convinced they have made a wise choice, warning his son that at *this* place if he misbehaves he'll not only get bad grades—he'll go to hell. Out front, there is a benign looking statue of the school's namesake, a gentle, robed friar. At the base, however, is a mixed message: "St. Jerome Suffered for Our Sins, Now It's YOUR Turn." Bart wears a uniform—bow tie, white shirt, blue shorts—as he takes his seat and is introduced by his teacher, Sister Thomasina. The new student is otherwise nonconforming, as he mumbles an introduction and walks back to his desk playing a GameBoy. But just as he sits down, the device is snatched from his hands. He mouths off to the nun, who rewards him with two hits from a yardstick, an advance over the more traditional ruler across the knuckles. And that isn't all. He is sent to the hall for a lecture from the angry teacher about sassing.

In another page from the past, perhaps familiar to older Catholic readers, Bart is told to stretch out his arms, "like our Lord on the cross," and hold a heavy dictionary in each hand. Sister tells him to think what it would be like if he had nails in his hands. Incorrigibly, Bart replies that the nails might help him keep the books up, which earns him another swat from the teacher, who returns to the classroom. The boy mutters that he is being persecuted by this stupid Catholic school for his hip attitude: "I'm the *real* Jesus here."

This sacrilege attracts the attention of a young, red-headed priest strolling down the hall. Father Sean chuckles, telling Bart he "used to be a wee ornery cuss" himself. At this point, a stream of Irish stereotypes kicks in. For the boy's benefit, there is a flashback to a drunken brawl between Sean and his father outside a pub on the Emerald Isle. The old man decks his son and then insults him by saying he's just like his mother—can't take a punch. As Sean leans over the gutter, St. Peter appears to him out of a street lamp, floating above the pavement and telling him to repent of his wicked ways. Then the saint spits in his eye. That, Sean tells Bart, is how he came to the church. The boy is not impressed, complaining that he has been enrolled in the Catholic school because of a prank he didn't do. Perhaps recognizing a kindred spirit, the priest says he believes him, observing that lots of church types, like St. Augustine, started off as troublemakers. Father Sean gives him a "lives of the saints" comic book and escorts him back to class, falsely telling his teacher that he has just given the boy a thrashing.

Bart is intrigued with the comic and opens it inside his math book—which uses guilt-ridden Catholic theology to frame exercises. The first story he turns to is the bloody martyrdom of St. Sebastian, a Roman soldier who is executed by order of the emperor for being a Christian, his body pierced by arrows. "This stuff is great!" the boy says. At home, he shares his enthusiasm for his new friend and his new school with his family at the dinner table. Father Sean quotes the rap artist Eminem in his sermons and plays drums in a rock band with other priests. (There are many real-life counterparts to such clerics, such as Father Ricardo Xavier-Zatwon Bailey, a priest at Holy Spirit Roman Catholic Church in Atlanta, who broadcasts as "Father Crunk" on a local rock station.) In art class, Bart paints the burning of Joan of Arc. "Catholics rock," is the boy's conclusion. But Marge is concerned. She is glad he is having fun but warns him about getting too involved in the Catholic Church, with all that sitting, standing, and kneeling, "like Simon Says, without a winner." Now it's Bart's turn to condemn blasphemy, and he begins to pray the rosary for her, but his mother snatches it away before he can touch the first bead. Marge worries aloud that Catholics can be a peculiar bunch—no birth control, no meat on Fridays. Next the boy asks to say grace, crossing himself and praying in Latin. That does it for Homer, who vows to jump in the car and pull his son out of "that crazy school."

As Homer arrives at St. Jerome's, people are streaming up the front steps. He shoulders his way to the front and confronts Father Sean, who is standing in the doorway. Homer identifies himself as Bart's dad and declares, "I'm sick of you teaching my son your time-tested values." But before the priest can answer, Homer is distracted by the aroma of pancakes—the reason for the crowd—and the priest invites him to stay for dinner. The two sit together and, before Homer can resume the conversation, it's time for bingo, and he ends up with a bag full of prizes. Sated and relaxed, he finally gets to talk to the priest about Catholicism. He asks the priest about the greatest sacrifice he has to make, which Father Sean assumes is celibacy. Of course, Homer is referring to no meat on Fridays (except during Lent this is no longer required). Then the priest explains the sacrament of confession, which gives absolution "if you truly repent." Grasping the concept instantly—if imperfectly—Homer says, "Let's make some magic," and begins to list his sins (some of which he says he intends to repeat), first in the hallway and then in the confessional, which induces eye-rolling on the part of Father Sean. Homer exits in what he believes to be a state of grace, exultant. "In your face, Lord!" he says, missing the point. Then the priest informs him that in order to be absolved of his sins, he must first become a Catholic. Homer is game, asking what he needs to do—beat up some Unitarians? It's a little harder than that, Father Sean says; it begins with introspection but ends with bread and wine. Homer agrees.

Slipping into the kitchen the next morning, after being out all night, Homer has a look that Marge recognizes immediately, "like you've accepted someone as your personal something." Under duress, he tells her of his visit to the Catholic church. "I knew they'd try to convert you," she says, voicing typical Protestant suspicion. "That's what they do." Marge informs him, as she did in an earlier episode, that she has no intention of having another dozen kids. Homer insists that the church would only require another nine or ten offspring, passing his wife a pamphlet called "Plop 'Til You Drop." Forget it, she tells him, starting to list other grievances she has. Once she went to a Catholic wedding and the incense ruined her pantsuit. Homer wonders why she is so upset; his and Bart's conversion is no big deal. But in Springfield it is. A headline from the local paper screams, "Local Father, Son May Switch Religions." A montage follows, of Bart and Homer lighting candles, praying the rosary together, eating pancakes and playing bingo, and going to an all-you-can-eat seafood restaurant with Father Sean. There is also a shot of the father and son firing tommy guns as mafiosi in 1930s Chicago.

Marge shows up as usual on Sunday morning at the First Church of Springfield, but she is alone, and she can hear the disapproving whispers. On the way out after the service, she tries to avoid Reverend Lovejoy, without success. He asks if she is by herself, and she dissembles, telling the minister that the other members of her family are under the weather. "Or under the spell of a man in a pointy white hat?" he asks. Marge confesses that her husband and son are at the Catholic church and asks for Lovejoy's advice. He suggests a meeting of the church council—himself and Flanders— and they convene at Stuckey's, next to the interstate. The men agree that they cannot allow Bart and Homer to "go Catholic." Protestants and Catholics have been divided, Ned says, since the Schism of Lourdes in 1573—another bogus and trivializing religious reference—over whether or not it is right to come to church with wet hair. Marge admits she is torn, recognizing that it is a good thing that her son and husband are interested in spirituality. Lovejoy says that spirituality is a great thing—"I'm Mr. Spirituality"—but the reality is that having a different faith means a different afterlife.

Marge daydreams about heaven. She arrives alone, finding St. Peter at a podium, perched on a cloud, and is welcomed to Protestant paradise. Preppy people, men in golf shirts with sweaters tied around their shoulders, are playing croquet and badminton, as ersatz classical music plays. Things are a lot more lively over in Catholic heaven, where the Mexicans are singing and dancing; the Italians are sitting around a long table with a red-and-white checkered cloth, enjoying a meal; and the Irish are fighting and dancing. Homer and Bart are there, swinging at a piñata and then joining the Riverdance gang. Marge wishes her family could be with her, but one of the Protestants informs her that Catholics are "not our sort," a demeaning expression used for decades by upper-class WASPs. Marge says she needs to speak with someone, but the preppy tells her that that person—Jesus—has "gone native," which is to say, to Catholic heaven. Sure enough, in one of his rare appearances in *The Simpsons*, Jesus is being tossed on a blanket by Bart and Homer. Even rarer for the series, Jesus is laughing and speaking, although the only thing he says is "Stop it!" Marge awakens with a scream, and Lovejoy assures her they will get her family back.

At the Catholic church, Homer and Bart are in Father Sean's class, First Communion 101. Although he is the only adult in the class, Homer is also in uniform. He is able to answer one of the more difficult questions only because he has written the answer—"Transubstantiation"—along one arm. On the other he has written more basic theology: "God: Good, Devil: Bad." Marge, Lovejoy, and Ned peer through the window in the classroom door, horrified. Flanders says they have to make their move now, because "once they seal the deal, there's no turning back," comparing it to Jewish circumcision. They barge into the room, and Marge tells her son he is leaving with her. Theology is not the only part of the ethos of the Catholic Church Bart has assimilated already. Sorry, he tells his mother, "this is the Catholic Church. Chicks don't have any authority here." Father Sean assures them that if there is a problem, they can work it out, but Lovejoy tells the priest to back off, calling him "Pope-y Le Pew." Homer asks Marge what she is doing. She tells him that *his* soul is *his* business but that she didn't change Bart's diapers to see him become a Catholic. Then she grabs him and takes off in Lovejoy's van.

The old VW minibus is painted in bright, psychedelic colors and big letters that read "The Ministry Machine," apparently a reference to "The Mystery Machine" in the Scooby Doo cartoons. Inside, Bart is angry about the intervention. "You're always nagging me to go to church and now that I am," he says, "it's the wrong one." Marge says that she just doesn't think Homer is the right person to pick out a religion for the boy. Okay, Bart says, I'll pick Judaism, and then he breaks into a personalized version of "Hava Nagila." It is Lovejoy who has to explain the situation to the boy. "We're here to bring you back to the one true faith—the Western Branch of American Reform Presby-Lutheranism." The allegation is a familiar one to Christians: "sheep stealing," or the luring of believers from one flock to another. At this moment, Homer calls from home, where he is with Father Sean and Lisa. "Once you go Vatican, you can't go back again," he declares. Marge claims that winning Bart over wasn't a fair fight; the Catholics "suckered him in with gory stories." She vows she will show Bart that "Protestants can be hip, too." Father Sean says he doesn't want to lose the young convert. If he does, he'll be the worst priest ever—then he pauses for a moment, wordlessly reminding himself of the obviously worse Catholic clergymen. There is an awkward moment of silence, as the same thing occurs to Homer.

The minibus pulls up to the Springfield fairgrounds, where a Protestant youth festival is underway. At first, it seems extremely lame, despite Marge's forced enthusiasm. "Isn't this the kind of religion you'd like to be a part of for all eternity?" she hopefully asks Bart. The MC at the main music stage is a middle-aged white man in a suit and tie, who introduces an aging rock group that has just converted to Christianity, changing their name from "Quiet Riot" to "Pious Riot." Their bland fare entrances Marge and the other adults. A young woman in the crowd, sitting on the shoulders of a young man, raises her shirt to flash, not her bare chest, but a tee-shirt with a picture of Jesus on it. Bart is not impressed, grumpily folding his arms. What's wrong, his mother asks. "You love youth culture." In an exchange that rings absolutely true, the boy replies, "A religion isn't cool just because they've glommed onto some crappy rock band from the 1940s. . . . You just don't get it. I've made a sacred commitment to the church and . . ." The principled convert then spots an attraction he cannot resist: "Onward Paintball Soldiers." For Bart, the violence is irresistible, and Marge smiles. The targets inside include a cut-out Adam and Eve, the Three Wise Men, and one of the Flanders boys, whom Bart blasts into eternity. "I knew one of these dumb things would work," Marge says.

The religious war is not over. Father Sean arrives on a motorcycle, with Homer in the sidecar, wearing a World War I German helmet with a cross on top. They are firing their own paint guns. Homer tells Bart to jump aboard. "We'll show your mother our God kicks their God's butt!" But Reverend Lovejoy and Ned, with their paint guns, join the fray. "Back off, you servants of the Holy See!" Flander says. Everyone pumps their weapons, prepared to refight half a dozen post-Reformation European wars. Unexpectedly, it is Bart who calls on the "church-o's" to curb their zeal, telling them he has something to say. "Don't you get it?" he asks.

"It's all Christianity, people. The little, stupid differences are nothing next to the big, stupid similarities." Ned agrees. "Can't we all get together and concentrate on our real enemies—monogamous gays and stem cells?" Well said, Father Sean chimes in. Bart, Reverend Lovejoy says, "you've taught us an important lesson. We Christians have been niggling over details for too long."

Originally, this episode—"The Father, the Son, and the Holy Guest Star"—was to air on April 10, 2005, eight days after the death of Pope John Paul II, and so it was bumped until May 15. The episode did not generate much controversy on this side of the Atlantic, perhaps because Catholic viewers were distracted by the death of the old pope and the election of a new one. However, in Ireland—where sectarian feelings have run high, and sometimes violent, for hundreds of years—the episode was the subject of comment after it aired in North America but before it appeared in Europe. Both Protestant and Catholic churchmen had something to say. The former Church of Ireland archdeacon of Dublin, Gordon Linney, told Sylvia Pownall of the *London Mirror* that he found the depiction of Protestant heaven "hugely offensive," adding that "it made us sound boring. . . . It is wrong for anybody to set out intentionally to cause offense, especially in religious matters." However, he told the paper that he still had a sense of humor—and perspective. "Sometimes religious people take themselves far too seriously and take offence too easily. . . . We have survived screen and strife for more than 2,000 years, so we're not going to get upset about a cartoon." The editor of the *Irish Catholic*, Garry O'Sullivan, made a similar observation: "In fairness to *The Simpsons*, they have given every major religion a fair whack. . . . The Catholics will probably laugh at the croquet in the Protestant heaven and laugh less at the drinking and fighting in the Catholic heaven, but at the end of the day it's just a bit of fun. . . . Catholics take it on the chin, it is anything goes for them. But at the same time Catholics should be able to sit back and laugh at themselves and allow others to poke fun at us."

Even Catholic temperance leaders seemed willing to overlook the alcohol in heaven. "If *The Simpsons* episode helps to portray heaven as a happy place, I have no problem with it," Father

Micheal MacGreil, the chairman of the Pioneer Total Abstinence Association, told the *Sunday Times* of London. "The real heaven, according to Catholicism, is seeing God's face and beauty in the presence of the saints. Nobody on earth could imagine what that is like. . . . I wouldn't take any notice of the Irish stereotypes. The Irish are a jovial people and emotionally expressive, and let's just say that other religions and peoples are more reserved. But we should remember that a sober heaven can be very jolly too." The Irish papers also pointed out that the episode had a back story. Liam Neeson, the Irish actor who provided the voice for Father Sean, was raised in the predominantly Protestant town of Bally-mena, in Ulster. In 1999, the actor told an American magazine that he felt "second class" as a Catholic growing up in the town, which drew a sharp rebuke from another Ballymena native, the demagogic Protestant politician Ian Paisley, who was still frosted at Neeson's film portrayal of the Irish rebel hero Michael Collins.

Some observers felt that the show's writers missed a good opportunity, that they pulled their punches. The biblical scholar John Dominic Crossan, himself a native of Ireland and a former Catholic priest, said, "The level and accuracy of satire in the episode would have been very appropriate against classic movie targets like *Going My Way* and *The Bells of St. Mary's* in the 1940s. But as contemporary Roman Catholic and/or Protestant satire, I found it too shallow. That is, too weak rather than too strong. The abuse of power by Roman Catholic authorities in the name of papal infallibility and by Protestant authorities in the name of biblical inerrancy deserves far more precise and lethal satire than anything *The Simpsons* dared to do in this episode."

Nine

The Jews: "Mel Brooks Is *Jewish*? . . . Are *We* Jewish?"

One night while working on this book, I heard my daughter reading aloud to my wife a story by Isaac Bashevis Singer, the great Jewish writer and Nobel laureate. It was a classic tale that provoked gales of laughter from both of them, and suddenly a thought struck me: *The Simpsons'* Springfield is a lot like Chelm, Singer's celebrated Eastern European village of Jewish fools, buffoons, and dunderheads, except that in Springfield, most of the fools are Gentiles (or seem to be). This transposition is not surprising, given the background and viewpoint of *The Simpsons'* writers and producers. "There have always been a lot of Jewish writers on *The Simpsons*," says longtime writer Mike Reiss. "We bring that comedy to it."

It is also not surprising that Judaism, although a target of satire like other faiths, denominations, and institutions in the series, is accorded considerable respect. As with most Hollywood productions, there is good representation of Jews on the creative side. "Jews play a disproportionate role in several key sectors of American society," including the media, according to Jack Wertheimer, provost of the Jewish Theological Seminary. "Jews have achieved respectability, and Judaism is treated with a great deal of acceptance within American society," he said at a seminar sponsored by the Ethics and Public Policy Center.[1] Despite their atheism or secularism, the Jewish writers on *The Simpsons* represent their faith well. Jewish humor, says Rabbi Harold W. Schulweis, the longtime spiritual leader of Valley Beth Shalom synagogue in Encino, California, "is not just funny—it's philosophical." Comedian Mel Brooks, who appeared as himself in an episode, observes that, for the Jews, "humor is just another defense against the universe."[2]

The many jokes squeezed into each episode of *The Simpsons* weave together two distinct strands of humor: on the one hand, the snarky, iconoclastic nastiness embodied by Harvard University's *Lampoon* magazine; and on the other, the dark, rapid-fire angst of Borscht Belt *tummlers* ("roisterers") and *shpritzers* ("sprayers") such as Lenny Bruce and Don Rickles. None is more typical of this Jewish strain of humor than the exchange between Bart's friend Milhouse and Lisa in the Exodus segment of the episode "Simpson Bible Stories." In this dream sequence, Milhouse is Moses. He has just led the Israelite slaves across the Red Sea, only to learn that what lies ahead is forty years of wandering in the desert. But after that, he asks Lisa hopefully, "it's clear sailing for the Jews, isn't that right?" Lisa, unwilling to break the news of what the next three thousand years holds for the Chosen People, smiles tightly and says, "Well, more or less."

There is an Orthodox synagogue in town, with the improbable name of Temple Beth Springfield (Jewish congregations are usually either "Temple" or "Beth," followed by a Hebrew name), located not far from Reverend Lovejoy's First Church of Springfield. The two houses of worship are so close, in fact, that once the church marquee carried the decidedly non-ecumenical message: "No Synagogue Parking." Without further comment on the subject in the episode, one can reasonably surmise that the incident might have occurred in a year when the Jewish High Holidays coincided with the church's Sunday morning service. This can be a sore point where synagogues and churches are neighbors. Otherwise, relations between Lovejoy and Rabbi Hyman Krustofski are cordial. The rabbi, bearded and dressed in the black garb of the Hasidim, is a regular on the minister's weekly call-in radio show, "Gabbin' about God." Orthodox rabbis are often wary of such interfaith dialogues, but Krustofski does not conform to this stereotype. According to *The Simpsons Guide to Springfield*, the rabbi plays basketball against Lovejoy in the annual "Springfield Two-Man Interfaith Jimmy Jam." Each Friday, according to the same guide, the synagogue offers a regular Friday Sabbath dinner that includes gefilte fish and Manischewitz wine, although this is highly unlikely since such meals are traditionally held in Jewish homes.

Jewish references thread through *The Simpsons*, and they sometimes reinforce stereotypes. One character observes that a grizzly bear can tear through a tree "like a Jewish mother through self-esteem." The local Jewish hospital is considered the best, if the most pricey, according to an ambulance driver. An unnamed Jewish child can be seen in an occasional suburban crowd scene, called in from the playground to practice his music. There is still an "old neighborhood" downtown, Springfield's Lower East Side, where Jews lived before moving to the suburbs. This is where Krustofski's synagogue is located and where visitors can dine at restaurants such as Tannen's Fatty Meats and Izzy's Deli. In real life, if there were enough Jews in Springfield, the synagogue would have followed the migration from the urban center to the suburbs, the pattern in most American cities of any size. Thus, the town's small Jewish community is marginalized and often misunderstood in ways that are still common in small Protestant communities in the American heartland. Related problems facing modern American Jewry in such towns—assimilation and how to fit into an overwhelmingly Christian society—are raised in various ways in *The Simpsons*. Thus, we learn that Kent Brockman, the local television news anchor and member of Springfield Community Church, started his broadcasting career as Kenny Brockelstein, and still wears a pendant around his neck with the Hebrew word *C'hai* (life). A tee-shirt pops up in one episode, reading "Jews for Jebus," the name Homer sometimes mistakes for Jesus. Costington's department store advertises "Christmas presents at Hanukkah prices."

This environment gives rise to a kind of unconscious anti-Semitism. For example, Lovejoy keeps the rabbi's address and phone number on his "non-Christian Rolodex." At the elementary school, Principal Skinner is heard fielding an angry call from the superintendent. "I know Weinstein's parents were upset," he stammers. "But, but, ah, I was sure it was a phony excuse. I mean, it sounds so made up: 'Yom Kip-pur.'" The Day of Atonement, the holiest day of the year for Jews, is completely unfamiliar to the school principal. When Homer needs fifty thousand dollars for a heart bypass, he goes to the rabbi, pretending to be Jewish in the only way he knows how. "Now, I know I haven't been the best Jew, but I have rented *Fiddler on the Roof* and I will watch it," he says. All he gets from the rabbi is a dreidel. In another episode, while visiting New York City, Bart mistakes several Hasidic rabbis— black-clad and bearded—for the Texas rock group ZZ Top, who favor the same attire, plus sunglasses. Finally, Bart works a sympathy scam in the shopping mall wearing a yarmulke, pretending that his bar mitzvah cake has just been smashed.

Just as Ned Flanders and Reverend Lovejoy embody Protestant Christianity on *The Simpsons*, the character Krusty the Clown represents the Jews. The host of a popular children's show on the local television station, Krusty was introduced during the 1989–1990 season in a short for *The Tracey Ullman Show*. Series creator Matt Groening, who wrote the episode, said in an interview that Krusty came as "a sudden inspiration on the part of a couple of writers" for the show. Groening told *TV Guide* that the braying, self-centered clown, who always appears in brightly colored hair, red nose, and makeup, was based on a clown named Rusty Nails in Groening's hometown of Portland, Oregon. Rusty Nails "was actually a very nice Christian clown [who later became a minister] who showed old Three Stooges shorts. But I couldn't get past the idea that this was a nice clown with the scariest name possible."[3] Writer and producer Mike Scully has similar memories. "For my generation, Krusty is every Saturday-morning TV clown. Everybody had a Krusty in their town." Cast member Dan Castellaneta, who does Krusty's voice, says he used the voice of Bob Bell, who played Bozo the Clown on Chicago's WGN-TV for many years, as a model for his characterization.

Krusty's show on *The Simpsons* features live gags and routines before an audience of kids, along with violent cartoons starring a cat and mouse named Itchy and Scratchy, obviously patterned on Tom and Jerry. Commercials promote a full line of Krusty merchandise: posters, lunch boxes, cereal, and appliances of dubious utility and reliability. There is a chain of fast-food restaurants featuring Krusty Burgers and a disreputable summer camp where overweight kids can avail themselves of his "exclusive program of diet and ridicule." In 2000, Krusty released a biography, *Your Shoes Are Too Big to Kick Box with God*, ghost written by novelist John Updike. And Krusty is Jewish, *very* Jewish. His picture forms a stylized Jewish star on his dressing room door. Yet Dalton, Mazur, and Siems, in *God in the Details*, see Krusty as "a gross caricature of a stereotypical secularized Jew corrupted by wealth and fame" who "dislikes children (and) finances his lavish debt-ridden lifestyle by over-marketing his own image unabashedly."

Krusty and Judaism are the center of a 1991 Emmy-winning episode entitled "Like Father, Like Clown." The show's premise is a reworking of the 1927 movie classic *The Jazz Singer*, which starred Al Jolson and was made again, with considerably less success, in 1953 (starring Danny Thomas) and in 1980 (starring Neil Diamond). The film tells the story of a Jewish cantor who disowns his son because the young man chooses to be an entertainer. Rabbi Lavi Meier and Rabbi Harold Schulweis, a leading thinker of Conservative Judaism in America, served as "special technical consultants" on *The Simpsons* version. The two rabbis' expertise and guidance is apparent throughout the show, which ranks in religious significance with episodes such as "Homer the Heretic" and "Lisa the Skeptic." Unlike most *Simpsons* episodes, there is no subplot in "Like Father, Like Clown," which means the full twenty-two minutes are devoted to a single narrative.

Schulweis said he was not a fan of *The Simpsons* when someone from the show called and asked if he would be willing to look at a draft of the script. He agreed to help, and said he was surprised to find how genuine it was. "I thought it had a Jewish resonance to it. It was profound. I was impressed by the underlying moral seriousness." The show's writers, he said, "have a Yiddish spark in them." Schulweis said he made some corrections to the script, and then he told the show's writer a Hasidic story about the honored role of the jester, called a "badchan." Such a person, who brings joy and happiness, would have a share in the world to come, the sages said, because "God loves laughter." When the episode aired and Schulweis's name appeared on the closing credits, the impact in his congregation was immediate and profound: "I became an instant hero among my young people. I was cool."

In the episode, members of the Simpson family are so oblivious to Judaism that they are shocked to discover that Krusty is Jewish. Having been invited to dinner, the clown is asked by Marge to offer a grace before the meal. Apologizing for being rusty, Krusty folds his hands (not a Jewish practice) and proceeds to recite the traditional blessing over bread, the "hamotzie," in Hebrew. Homer bursts into laughter, calling the blessing "funny talk." Lisa corrects her father, recognizing the language and making the connection that Krusty is Jewish. Naturally, clueless Homer is shocked at the notion of a Jewish entertainer, only to be informed by his daughter that many show business people are Jews: Lauren Bacall, Dinah Shore, William Shatner, and Mel Brooks. The revelation that Brooks (whose humor is in fact nothing if not Jewish) is Jewish dumbfounds Homer. Suddenly, Krusty collapses into tears, as a clarinet plays European klezmer music. Reciting the blessing—the "bracha"—brings back painful memories involving his father, he tells the Simpsons.

The clown reveals to family members that his real name is Herschel Krustofski and he is descended from a long line of rabbis, ending with his father, Temple Beth Springfield's Rabbi Hyman Krustofski. Krusty's story flashes back to his youth, when his father —voiced in an unmistakable Yiddish accent by comedian and former rabbi Jackie Mason—was a respected leader of Springfield's Lower East Side's Jewish community, dispensing all manner of wisdom on issues both profound and trivial. A man asks if he should finish college, and the rabbi answers that "no one is poor except he who lacks knowledge." A woman with an infant in her arms asks whether she should have another child. The rabbi says that she should, that another child would be a blessing. But when a man asks whether he should buy a Chrysler, Rabbi Krustofski requires him to rephrase the query as an ethical question, the approach favored more recently by Dr. Laura Schlessinger, another Orthodox Jew with a penchant for giving advice. Asked whether it would be "right" to buy a Chrysler, the rabbi says it would, "for great is the car with power steering and Dyna-flow suspension."

As sometimes happens in clergy households, however, the rabbi's wisdom does not extend to his own family. Young Herschel, who wears a yarmulke on the street, yearns to go into comedy to be a clown: "I want to make people laugh," he says. Because a clown is not a respected member of the community, the rabbi forbids the boy to consider such a career. Life is not fun, the rabbi says—life is serious. "Seltzer is for drinking, not for spraying," the father admonishes. "Pie is for noshing, not for throwing." He threatens to give his son "such a *zetz*" (a hit) if he pursues his ambition rather than becoming a rabbi like his father.

But, Krusty tells the Simpsons back at their dinner table, "the Lord works in mysterious ways." The father's threat does not deter the boy, who gets his first laugh imitating his father in his yeshiva class, and the rabbi's efforts to extinguish his son's love of comedy fail. Soon, Krustofski discovers his son in the bathroom, a turn on a Neil Simon comedy, squirting himself with seltzer, prompting the rabbi to cry out, "*Oy gevalt!*" (O, horrors!).

Time passed. Older, but still unabashed, the young man donned what would be his trademark Krusty the Clown costume and makeup and accepted a paying gig entertaining rabbis at a Talmudic conference in New York's Catskill Mountains—his first big break. The act, which featured Israeli folk music and colorful balloon sculptures of a Star of David and a menorah, was a hit, even with his unsuspecting father who was in the audience. To compound the irony, as Krusty performs, Rabbi Krustofski brags about his son to a colleague, saying he was first in his yeshiva class and voted "most likely to hear God." The fellow rabbi accuses Krustofski of being so proud of his son that he exaggerates. No, insists Krustofski, "a rabbi never exaggerates. A rabbi composes. He creates thoughts. He tells stories that may never have happened. But he does not exaggerate!"

Just then, a rowdy rabbi in the audience gets carried away with the clown's performance and squirts Krusty with seltzer, dissolving his makeup and revealing his true identity. His father is crushed and shouts, "*Oy vey is mir!* ("Woe is me!"). He denounces his son, saying he has "brought shame on our family! I never want to see you again, you clown!" A joke within a joke follows, in typically brilliant *Simpsons* fashion, reminding knowing viewers of the episode's cinematic reference. "Oh, if you were a musician or a *jazz singer*, this I could forgive," the rabbi proclaims. But not this, and from that time on the clown has not seen or spoken with his father. Despite the twenty-five-year estrangement that has followed, Krusty tells Bart that he thinks about his father almost all the time—"except when I'm at the track. Then I'm all business." Similar estrangements, provoked by less profound differences, are common in the Jewish community, rabbis today will testify.

After completing his tale, Krusty leaves the Simpson household, telling the sympathetic family not to worry about him, because he is a survivor. Yet he is in fact tortured by the memories and wanders the rainy streets of Springfield after midnight. He passes a newsstand where his eyes fall on a magazine called *Modern Jewish Father*, featuring a bearded father and young son happily working together in front of a computer, an image that causes him to burst into tears. All this reminiscence and rambling prompts Krusty to try to reestablish contact with his father. He phones the rabbi at home, yet he cannot speak. "Hello, hello?" Rabbi Krustofski says, awakened from sleep. "Anybody there? What's this? I hear the phone ring and suddenly there's nothing. I'm listening and there's no talking. Hello, mister, who are you? Why would they call if they don't want to talk to you?" The rabbi hangs up, and the next day Krusty continues to disintegrate, this time on screen during his show. After a violent cartoon that includes tender scenes between a mouse and a cat and their respective fathers, Krusty weeps.

Lisa and Bart, watching in horror on their couch, decide they have to intervene to bring father and son together. Through Reverend Lovejoy, who shares a radio show with Rabbi Krustofski, they get his address and pay him a visit. The children knock on the door of his book-lined study. He is studying from a scroll, muttering words including, *"rebonno shel olam"* ("Master of the universe"), a reference to God. The rabbi asks what he can do for his "young friends," and the two children tell the rabbi they want to talk about his son. Repeating a line from countless plays, movies, and television shows about parents and alienated children, Rabbi Krustofski says, "I have no son!" and slams the door in their

faces. Bart, clearly his own father's son, takes the statement literally and assumes, "We came all this way and it's the wrong guy."
Krustofski opens the door to explain that his comment was
metaphorical—and then slams the door again.

The next airing of "Gabbin' about God" on KBBL-AM (K-
babble? The broadcast tower sometimes seems like the tower of
Babel in Genesis 11, with its "confusing tongues") offers another
opportunity to approach Rabbi Krustofski on the subject of reconciliation. First, Krusty calls, but again he is unable to speak.
"Anybody there?" the rabbi asks. "I hear breathing but I don't hear
talking. . . . Some people got nothing to do but call people and
hang up. There's all kinds of *mishegoyim* in the world." *Mishegoyim*
can be translated "crazy gentiles," but the voice at the end of this
particular line belongs to a distraught Jew. Bart then calls the
show, identifying himself as "Dimitri." He asks all three religious
leaders, "If a son defies his father and chooses a career that makes
millions of children happy, shouldn't the father forgive the son?"
The priest and the minister say he should, but the rabbi goes bal-
listic. "No way! Absolutely not! Who screens these calls? Who's
in charge here? There's nobody in charge here!"

Bart and Lisa are undeterred. The boy goes to Springfield's
Lower East Side to a shop called Yiddle's that specializes in "practical jokes, magic tricks, and medical supplies." He buys a fake
beard, eyebrows, and earlocks, and a set of black clothes, white
fringes, and a broad-brimmed hat favored by Hasidic Jews. Thus
disguised, the boy slips into a circle around the rabbi, who is in the
park, in the midst of a discourse on the nature of philanthropy, as
more Jewish music plays. Krustofski quotes the medieval philosopher Maimonides, that "the best charity is to give and not let anybody know." (Or, as Jesus puts it in the Sermon on the Mount,
"When you give to the needy, do not let your left hand know what
your right hand is doing, so that your giving may be in secret. Then
your Father, who sees what is done in secret, will reward you"
[Matt. 6:3–4].) A man in the circle questions this view, just as the
ancient rabbis did, wondering if the public example might not
encourage others to give to charity. Before the debate can continue, Bart interrupts, saying, "speaking of charity," shouldn't

Krustofski forgive his son? The rabbi rebuffs him. "Don't you understand that my boy broke my heart? He turned his back on our traditions, on our faith and on me." He exposes Bart's disguise, denounces him as a "little *pisher*" (squirt) and tells him to go away.

Lisa suggests they try to outsmart the rabbi by using another approach to bring father and son together. First, they call the rabbi and pretend to be the Nobel Prize–winning author Saul Bellow, requesting a meeting at Izzy's Delicatessen. Then they call Krusty, impersonating former French president François Mitterand, and request a meeting at the same place and time to present the clown with the Legion of Honor, another sly reference, this one to the unfathomable popularity in France of another Jewish comedian, Jerry Lewis. Disaster ensues at the restaurant, which we soon learn is Jewish but not kosher. The rabbi is offended and storms out after seeing a Krusty the Clown sandwich on the menu, which consists of ham, sausage, bacon, and mayonnaise on white bread—as Gentile a combination as can be imagined.

Lisa won't quit and tells her brother that the way they have been approaching the problem is all wrong. "What's the one thing rabbis prize above everything else?" she asks. (She might just as well be asking, "What's the one thing Jews value above everything else?") For comic relief, Bart guesses, "Those stupid hats?" The correct answer is "knowledge," and Lisa pledges to "hit him where it hurts—right in the Judaica." Easier said than done. They don't know it yet, but the good-hearted, well-meaning Simpson kids are in way over their heads. At the Old Springfield Library, Bart and Lisa begin their research. While her brother focuses on Bible pop-up books, Lisa dives into weightier fare, including the Babylonian Talmud, *The Big Book of Chosen People*, *Views on Jews*, and *Jewishness Revisited*. Using Lisa's crib note, Bart returns to the rabbi's study and, before he can be driven off once more, asks if the Babylonian Talmud does not say, "A child should be pushed aside with the left hand and drawn closer with the right." Krustofski agrees. "Then doesn't your religion command you to make up with Krusty?" Bart asks. The rabbi easily bats this away, citing the Fifth Commandment (Exod. 20:12): "Honor thy father and thy mother," he tells Bart. "End of story." This round goes to the rabbi.

But this argument is a profound one, according to Rabbi Sholom Dubov of Congregation Ahavas Yisrael in Maitland, Florida. Some talmudic scholars have suggested that when Jesus confronted the rabbis in the first century he too should have been pushed aside with one hand but drawn closer with the other, rather than driven away. One historic strain of rabbinic Judaism that survives to this day—exemplified by Rabbi Krustofski—characterizes some sins as so unforgivable that the sinner must be abandoned. Other strains, like the Orthodox Lubovitch Hasidim of which Dubov is a part, strive for a more inclusive approach. "For us, that means unconditional acceptance of the person on one hand, and absolute rejection of the bad behavior on the other," he says. "The Talmud says you should be capable of having both feelings at the same time. Unfortunately, some parents and some rabbis, like Rabbi Krustofski, are unable to adopt this seemingly contradictory approach. There's no reason why Krusty can't be a kosher clown."

Lisa sends Bart back with what she says is dynamite material, this time from Rabbi Simon ben Eleazer, a second-century talmudic scholar. This time the forum is a steam bath—the *schvitz*—where the learned men gather to discuss ethical issues wearing nothing but towels. "At all times," says Bart, to the approval of other sweating rabbis, "let a man be supple as a reed and not rigid as a cedar." Krustofski, now addressing Bart as "my learned short friend," replies from the book of Joshua, "You shall meditate on the Torah all day and all night" (1:8). Again, the round goes to the rabbi.

Almost asleep in the library, Lisa is running out of answers, but she tries once more. Bart again attempts to win over the rabbi, interrupting him without success in the midst of a circumcision. He asks if it is not written in the Talmud, "Who will bring redemption? The jesters." Krustofski says he is not convinced, adding, his blade poised over the male infant, "This is hardly the time or place to discuss it."

Short of learning ancient Hebrew, Lisa has only one long shot idea remaining. Back in the park, Bart engages Rabbi Krustofski in another Jewish arena, a chessboard. Bart quotes a source he identifies as another "great man," without further citation. "The

Jews are a swinging bunch of people," the boy recites. "I mean, I've heard of persecution, but what they went through is ridiculous. But the great thing is, after thousands of years of waiting and holding on and fighting, they finally made it."

This time, the rabbi is clearly impressed. "Oh," he says, "I've never heard the plight of my people phrased so eloquently." He asks Bart if the citation is from a sage like Rabbi Hillel, Judah the Pious, Maimonides, or the Dead Sea Scrolls. The boy trumps the rabbi, telling him the quote is from *Yes, I Can*, the autobiography of Sammy Davis Jr.—"an entertainer, like your son." (Davis, an African American and a convert to Judaism, was known as "The Candy Man," the title of one of his hit songs.) "The Candy Man said that?" the rabbi says, incredulous. "If a performer could think that way, maybe I'm upside down on this whole problem." But of course no Jewish dilemma could possibly be resolved without a healthy dose of guilt and a lament. "Ah, all the years of joy that I've lost. Why? Because of my stubborn ways." He weeps, consoled by Lisa, who tells him it is not too late to make things right.

Meanwhile, still dispirited and listless over his relationship with his father, Krusty is barely going through the motions on his television show. He lights a cigarette while a cartoon rolls. Suddenly Bart and Lisa lead Rabbi Krustofski through the backstage door. From the shadows, a familiar voice admonishes, "Hey, such a filthy habit." Krusty snaps, "Who asked you?" The rabbi emerges from the shadows and is recognized by his son. They embrace and weep, calling each other "Papa" and "Boychick" (little boy). Krusty brings his father on stage and introduces him to the audience. The clown asks the band to strike up "some reconciliation music," and the two men sing a schmaltzy duet of "Oh, Mein Papa," a 1950s hit by the Jewish crooner Eddie Fisher that is a paean to a beloved father. To seal the bond, the rabbi takes a pie from Bart and hits his son in the face.

Mike Reiss, who was executive producer and show-runner for *The Simpsons* during seasons three and four, wrote the episode. He told Australia's *Encore* magazine in August 2005 that the episode— his favorite—"was a departure from the norm in that it focused on a 'peripheral character and his relationship with a father we've never seen before.'" It was, he told the magazine, "as thorough a debate on that topic as you're ever going to see on a cartoon on Fox. . . . Somehow we did it, and it came out so well that we were just flooded with calls after that. People were saying, 'I just talked to my father—we haven't spoken in 25 years.' That one is very special to me. I'm proud of it, and it tells you something about how we do *The Simpsons*. To write this thing we had three rabbis on the payroll. They were working with us all week to make sure we got it biblically correct. We love to do our homework on the show— when you see us cover a topic, we really research it to death."

"That's a great episode!" says Rabbi Daniel Wolpe, formerly of Congregation Ohalei Rivka in Orlando. "I thought the episode was brilliant, first of all, because of the use of real Jewish sources. Second of all, because it was an interesting take on the greatest of contemporary Jewish dilemmas, which is the battle between tradition and modernity." When "Like Father, Like Clown" first aired in reruns, Wolpe—himself the son and brother of rabbis and then living in Los Angeles—assigned the Hebrew high school class he was teaching to watch, prompting some puzzled phone calls from parents.

The on-camera denouement of "Like Father, Like Clown" was not the end of the story of the Jews of Springfield or of Krusty, their exemplar. The second act in *The Simpsons'* examination of Krusty's Judaism came in December 2003. Despite his reconciliation with his father, the clown is again living a bored, lonely, dissolute, and narcissistic life. Beneath a knockoff of the famous Andy Warhol four-panel lithograph of Marilyn Monroe—this version features Krusty in four colors—he is channel surfing on his huge, flat-screen TV and downing a cocktail of champagne and a weight loss drink. Bart and Lisa come to his door and talk him into taking one of their litter of puppies. Later, while walking his new pet, he wanders back to the old Jewish neighborhood, strolling past a feast of storefront sight gags. It hasn't changed a bit, he observes. The butcher shop is a K Mart, with the K in a circle, the seal indicating the meat is kosher. L. L. Beanie advertises a bargain basement for yarmulkes. The bakery window raves,

"I can't believe it's not Trayfe!" Fantastic Schlomo's barbershop offers to trim two ear locks—*payos*—for the price of one. Push-carts, manned by rabbinic-looking entrepreneurs, hawk every-thing from DSL service to Brazilian wax.

Krusty comes up short when he turns a corner and encounters the "Jewish Walk of Fame." The puppy is sniffing around, so the clown tells him to pee on Sandy Koufax's star—since he lost $10,000 when the Dodger ace famously wouldn't pitch on Yom Kippur. By contrast, the irreligious clown recalls, "I did five shows that night." As he walks down the row he notices the names: comedian Joan Rivers, Albert Einstein, *Saturday Night Live* cre-ator Lorne Michaels, and the puppeteer Shari Lewis, whose cre-ation Lamb Chop has her own star. Then he comes upon the star for the novelist Chaim Potok, a name he fails to recognize. "What is he, some kind of Klingon?" More to the point, Krusty insists that he is a bigger name than the author of *The Chosen* and *My Name Is Asher Lev*, so why isn't there a star for him? Determined to get to the bottom of this puzzle, he goes to the offices of Spring-field's "Jewish Walk of Fame, Where the Chosen Get Chosen."

The curator assures him that he certainly deserves to have his star on the walk, but he proceeds to ask Krusty a few questions. Krusty gives his full name, including one of his middle names, Pin-cus, and confirms that he is circumcised. But when he is asked the date of his bar mitzvah, he fumbles and then confesses that he never had a ceremony. In that case, the curator pronounces, "In the eyes of God, and the Springfield Jewish Walk of Fame committee, you are not a Jewish man." For this episode, apparently, no rabbis were consulted, since this statement is false. At age 12 for girls and age 13 for boys, young Jews are automatically adult members of the community and subject to religious law. No ceremony is necessary. In any event, Krusty is crushed after his weak attempt to bluff his way to a star by falsely claiming a record of Jewish philanthropy.

Out on the street, the disconsolate clown runs into Bart and Lisa, who ask what the trouble is. Krusty tells them he has just learned that he is not Jewish. "I was turned down by all those country clubs for nothing," he says. "Everything's changed. I thought I was a self-hating Jew, but it turns out I was just a plain old anti-Semite." Just then, *The Simpsons'* stand-in character for Arnold Schwarzenegger, the Germanic Rainier Wolfcastle, passes by, overhears him, puts his arm around him, and says they have "much to discuss." Krusty slouches on a park bench, dejected. "Now I know the reason my life is so empty. I never had a bar mitzvah." Bart is puzzled, so Lisa explains the significance—imperfectly: "The bar mitzvah is the most important event in a Jewish boy's life. It's when he reads from the Torah and becomes a man." Krusty confirms this interpretation. "The sweet little shiksa's right," he tells Bart. "Without a bar mitzvah, I'm just a boy." Lisa suggests that since Krusty's dad is a rabbi, and they are in the neighborhood, they ask him why the clown never had a ceremony. "My father will put this in a spiritual-philosophical context," Krusty says.

No such luck. Rabbi Krustofski replies with a vulgar Yiddish epithet. You had no bar mitzvah, he tells Krusty, "because you're a *putz*. Everything is a joke to you. I was afraid you'd make a mockery of the whole ceremony." At this, the clown breaks into tears. "Without a bar mitzvah, I'm nothing," he wails. Lisa suggests an adult bar mitzvah. Krusty wants to know if such a thing is possible. "Nothing in the Talmud forbids it," she says, this time correctly. In recent decades adults who did not have a bar or bat mitzvah, and converts as well, have gone through the study process and had a ceremony, sometimes in groups. Again, Bart wants to know how his sister knows all this. "I have a Jewish imaginary friend, Rachel Cohen, who just got into Brandeis," she explains, as Rabbi Krustofski gives his blessing to his son's commitment.

As Krusty begins studying with his father, he shares—inflicts?—his rediscovered Jewish identity on viewers of his children's television show. The clown, now wearing a yarmulke, tells the kids he's a Jew and from now on he's going to embrace his faith. He explains that he intends to teach his faith's traditions "the way my people have passed them down for centuries—through animation." An Itchy and Scratchy cartoon about circumcision follows, in characteristic Grand Guignol fashion, called "A Bris before Dying." Scratchy, the cat, recites a Hebrew blessing before using the scalpel. Itchy, the mouse character, jumps off the table and mayhem ensues. It concludes with the cat dismembered and ground up, transformed into a glass wrapped in a napkin, which is then crushed—a custom at Jewish weddings. Newly observant, Krusty tells network executives he can no longer tape shows on Saturday, the Jewish Sabbath. But he wants a guest host who won't upstage him—so he recommends Homer.

At home, sitting among a pile of open books, Krusty is taking his studies with his father seriously. The rabbi, pacing behind his son, goes over the tenets of Judaism: don't mix milk and meat at meals, don't eat pork products, and be sure to eat Chinese food on Christmas (they're the only restaurants open that day). Krusty complains about having to learn all these rules. The clown also reads from the Torah scroll—sitting down, which a rabbi wouldn't permit. Rabbi Krustofski is so pleased with his son's progress that he offers him a Jewish elixir, Dr. Brown's soda. But the news is not all good. Krusty's commitment to his faith has come at a cost. Homer's talk show has been so successful on Saturdays that station executives have decided to replace the clown permanently. Krusty is so desperate to keep his television career alive that he resorts to pitching Fox—"known for taking a chance on crap"—at its world headquarters in a lone trailer in the windswept desert. After rejecting a series of half-baked ideas for shows, they leap at his suggestion of a live broadcast of his upcoming bar mitzvah.

The spectacular takes place at Isotope Stadium, where Springfield's minor league baseball team plays. Above the entrance, huge letters proclaim, "Krusty's Wet 'N' Wild Bar Mitzvah," with the warning below, "First Two Rows May Get Converted." An organ plays music identical to that played at professional baseball games, as Krusty's sidekick, Sideshow Mel, appears on the stadium's Jumbotron screen, welcoming the crowd—all wearing yarmulkes —with "Shalom, Springfield." Backstage, Krusty is practicing guttural scales for his Hebrew chanting. To set the mood, the Beach Boys sing an appropriate song, about using two sets of dishes (required for a kosher home) and a church "with no steeple, for God's chosen people." The master of ceremonies is Mr. T, who exchanges his trademark Mohawk for a yarmulke and his shaven sideburns for traditional ear locks. "Let's scroll," he shouts, bringing the crowd to its feet. Mr. T, who is not Jewish, holds the sacred Torah in both of his muscular hands (not permitted by Jewish practice) and appears to read the scripture, although he is actually reciting a transliteration of the preparatory blessing from the prayer book. Krusty then proceeds to introduce the world's largest latke (potato pancake) and the cast of the Broadway show *The Lion King.* For the grand finale, Mr. T is lashed to a large menorah, which spins as fireworks shoot from the candleholders.

Krusty looks to the stands, where his father is sitting, in search of approval, but Rabbi Krustofski only shakes his head sadly. This is exactly the reason he didn't let his son have a bar mitzvah when he was 13: he has made a joke and televised mockery of the ceremony. Still, the father comes backstage after the show, which did well in the ratings, and puts his arm around his son. Without being berated or accused by his father, Jewish guilt gets the better of Krusty. "There's one thing that's still nagging at me," he admits. "I want a real bar mitzvah at the temple." Wonderful, his father says, without sarcasm. The next scene is at the modest synagogue, with Krusty on the pulpit, dressed in a suit and tie, wearing a *tallit*, the prayer shawl, and flanked by two rabbis. With the Simpsons sitting in the front pew, Krusty reads the Torah and says, "Now I am a man," as hundreds of thousands have said before him.

Still, the clown remains clearly ambivalent about his religion and heritage. At his fifth "retirement" show, Krusty tells the audience, "I'd like to thank God for all my success, even though I never worshiped or believed in him in any way." In another episode, Lisa accuses him of being ashamed of his Jewish roots, and with some justification. In a kitchen segment of his show, "Cooking with Krusty," the chef surprises the clown with the news that he has gotten Krusty's mother's recipe for a traditional Passover breakfast fare, called "matzoh brie." Krusty snaps, "I don't do the Jewish stuff on the air!"

Like many of his coreligionists, Krusty is extremely conflicted about Christmas. At Hanukkah, Krusty has a menorah in the window, and when neighborhood kids come to carol for him, they sing to the tune of "Hava Nagila." "A Krusty Kinda Kristmas," a television special on which Christmas merchandise is advertised, later gives way to a "nondenominational Holiday Fun Festival," with God as "our sponsor." During the holiday season, Krusty Burger restaurants have menorahs and Stars of David in their windows. A sign in front of Temple Beth Springfield advertises the coming Saturday sermon as "Coping with Christmas," although the "December dilemma" does not usually trouble Orthodox Jews.

Jewish dietary laws are another recurring theme. Given the Simpson family's love of pork products, Krusty was lucky that dinner in "Like Father, Like Clown" was meatloaf. In another episode, a row of rapping rabbis dressed like Hasidim appear on a local television show, "Eye on Springfield," singing, "Don't eat pork, even with a fork." Yet Chunky the Pig is a regular character on Krusty's show. And while pushing his own signature line of sausage and bacon products on the air in the 1980s, the clown suffers a near-fatal heart attack and is saved only by both a triple bypass *and* a pacemaker. A divine message, perhaps?

Krusty has had a checkered career in show business, which took him from work as a street mime in Tupelo, Mississippi, to the self-designated titles of "Sultan of Seltzer" and "Prince of Pies." He is considered to be a god by Bart and the other children of Springfield. But his show has been canceled at least once, and he failed at foul-mouthed stand-up comedy for adults. When he is framed for armed robbery, his arrest sparks a campaign against all of his products, led by Reverend Lovejoy. The minister denounces him as the "Clown Prince of Corruption" and organizes a bonfire of the merchandise. The subtext of the minister's drive is clear, and familiar to students of anti-Semitism: "lascivious Jew." And Krusty, who has a frequently referred-to weakness for pornography, has been ordered to do community service for unspecified offenses. His television biography (portrayed in *The Simpsons* as airing on the WB network, a Fox rival) was titled, "The Krusty the Clown Story: Booze, Drugs, Games, Lies, Blackmail, and Laughter," starring the Jewish actor Fyvush Finkel.

Although he lives alone, he is not totally without honor in his own land. On Springfield's Lower East Side there is a Krusty the

Clown Birthplace Tour & Gift Shoppe, known as "the Graceland of Jewish clown fans." During the Gulf War, he was invited on a USO tour to the Persian Gulf. And he is philanthropic. He goes door to door, collecting money for the Brotherhood of Jewish Clowns. "Last year, tornadoes claimed the lives of seventy-five Jewish clowns," he tells Homer. "The worst incident was during our convention in Lubbock, Texas. There were floppy shoes and rainbow wigs everywhere. It was terrible!"

How unlikely is the premise of such a gathering? Given the heavy burden placed on Krusty—to represent the Jewish people—it is fair to ask, Are there *really* Jewish clowns? Of course there are, just as there are Jewish bullfighters and cowboys and American army generals. Perhaps the most famous Jewish clown was Max Patkin, known as the "Clown Prince of Baseball" and a member of the Philadelphia Jewish Sports Hall of Fame. The rubber-faced, double-jointed comic began as a minor league pitcher but became famous for dressing as a ball player and imitating real athletes on the field. Patkin, who died in 1999 at the age of seventy-nine, had a cameo role in the movie *Bull Durham*.

There is, in fact, a national (if informal) organization of mostly amateur and part-time Jewish clowns, called "Clowns for Judaism," founded in 1999 by Bruce and Kim Bayne of Colorado, both of whom have clown forebears. Their Web site is "dedicated to reaching out to Jewish families through Jewish humor" and "incorporating Jewish heritage into public performances." Bruce Bayne performs under the name of "Poppy Hamentashen" and teaches kindergarten at Temple Shalom in his home town. Perhaps because the issue is too close to home, or too painful, no one from the discussion list would comment on Krusty's portrayal.

Having covered the contemporary issues of Jewish identity, assimilation, and theology, *The Simpsons* writers reached into the world of mysticism in the 2006–2007 season. Appropriately enough, the foray takes place in the annual Halloween special, the *Treehouse of Horror*, a fantasy episode. Their subject is the legend of the golem, a kosher cross between the Mummy, the Hulk, and Frankenstein's monster. The giant creature was said to have been made in 1580 from mud from Prague's River Moldau, by Rabbi Judah Loew and two assistants, using incantations from the Kabbalah. Most of the time the mute creature's role was to do household tasks for the real and revered rabbi, who lived from 1513 to 1609. But from time to time the golem was also called on to defend the Jews of Prague's ghetto from priest-led, anti-Semitic mobs who believed the "blood libel," the charge that the blood of Christian children was used to make matzoh for Passover. Named Jossele— "Joey"—the golem was animated by a parchment inscribed with one of God's names that was put in his mouth. Fridays at sundown, Rabbi Loew would remove the paper so the golem would have rest. But one Sabbath eve, the rabbi forgot to remove the parchment and the golem ran amok. The rabbi managed to remove the paper, and the golem was no more. The clay figure was hidden in the loft of Prague's historic Old-New Synagogue. The rabbi was so concerned about what he had done that he removed the steps to the loft and forbade anyone to go there. Some think the story inspired Mary Shelley to write her own version of the story, namely, *Frankenstein*.

In the twentieth century, the story has attracted many writers, including Gustav Meyrink, Isaac Bashevis Singer, Elie Wiesel, and Pete Hamill. In *The Simpsons* version, the golem ends up in Krusty's prop room, after a brief career of shooting hecklers at the clown's nightclub act. The creature in the episode is an exact replica of the golem in the 1920 German film of the same name, considered a classic of German expressionism. After one of his shows, Krusty explains to Bart that the golem is "the legendary defender of the Jewish people—like Alan Dershowitz, but with a conscience." In telling the story, the flashback includes historically accurate scenes of the Old-New Synagogue. However, there are a few alterations. In Krusty's version of the tale—a fantasy of a legend—this golem is given specific instructions on the parchment, which he is obligated to carry out. Also, he kills the ancient European enemies of the Jews with a western carbine, like the hero of the 1960s television show *The Rifleman*.

Bart immediately recognizes the golem's potential for intimidation and slips a note into his mouth telling him to come to the boy's room that night. The creature arrives and follows his first order: kick Homer in the groin. Next he accompanies Bart to the schoolyard to confront the trio of bullies. Bart's surprise is ruined when the Jewish bully recognizes the golem, which does not spare him and the others from a thrashing. Next the creature tears Principal Skinner in half. In light of this mayhem, Lisa approaches Bart and asks him if his "mystical Jewish monster" is responsible. Her brother is offended by the (true) accusation: "Oh, it's always the *Jews'* fault."

Lisa tells Bart she thinks that the golem doesn't like hurting people, and to prove her point she writes the word "speak" on a piece of paper and puts it in his mouth. Out comes the voice of comedian Richard Lewis, who most recently played a neurotic rabbi in the series *7th Heaven.* He's feeling bad, the golem says. "My stomach feels like it's hosting a Chabad telethon," he kvetches, barfing up a load of old parchment requests. "Kill the czar—now that's an old one," he observes, adding that he feels guilty for the people he has recently killed. Lisa—clearly unfamiliar with angst-ridden, modern comic book superheroes—comments that he seems neurotic for a monster. But the Simpson family soon has a pleasant surprise for the golem: have they got a girl for him! In their backyard, they have built from multicolored Play-doh a female counterpart. The golem can't believe his good fortune; Hanukkah has come early this year. Lady Golem opens her mouth, and Fran Drescher's voice begins doing lame stand-up. Homer wants to chop her up and start over, but it is clear the two creatures are made for each other.

In the final scene, Rabbi Krustofski is in the synagogue, pronouncing them "monster and whatever you are." The golem declares his bride a "shayna punim," Yiddish for "beautiful face." However, before he can crush the goblet and make everything official, Chief Wiggum and his officers burst in to the sanctuary with guns drawn, to charge the golem for his Springfield rampage. Not to worry—the rotund officer dismisses the charge in exchange for *latkes,* fried potato pancakes.

Yiddish expressions, usually voiced by Krusty, abound: *tucchus* (butt) and *yutz* (empty head), *plotz* (burst), *bupkes* (nothing), *ferkakteh* (execrable), *schlemiel* (bungler), and *schmutz* (mess). The clown refers to his long-lost daughter as "my lucky little *hamentaschen*," a reference to triangular pastry eaten on the holiday of Purim. Other Yiddish words and puns and double entendres also pop up. Springfield's miniature golf course is sometimes (but not always) called "Sir Putts-a-Lot." The Yiddish word *putz* means penis. Another of Krusty's middle names is "Schmoikel," which sounds like the diminutive of another Yiddish term for penis. "What's a good Jewish word Krusty can use here?" Gentile writers would ask Mike Reiss. And it usually would be Gentile writers who would seek such words. "Not even a majority of the stuff comes from the Jews."

There are other in-jokes that were obviously written by Jews for other Jews. A casino boat travels from Springfield beyond the territorial limit to allow activities forbidden by U.S. law. In a fleeting shot, a man in a tuxedo, under a canopy, is seen marrying a cow in what is clearly a Jewish wedding ceremony—then the groom smashes with his foot a glass wrapped in a napkin.

The Jewish content of *The Simpsons* inspired one fan, Brian Rosman, a health policy researcher at a Brandeis University think tank, to create a Web site that features still shots from "Like Father, Like Clown" under the heading, "Jewish Life in Springfield." It also uses Homer Simpson to help Jewish viewers with the observance of Lag B'Omer, the counting of the sheaves between Passover and Shavuot, the Feast of Weeks, and a bilingual pun on Homer's name. Rosman believes that

> *The Simpsons* does the funniest, most authentic parodies of Jewish life among all the comedy shows on TV, certainly compared to shows that are considered more "Jewish," like *Seinfeld*. The *Simpsons* demonstrates a more intuitive understanding of American Jewish history, Jewish religion and culture, and Judaism's place among all the other varieties of belief and identity in America. I only wish there was more Jewish content on the show, because when they do it, they do it very well.

Actually, there may be more than even Rosman realizes. Apart from Krusty, *The Simpsons* from time to time suggests an underlying element of what might be called "crypto-Judaism." In one of the opening chalkboard sequences, Bart writes, "I am not the reincarnation of Sammy Davis Jr." While watching the "Rapping Rabbis" on television, Homer asks Marge, "Are we Jewish?" Sight gags in the series also extend this conceit. A menorah—the Hanukkah candelabra—is seen in the Simpsons' family storage closet, without comment on how or why it got there. There are other hints. Watching the cross-dressing movie *Yentl* puts Homer in an amorous mood—at least when he's delirious—especially the part when Barbra Streisand, the title character, is in the yeshiva. In another episode, Homer, lightheaded from donating blood, raves, "Jewish? No, I'm not Jewish." And Jews pop up in unexpected places. Along with Duff Man, the local beer company mascot, one of the regular trio of teenage toughs is also Jewish. He excuses himself from one incident of troublemaking to go to Hebrew school, donning a yarmulke and a prayer shawl and walking away chanting a Hebrew blessing.

In *The Simpsons* comic *Holiday Humdinger*, Bart takes a step further. At Hanukkah, he learns from a Jewish friend about the eight nights and eight gifts, and naturally Bart decides to convert, noting the additional benefit of holidays off school. Homer asks if his son is certain he wants to "abandon the faith you happened to be born into," the reason most people worship where they do. Bart, now wearing a skullcap all the time, replies that he'd rather be on Krusty's team than the Flanderses'. Following the sometimes traditional practice for those who want to convert to Judaism, Rabbi Krustofski turns Bart down several times—to be certain he is serious—before agreeing to take him on for classes. Bart argues that if he became Jewish, he'd be a "trash-talkin' Spiky-haired Seinfeld with a Fox attitude." Even so, the rabbi is unconvinced, predicting the boy would not like the religion because "so much Judaism is like opera, the Lincoln Douglas debates, and the Atkins Diet, all rolled into one." Bart is plainly in it for the toys, which his parents supply each night of the holiday (along with gingerbread rabbis), but sister Lisa is optimistic that her brother may be undergoing a spiritual awakening. Her gift, after lighting the menorah, is a book about Jewish history, humor, and "food-oriented Yiddish phrases" that

Bart uses as a TV tray, holding Dr. Brown's Cream Soda and low-carb *hamentaschen*. The boy also announces he can't do chores around the house on Saturdays because he has become a strict Sabbath observer. As a convert to Buddhism, Lisa despairs at her brother's antics. "I thought we finally had something in common," she says. "That we followed our hearts because of what we believe in. But as usual, the only thing you believe in is self-gratification." In the end, Bart spends enough time with the rabbi to make the right decision and not convert. "Love the religion," he confesses to Lisa, "but, *oy* . . . I can't handle the guilt."

Several other characters in the show, ostensibly *not* Jewish, can be read by their names and their view of life as otherwise distinctly Jewish: Homer's father, Abe; and Marge's twin sisters, Selma and Patty Bouvier. In manner and disposition, Abe, a child immigrant from "the old country," is every *alta kaka* (old fart) sitting around a swimming pool in Miami Beach, complaining about his declining health and the ungrateful younger generation. His absent wife, Penelope Olsen, Homer's mother, is a '60s radical and free spirit whose anti–germ warfare activities forced her underground for twenty-five years. Her Scandinavian name notwithstanding, she *could* be Jewish; she fits the profile. The Bouvier sisters are also familiar types: sharp-tongued unmarried aunts and sisters-in-law, their dialogue taken directly from the late Selma Diamond or Fran Leibowitz or Sandra Bernhard. And according to Matt Groening's *The Simpsons Uncensored Family Album*, Montgomery Burns's sister, Cornelia, has five grandsons named Bernstein: David, Levi, Moshe, Murray, and Saul.

So, latent or blatant, is the portrayal of Jews in *The Simpsons* on balance a positive one, likely to encourage understanding among society at large? The rabbis seem to think that it is, although not entirely without qualification. Rabbi Steven Engel of the Congregation of Reform Judaism, in Orlando, says, "For Jews, humor has always been as reflective as our holy writings and sacred liturgy in expressing our feelings, concerns, aspirations, and in bringing to light the realities we face. Our general understanding is that humor has contributed to our ability to survive as a people. There is no question that *The Simpsons'* Springfield in many ways accurately reflects the feelings, concerns, aspirations, and realities of contemporary Jews. It is certainly funny stuff and does make people laugh. But is it good for the Jews? I suppose that depends upon who is doing most of the laughing, why they are laughing, and to whom the laughter is directed."

Ten

Buddhism: Lisa Changes Teams, Sort Of.

A narrative conceit of *The Simpsons* is that no one ever ages, and nothing ever changes—at least from one episode to another. There have been some exceptions, like when the barfly character, Barney, stopped drinking for a while. Or when a few minor and supporting characters died: Dr. Marvin Monroe, Bleeding Gums Murphy, and Maude Flanders. Some would argue that over time Bart has become less bratty and Homer less oafish, but Lisa's conversion to Buddhism may be the greatest exception to the show's continuity rule.

Christianity, Judaism, and Hinduism are well represented in *The Simpsons*, as described in other chapters, and Islam remains virtually invisible. Buddhism is present in the series, but the predominantly Asian faith is a relatively late entry, almost a footnote. There have been scattered references to the religious philosophy, both before and after Lisa's conversion in 2004, yet almost always as an afterthought or a throwaway image or line of dialogue. For example, in a subsequent episode when Homer and Bart briefly convert to Catholicism, Lisa defends their freedom to choose their faith, citing her decision to become a Buddhist. A visiting Catholic chuckles condescendingly and says, "I guess lots of kids have imaginary friends."

Often these seemingly random images and lines of dialogue— brief but explicit nods to Buddha and Buddhism—pop up in conjunction with other divine figures, often showing Buddha as a proponent of mercy. In "Left Below," a Simpsons spoof of the *Left Behind* novels and movies based on the Apocalypse, a world-ending flood catches a Buddhist monk unawares: "I thought all religions

were a path to God—I was wrong!" (Lama Surya Das, who wrote
AskTheLama column at Beliefnet.com, observes, "No Buddhist
monk in the world would make that statement.") In another
episode, Homer prays, "Jesus, Allah, Buddha, I love you all!"
Sideshow Bob, the homicidal television host, suggests that Homer
is forgetting "the first two noble truths of the Buddha . . . [:] 'Existence is suffering' and 'The cause of suffering is desire.'" Homer
protests that he has not forgotten them.

There's a Chinese restaurant in Springfield called Bob's Big
Buddha. Buddha himself makes several fleeting physical appearances as well. Trapped in the trunk of a car with lava from the
eruption of Mt. Springfield bearing down on her, Lisa utters her
own version of Homer's mantra. Desperate, she prays to "Buddha, Jesus, SpongeBob—there's no time to be picky!" Buddha,
sitting on a cloud with Jesus and SpongeBob SquarePants, the
children's cartoon character, says, "Perhaps we should help." But
SpongeBob replies, "Nah, screw her!" and laughs maniacally.

Similarly, when Homer brings down a wrathful flood on
Springfield, Lisa tries to attribute it to various natural phenom-
ena. Bart then asks how to account for the sunshine immediately
following Reverend Lovejoy's prayer. Lisa, momentarily stumped,
mutters, "Buddha?" Sure enough, sitting next to God, who is in
standard issue attire of flowing white robe and Birkenstocks, is a
small, plump Buddha, who once again suggests that the mortals
below have suffered enough.

Early in the show's run, Homer enters his son in a miniature
golf tournament against Todd Flanders. Bart is anxious about the
upcoming contest, so Lisa offers to help. She starts at the library,
where she borrows books on putting but also the *Tao Te Ching*, by
Lao Tzu. The brother and sister go to the woods, where Lisa
introduces Bart to the way of Zen. The first steps are easy for her
brother: shutting off the logical part of his mind, embracing noth-
ingness, and becoming like an uncarved stone. Atop a mountain—
yet another Buddhism cliche—Lisa then tries the classic koans,
which are humorous, paradoxical riddles. She asks Bart to imagine the sound of one hand clapping. Bart undermines the paradox
by clapping with one hand, slapping his fingers against the base of

his palm. Lisa then asks him whether if a tree falls in the forest and no one is there to hear it, it makes a sound. Finally, golf club in hand, Bart assumes the "crane" position made famous by the movie *The Karate Kid*. Nothing works for her brother, so Lisa gives up.

The main representation of Buddhism in *The Simpsons* deals with Lisa's flight from Christianity. Her move to Buddhism grows out of her sense that her mainline Protestant church has become spiritually bankrupt—a direct result of it also being nearly financially bankrupt. Bart and Homer launch a huge model rocket that goes off course and hits Springfield Community Church, leaving it a burned-out shell. Reverend Lovejoy convenes a meeting of the church council, where he prays for divine intervention for money to rebuild the structure. Dejected at hearing only silence from above, he declares, "All right, we'll help ourselves—yet again." The congregation agrees to a proposal from Mr. Burns and his consultant to "rebrand" the congregation, in exchange for rebuilding.

The rebranding plan for the congregation is ironic, since, like many mainline Protestant churches, the congregation already has an updated brand. For years, church consultants have been saying that congregations with denominational identification no longer attract new, young members. Thus, instead of "Methodist" or "Presbyterian," new churches prefer to use the more generic word "community" in their names. The best example of this phenomenon is Rick Warren's Saddleback Community Church in Orange County, California. This megachurch is affiliated with the Southern Baptist Convention, but a new worshiper would be hard put to know that. In the case of the Simpsons' church, whose worship style is either Presbyterian or Lutheran, the decision to play down the denominational identity was made long ago. Still, Burns's consultant says, the church is "skewing pious. We prefer a faith-based emporium teeming with impulse buy items"—and, of course, new revenue streams derived from saturation advertising and product placements.

The latest incarnation of Springfield Community Church (alternately known as the First Church of Springfield) features a lighted marquee outside and a huge, Las Vegas–style, neon Jesus waving one arm in welcome and holding a lasso in the other. Inside, the walls are plastered with ads for local businesses, including one for Pep Boys (whose namesakes, Manny, Moe, and Jack, were Jewish). There is even a money-changing kiosk, Jesus' admonition notwithstanding. The front of Lovejoy's podium flashes changing promotions, and he manages to work other paid plugs into his sermons. Lisa is unhappy with the changes, which is made plain when she appears on the sanctuary's new oversized television screen "Godcam" with the caption, "Pouting Thomas." For her, the last straw is an appearance by the Domino's Pizza character, the Noid. Lisa accuses Lovejoy of going well beyond his claim to having dressed the church up a little; instead, she believes he has tarted it up like the Whore of Babylon—at the price of its soul. That night at home, Lisa prays by her bed for guidance. "Lord, I'm not turning my back on you," she says. "I just need to find a temple that is free of corruption." Marge, who has been eavesdropping from the other side of the bed, is worried that her daughter may lose the family's only realistic shot at heaven. "I still believe in God," Lisa assures her. "I just think there's another path to him—or her."

After Lisa rejects Bart's first preference—that she join a religion that eats human hearts—her brother suggests the Methodists. This is the setup for another fast-moving, typically *Simpsons* joke, what writers of animated comedies call a "one percent gag," since that is the estimated fraction of viewers likely to pick up on them. Lisa rejects that suggestion with the punch line, "I'm not just going to pick a religion that seems cool." (No one would ever suggest that being a United Methodist in the current era is cool.) She also ignores Bart's idea that she choose Judaism because of the bat mitzvah payday when she hits thirteen. (A similar scenario, with a similar outcome, is the cover story of a *Simpsons Comics* issue called "Money to Burns!" In that version, the congregation is debauched, but it is Flanders who leaves, sampling Judaism, Hinduism, snake handling, and a generic cult before inadvertently stumbling into a Satanist coven.)

Lisa roams the streets of Springfield in search of a new faith, passing signs for Baha'i and Amish houses of worship, as well as

one for a Church of Latter-Day Druids. The sequence notwithstanding, most seekers say they convert *to* a new faith that engages
them, rather than *from* an old one they don't like. Still, it is not surprising that Lisa is attracted when she comes upon the Springfield
Buddhist Temple, announced by the sound of an unseen gong.
Inside, she is startled to find Homer's coworkers Carl and Lenny
burning incense and meditating in the lotus position before the
statue of a large, bald, big-bellied Buddha. Carl explains, "If I didn't
have inner peace I'd completely go psycho on all you guys all the
time." Lisa explains that she is looking for a new faith, one that isn't
so materialistic. As it happens, the temple is either ecumenical or
generic: the building's architecture is Chinese, but inside there is a
Japanese rock garden. And the person raking the sand is the actor
Richard Gere, a devotee of Tibetan Buddhism. Hearing what she
is searching for, he says that the girl has come to the right place.
"Buddhism teaches that suffering is caused by desire," he explains.
When Lenny identifies the speaker as the world's most famous
Buddhist, Gere cringes, suggesting that the title is held by the
Dalai Lama. Carl explains to his friend that the Dalai Lama is
descended from the Buddha, prompting Lenny to ask who Buddha
is. Gere then has an opportunity to goof on his own spirituality.
"It's a good thing Buddhism teaches freedom from desire," he says,
"'cause I've got the desire to kick your ass."
  Lisa tells Gere that she is hoping that Buddhism can provide
her with inner peace, then asks if that is just a pipe dream. The
actor replies that we all have dreams; and that his is for a free
Tibet—guaranteeing that this episode of *The Simpsons* will never
be broadcast in China. Gere, handing Lisa a pamphlet from
his back pocket, then begins a concise explanation of Buddhism.
"All things are impermanent," he says, "and are empty of inher-
ent existence."
  Later that evening, Lisa goes over the pamphlet and, in the
process, extends the lessons on the tenets of Buddhism. "Nirvana
is achieved through right views and right speech," she reads aloud.
"Positive actions lead to happiness, and negative actions lead to
unhappiness. No creator gods—just the pursuit of enlightenment." Lisa is convinced—and converted. She goes to the window

and shouts, "I'm a Buddhist!" Admittedly, the ground has already been well prepared for Lisa's conversion, predating her disenchantment with her church, since we know from previous episodes that she is already a pacifist and a vegetarian.

Those around Lisa are not so happy for her. Next door, Ned Flanders tells his sons his "Satan sense is tingling," so he scoops the boys up and heads for the root cellar. At the Simpsons' dinner table, the reception is equally hostile when Lisa informs them that her spiritual quest is over. Homer assumes this is something she got in an Internet chat room. Marge tells her that Buddhists don't get desserts in their lunches. At school the next day, bullies needle Bart, telling him they heard his sister "dumped Christianity." Undeterred, Lisa throws herself into her new religion, even planting a Bodhi tree in her yard in hopes of meditating under it, like the Buddha. When her mother hassles her, the daughter chants her mantra. Lisa's conversion appears on the agenda of the church council, under the heading of "Marge Simpson's devil daughter." Lovejoy and Flanders suggest that, with Christmas coming, Marge leverage the presents issue: tell Lisa that Santa doesn't leave presents under a Bodhi tree. Marge wonders whether it is ethical to use bribery to bring her daughter back to church. The minister assures her that more souls have been saved by presents like skates and Easy-Bake ovens than with the Bible, which he describes as "this two-thousand-page sleeping pill."

In the first step in the campaign to win Lisa back, Homer jams a ceramic angel on top of her little Bodhi tree. The girl is not troubled by the addition, until it turns out to be motorized, swinging its arms and singing the barking dogs version of "Jingle Bells." On Christmas Eve, other family members serenade Lisa as she comes down the stairs and walks into the living room, where the Christmas tree and presents are. Since no one told Santa the girl had become a Buddhist, there is a present for her. Lisa starts to dismiss the ploy, saying she is not ruled by material desires—until she realizes that the present looks a lot like a real pony, heretofore her dearest wish. Torn, she flees to the temple for advice, so distraught that she interrupts Gere, Carl, and Lenny, who are meditating. Lisa apologizes, and the actor says it is all right, despite the fact that he was just about to achieve enlightenment. Gere tells her she shouldn't be upset at her parents' attempts to trick her. "Buddhists respect the diversity of other religions, as long as they are based on compassion," he says. "You can celebrate any holiday." Go home, he says. "I'm sure your family really misses you." Or, as the Dalai Lama says, "Contribute to others rather than convert others. Buddhist practices such as meditation can make you, whatever your beliefs, into a better whatever-you-are."

In fact, the family has missed her, and has been frantically searching the neighborhood. They discover her Christmas morning asleep in the living room, under the Christmas tree. Homer assumes that this means that she is "back on the winning team"— a common way of viewing religious commitment by some believers. Families of converts to new faiths are often upset, fearing that their relatives may be leaving their orbit. But that is not what Lisa intends. She explains that, while still a Buddhist, she wants to celebrate Christmas with her family. "So you're just going to pay lip service to our church?" Marge asks. Yes, Lisa says. "That's all I ever asked," Homer says, putting his imprimatur on the resolution.

In another episode, after Lisa's conversion, there is a "Free Tibet" rally at Springfield's Town Hall. As Springfield's youngest Buddhist, the girl gets to introduce the Dalai Lama, which she does, as the "Elvis of enlightenment . . . a lean, serene, chanting machine." His Holiness strolls onto the stage, accompanied by a Tibetan horn trio. Then Homer shows up as a masked character, "Pie Man." Homer has orders from Mr. Burns to hit the Dalai Lama with a pie—"All this talk of peace and love is honking off my Red Chinese masters," Burns explains—which Homer refuses to do. The Dalai Lama conveys his greetings to "fellow travelers on the road to enlightenment." Then he levitates and flies out the window to his next engagement—Buffalo. When the episode was first broadcast in Asia on Rupert Murdoch's Star World channel, the references and images to the Dalai Lama were deleted, to appease either Buddhist viewers or Murdoch's master in the Chinese government—or both. In another episode, Springfield's Dalai Lama Expressway has been renamed for Michael Jackson, perhaps for similar reasons.

On a subsequent Christmas, Lisa tells her father that "as a Buddhist I believe people would be a lot happier without presents." Homer takes her comment to heart, imagining Buddha, a Christmas sweater, and a convertible, which morph into an image of the Buddha wearing the sweater and driving the car. "Presents are material goods, and attachment to material goods kills the soul," Buddha tells Homer. At this point Buddha hears police sirens and speeds off, saying, "I'm not going to jail again." Nonetheless, he is seen in custody, shirtless, with tattoos as he is handcuffed against the convertible's hood. Buddha is uncharacteristically surly, demanding the officer's badge number and warning him and his partner that they better hope he never gets out of jail. The columnist Surya Das, author of the best-selling *Awakening the Buddha Within: Tibetan Wisdom for the Western World*, suggests it would be more theologically consistent to have him pulled over for driving too slowly.

Lisa's conversion doesn't make her any less of a Simpson, even as it is integrated into her character. After her initial discomfort with her daughter's decision, Marge uses it when necessary. When a string of pet cats dies, Marge is angry at God, but she comforts Lisa by saying, "You're a Buddhist, so you know your pet is reincarnated as a higher being," in this case a dog. In a subsequent episode, Lisa is seen meditating in the lotus position at a backyard koi pond. But Lisa is still vulnerable to manipulation. "As a Buddhist, I'd believe Buddha in a commercial," she says.

Surya Das is generally satisfied with the *Simpsons* episode that deals with Lisa's conversion. "This episode gives a nice, pleasant, agreeable—if stereotypical—representation of Buddhism as popularly understood in the West today," he says. "I don't think that, given the limits of the genre, there is anything very objectionable in it, except to nitpickers and brainwashed traditionalists. If it leaves out anything, it is the notion of reincarnation and karma, two closely interrelated ideas somewhat (though definitely not entirely) foreign to the Western mind. If there were a little more emphasis on nonviolence, altruism and lovingkindness, and nonsectarianism, it would've pretty much summed up my favorite 'ism' in a nutshell. Some modernists subscribe to the belief that

Buddhism is less a religion than an ethical and psychological way of awakening. That is, it has little or no dogma, no creed one has to subscribe to, no conversion ceremonies, no absolute deity or creator, etc. Its sole goal is enlightenment, both universal and personal." The goal of Buddhism, he says, "is the realization of enlightened wisdom and love."

Das also sees some shortcomings. "On the critical side," he says, "the idea that Buddhism teaches—that Buddha taught—in the two first Noble Truths that the cause of suffering is desire may not be the best, most well-rounded, or even useful translation of the original concept of 'dukkha.' I would say the first truth is that life is difficult, and the second is that its cause is ignorant attachment or unwise desire. Moreover, my understanding and teaching regarding the Buddha's first truth is always that unenlightened life is full of confusion and suffering. It causes ignorance and attachment to and desire for things that don't help very much, in either the short or long run—looking for love (and happiness) in all the wrong places, as the song more or less goes. Also, I thought the way the phrase 'no creator god' is thrown in (in Lisa's summation of Buddhist tenets) seems oversimplified. No separate eternal deity or creator would be more accurate, since karma is the creator of all things."

Mario D'Amato, a specialist in Buddhist studies at Rollins College in Winter Park, Florida, agrees with Surya Das, but is somewhat more forgiving of the portrayal: "Regardless of whether or not the episode accurately represents Buddhism (or accurately represents one's preferred form of Buddhism), it's great that the episode allows even Buddhist viewers to see some humor in the religion. I don't believe that it's antithetical to Buddhism to be able to laugh a bit at Buddhism itself—this might even be helpful in breaking one's own attachments, including attachments to religion. After all, according to an ancient metaphor, Buddhism itself is only a raft which should be left behind when the goal is reached. Buddhism is perhaps one of the most humorous traditions among the world's major religions. Doses of humor may be found throughout the religion. From the subtle hint of a smile seen in many artistic depictions of the Buddha, to humorous stories in Buddhist scriptures, to the crazy antics of Chinese Zen masters, it's hard not to see bits of humor in Buddhism.

"American Buddhist viewers should feel proud that Lisa Simpson converts to their religion, primarily because she is one of the most lovable characters on the show. Whether or not the episode gets all the details of 'basic Buddhism' straight is not as important as the fact that Lisa converts to Buddhism: While viewers might not remember much about the teachings as presented in the show, they will remember that Lisa, a favorite of many, converted to Buddhism. Lisa is open-minded, reflective, ethical, and interested in improving herself in various ways, while still preserving a child-like sense of innocence (she is, after all, eternally a child!). These are all excellent qualities, ones which are espoused by many Buddhist traditions. So American Buddhist viewers should be pleased to have their religion represented by one of the most lovable and intelligent characters on television."

Given the spectrum of possibilities for satire, Buddhism is fairly and positively represented in *The Simpsons*, at least from my outsider's perspective. And because it is as much a philosophy as a religion, there is nothing in Lisa's conversion that prevents her from continuing to speak for the prophetic voice of Jesus as well as for the reflective Buddha.

Eleven

Miscellaneous: "Hindu! There Are 700 Million of Us!"

In the episode "Homer the Heretic," Springfield's multifaith volunteer fire department mobilizes to save the Simpsons' home—and Homer's life. Reverend Lovejoy explains to Homer that God was working through his friends and neighbors, including Ned Flanders, a Christian, and Krusty the Clown, a Jew. But the minister comes up short when he points toward the other firefighter, Apu Nahasapeemapetilon. After a nonplussed pause, the minister characterizes the convenience store operator's religion as "miscellaneous." This level of ignorance is too much for the normally mild-mannered Asian immigrant. Apu explodes: "Hindu! There are 700 million of us!" Corrected, Lovejoy replies with condescension, "Aw, that's super."

Despite a surge of immigration from the Indian subcontinent and a growing interest in beliefs outside the Judeo-Christian traditions, most Americans are as in the dark about Hinduism as Reverend Lovejoy. A few aspects of the faith have penetrated Springfield's consciousness: Lisa patronizes a New Age store called Karma-Ceuticals, which features a shrine to Vishnu and a *Kama Sutra* poster, and where the owner offers the traditional Hindu greeting, "Namaste." There is a Hindu priest in town, Sadruddin Mabaradad, host of an exercise show called "Yoga Party" on the Springfield television station and author of the ghost-written *The Unsinkable Sadruddin Mabaradad*. "Just let your head flop back and forward," the priest tells viewers. "Your neck is a well-cooked piece of asparagus." (Incidentally, Sadruddin is typically a Muslim, not Hindu, name.)

181

For other residents of the town, Apu is their introduction to Hinduism. *Simpsons* creator Matt Groening, a fan of obscure Indian music, initially suggested that the operator of the Kwik-E-Mart come from the subcontinent. "With Apu, that kind of character has not been seen on U.S. TV," Groening told a British magazine. At first, writer-producer Al Jean told *TV Guide*, "we were worried he might be considered an offensive stereotype."[1] Apu in the series was named for a character in a trilogy of Indian films made in the 1950s by famed director Satjayit Ray. In one episode, a photo on the wall of *The Simpsons* character's father is similar to that of the actor who played Apu's father in the Ray movie *Pather Panchali*, one of Groening's all-time favorites.

In many ways, the character *is* stereotypical of Asian immigrants to North America, and a model minority member. Born in Pakistan, Apu migrated with his family to Ramatpur in India and later studied at the Calcutta Institute of Technology ("CalTech"), where he graduated at the top of his class of seven million. In the 1970s, he came to the United States on a student visa to do graduate study in computer programming at the Springfield Heights Institute of Technology (try the initials). During his nine years at the school, he took a job at the convenience store to pay off his student loans, a choice that evolved into a career. Apu often works eighteen hours a day, seven days a week, and, on at least one occasion, worked ninety-six hours straight. He is frequently the victim of shoplifters and armed robbers.

However, not all of the stereotypes Apu embodies are positive. For example, he is apparently a Hindu nationalist: On the shelf in his apartment is a record album entitled "The Concert against Bangladesh," with a mushroom cloud on the cover, obliterating India's poverty-stricken, Muslim neighbor. He refers to Springfield residents with a different area code as "foreign devils." An obsequious shopkeeper, he is known for outrageous overcharging ($1.85 for a 29-cent postage stamp and $4.20 for $2.00 worth of gas) and for selling foods well beyond their expiration dates. "I think he really loves his job and the power that it gives him to frustrate other people," Groening says.[2] As Apu has prospered—

offering everything from flavored iced treats called "Squishees," to beef jerky, to *Playdude* magazine, to violent video games—he has been able to follow another immigrant pattern, that of bringing to America other members of his family.

Yet next to Marge and Ned Flanders, Apu is probably the most good-hearted and saintly character on *The Simpsons*, qualities presented on the show as an outgrowth of his Hindu faith and of his Indian culture. At his dinner table, with Homer and Marge as guests, he recites a grace that is clearly a parody of one familiar to the Simpsons: "Good rice, good curry, good Gandhi, let's hurry." Of course, the beloved independence leader and martyr Mohandas K. Gandhi, although worshiped by millions of Indians, is not a part of the Hindu pantheon. On another occasion, Apu swears by "the many arms" of the god Vishnu and keeps a statue of Shiva in his apartment, but his continuing allegiance is to a deity less well known in the West—Ganesha.

With four arms, a potbelly, and the head of an elephant, Ganesha is a god who bestows happiness and banishes sorrow—ideal for a character in *The Simpsons*. There are various explanations for how and why he came to have a pachyderm's head: he betrayed his father, Shiva; he defended his mother; he lost a race to his brother. Ganesha is popular in the west and south of India and is the focus of a joyous, annual ten-day festival in Bombay. Most statues of Ganesha, such as the one Apu places in a shrine in the Kwik-E-Mart's employee lounge, are two to four feet tall. In his first encounter with the statue, Homer is particularly scornful of Apu's devotion, in much the same way that some evangelical Christians still dismiss Hindus as "pagans" or "heathens." For offering the statue a peanut, Homer is ordered out of the store by the Indian. "No offense, Apu," Homer says, "but when they were handing out religions, you musta been out taking a whiz." Naturally, there is some theological sparring between Apu and Ned. In one episode, Flanders assesses his chances of winning a baking contest by saying he "wouldn't have a Hindu's chance in heaven." On a drive to Canada to buy cheaper prescription drugs, Ned tries to convert Apu, who tells him, "I don't believe in one God."

Over time, in small ways and large, and in more than a dozen episodes, Apu articulates essential elements of Hinduism, Indian culture, and the plight of immigrants, including:

1. Vegetarianism. Apu wears a tee-shirt with a red circle and slash, superimposed on a cow, with Bart's slogan, "Don't Have a Cow, Man!" and he secretly substitutes tofu for beef in the hot dogs he sells. The storekeeper is a vegetarian, but he acknowledges to Lisa that it is not easy. The girl lets slip that she includes cheese in her diet, which Apu says he does not, since it comes from an animal. Lisa concludes that he must think her a monster for this lapse. Indeed he does, Apu replies with a smile, in what is a clear distortion of Hinduism. "As any yogi or Hindu will tell you," says yoga instructor Ted Srinathadas Czukor, "we drink milk and eat ghee, yogurt, cheese, lassi, etc. This is why the cow is considered such an important animal in the Hindu culture."

2. Reincarnation. Sideshow Mel, one of Krusty the Clown's television sidekicks, says, "You only live once." Apu pipes up, "Hey, speak for yourself."

3. Meditation. Apu has a secret stairway in the Kwik-E-Mart that leads to a rooftop garden, where, he tells Lisa, "I go when I need some refuge from the modern world."

4. Pluralism. "I learned long ago, Lisa, to tolerate others, rather than forcing my beliefs on them," Apu tells the girl. "You know, you can influence people without badgering them always." *The Simpsons* writers used Apu to take a well-deserved swipe at anti-immigrant hysteria in California, which gave rise to a referendum called Proposition 187 in the 1990s that would have barred the children of undocumented workers from public schools and from all social services. In the episode, it is a proposed local ordinance called Proposition 24, which would expel all immigrants from Springfield in order to pay for patrols to guard against marauding bears. Homer is all for the measure until he figures out that it will affect Apu. Apu has overstayed his student visa by years, although the merchant has done everything he can think of to fit into American society, including going bowling and learning to square dance.

Things get out of hand when an anti-immigrant mob gathers outside the Kwik-E-Mart in support of Proposition 24. Apu attempts to placate the mob by feeding his statue of Ganesha Yoo-Hoo, a chocolate milk drink. "If you help me out, I'll give you the rest of the bottle," he explains to the deity, demonstrating that bargaining with the divine is not confined to the Judeo-Christian tradition. (Even for well-informed Indian viewers, there are inside jokes on *The Simpsons*. Six months earlier, in India, a craze swept the country as some Hindus claimed a "milk miracle" in which a Ganesha statue appeared to be drinking milk from a spoon. "The milk-drinking episode was witnessed by hundreds of thousands of people in dozens of nations," says Acharya Palaniswami, editor-in-chief of the U.S. monthly magazine *Hinduism Today*.)

When Apu's offering to the Hindu deity fails, the convenience store operator panics. He replaces his shrine to Ganesha with a periodicals rack, featuring magazine covers of movie actors Tom Cruise, a prominent Scientologist, and Cruise's former wife, Nicole Kidman. "Who needs Ganesha when I have Tom Cruise and Nicole Kidman to guide me?" he tells Homer. Still, his betrayal provokes a tearful flashback to his departure from India, where his parents urge him, "Never forget who you really are." Apu admits that, in an attempt to fit in as an American, he has turned his back on his faith. "I cannot deny my roots and keep up this charade," he says. "I only did it because I love this land, where I have the freedom to say, and to think, and to charge whatever I want!" In the end, Lisa realizes that Apu has been in the United States long enough to qualify for amnesty, which enables him to take—and pass—the citizenship test.

5. Assimilation. A member of the Brahmin caste (a Brahmin would never be a shopkeeper in India), Apu faces similar challenges to maintaining his minority faith when it comes time to marry. Like Jews who become Episcopalians and Koreans who become Baptists, the immigrant must decide what road to take. In the U.S., many modern immigrant parents still prefer arranged marriages, although they are more willing to make the process seem voluntary. Apu's mother arrives from India, wanting to know why he says he cannot marry the young woman to whom he was betrothed when he was eight (sealed with the promise of a dowry that includes ten goats, an electric fan, and a textile factory). Her arrival affords her an opportunity to explain to Bart and Lisa the meaning of the red dot, called a gopi or bindi, on her forehead.

The main reason Apu does not want to marry is that he has been having the time of his life playing the American field after starring in Springfield's Charity Bachelor Auction. A plot to convince Apu's mother that he is already married—to Marge—fails. Apu protests that one in twenty-five arranged marriages ends in divorce (compared to one in two U.S. "love matches"), but he eventually agrees to the match, to be held in the Simpsons' backyard. Upstairs before the ceremony, Apu worries about the custom of not seeing his future bride until the wedding ceremony, and wonders if the whole world has gone mad. Homer, Mr. Diversity, blames it on "your screwy country."

Alas, there is no Hindu priest (perhaps Mabaradad is out of town), so Reverend Lovejoy agrees to be drafted to conduct the ceremony. After all, as the minister observes, when it comes to performing a wedding, "Christ is Christ," and anyway Lovejoy has consulted a Hindu Web site to customize the service. The wedding goes forward, with Apu wearing a turban and riding an elephant, heralded by trumpets and guests wearing floral garlands. Homer attempts to break up the ceremony the best way he can think of, by dressing as Ganesha, complete with elephant head. He shouts that Ganesha is angered by the wedding and that all present will die unless it is called off, but he is subdued by an Indian guest and stuck up in a tree until the ceremony is completed. To his delight, Apu finds his bride Manjula beautiful and witty, and is reconciled to the match. The couple walks around the sacred fire hand in hand.

The course of the love that follows is not without interruption, as Homer and Marge learn when they are invited to the Nahasapeemapetilons' book-filled apartment for dinner. A fight erupts between the Indian spouses, and the Simpsons excuse themselves. As they leave the apartment building, a copy of the *Kama Sutra* comes flying out the window and lands at Homer's feet, provoking his interest in at least one aspect of Indian culture. For the most part, however, Apu is known to be so devoted to his wife that all the other husbands in Springfield fear he will make trouble for them on Valentine's Day. But later he has an affair, scandalizing the community.

In another episode, Homer sets off a series of events that culminates in a TV exposé of Apu's shady practices at the Kwik-E-Mart, and the merchant is stripped of his franchise. At first he is angry at Homer for causing this misfortune, but he realizes that his Hindu faith requires that he make amends to his customer. "I blamed you for squealing," Apu says, "but then I realized, it was *I* who wronged *you*." It is up to the Indian to work off his karmic debt to Homer, who shocks Apu by pointing out that "karma can only be apportioned out by the cosmos." There is but one way the matter can be resolved and Apu restored to his rightful place at the Springfield Kwik-E-Mart: Homer must accompany him to the chain's Himalayan mountaintop headquarters in India and plead his friend's case. As one might expect, when the pair arrives at the airport in India they encounter young Christian proselytizers rather than the Hare Krishnas familiar to American travelers. In any event, the debt is forgiven, and balance returns to the universe.

Like Catholics and Protestants, some Hindus have objected to their portrayal on *The Simpsons*. In the mid-1990s, Southern California Hindus protested the representation of Ganesha. The president of the Federation of Hindu Associations, Prithvi Raj Singh, called Fox Television to complain. A spokeswoman returned his call, Singh told *Christian Century* magazine, offering the network's standard response. "She said it was not a planned attack on Hinduism. . . . 'The show treats other religions humorously too,' she said."[3] Unlike the Catholic League and Media Action Network for Asian Americans, however, the Hindu group was not able to force *The Simpsons* to knuckle under.

With the help of *Hinduism Today*, I informally surveyed attitudes toward *The Simpsons*. What I found was that Indian immigrants and adolescent and teenage children of immigrants—especially orthodox Hindus—were generally offended by Apu and his stereotype. They also have specific complaints about what they feel is doctrinal error and distortion. "Hindu kids growing up in America have enough trouble adjusting during middle and high school, and they don't need *The Simpsons* fueling teasers with misinformed jokes about Hinduism," Amit Chatwani, then a Princeton University student, said. "I think that Hinduism is trampled to add more laughs to the show. People who don't know anything about Hinduism watch the show with the idea of a 'goofy, sacred elephant statue' that is Lord Ganesha. This skewed view then becomes their only knowledge of Hinduism."

By contrast, American converts to Hinduism, steeped in our culture of irony, seemed amused and unfazed by the portrayal of their faith on the series. "Unlike Hindus, *The Simpsons* have no sacred cows," said Fred Stella, an actor and yoga instructor from Michigan who identifies himself as an Italian-American adherent of Hinduism. "But more than making fun of Hinduism, the writers tend to mock people's perception of Hinduism. They do the same with Christianity."

Ty Schwach, an orthodox Hindu from Los Angeles, said that the humor involving Hindus and Apu "seems quite clearly to be poking fun more at the stereotypical ideas and preconceived notions of mainstream America regarding the Indian culture. The incidents involving Apu always leave me feeling a sense of respect for him and the way he responds to the provincial notions of his neighbors and friends who truly know very little about his culture and religion."

Bo Lozoff of the Human Kindness Foundation in Durham, North Carolina, agreed. "I like the way *The Simpsons* makes no effort to pretend that elements of Hinduism, like Ganesha, seem sensible. I trust that perspective, because we know where we stand with each other," he said. "What I enjoy about the show's religious plurality is that the bottom line gets back to the actions of the adherent and not the trappings of his or her religion that can seem weird or blasphemous to outsiders."

There are exceptions to the division between American and Indian Hindus—those Indian immigrants to the United States who said they see beyond the errors and the caricature. "Sure, it skewers us," said the Indian-born novelist and journalist S. V. Date, author of the satires *Deep Water* and *Smokeout*. "But *The*

Simpsons skewers everybody, and in the process, it's obvious that it likes us, and that's what makes it okay."

Kartik Mohan, an animator from Bombay studying at the School of Visual Arts in New York, said he is a huge fan of *The Simpsons* and watches episodes repeatedly and learns many by heart. "I don't think there is anything the least bit offensive about their treatment of the Hindu religion or their depiction of Indian people over and above the general irreverence towards all people and norms that makes the show so uniquely funny." He acknowledged that "there are a number of hot-headed Hindu fundamentalists who are defensive about their status as a newly emergent, highly successful immigrant group in the United States and are all too eager to take offense at anything even obliquely derisive of our culture."

Vikram Rangala, a Hindu who has taught a course on spirituality in popular culture at the University of Florida, said he is also a huge fan of the show, which he considers "the best television show on the air." It is "supportive of religion and even spiritual itself," although it does require "a depth of understanding beyond stereotypes."

"Apu is a sophisticated composite," says Sanjay Patel, an Indian American animator who worked on *The Simpsons* for a season, before joining Pixar in 1996. "My hat's off to the writers for the Sajit Ray reference. Kudos there. That's very heady. It's a really smart choice." Apu, he told me in 2006, five years after the first edition of this book was published, is "very truthful, a very clever composite, because it's relatable. But I want to get *The Simpsons* writers and artists by the ears and tell them this: That caricature has changed. There are a lot of Asians, Indians who are doing a lot more than running convenience stores. We are also affecting culture in terms of art, design, and music. And I want to raise my hand and say, 'Hey, I'm one of them.' It's a bit dated now."

For Acharya Palaniswami, the editor of *Hinduism Today*, the double-edged response to *The Simpsons* is entirely understandable: "It is often difficult for good, religious people to smile at their faith's foibles. That's natural. Religion is a serious matter for the devout, and when things they hold precious are held up to humorous scrutiny or even ridicule, they are offended. Among Hindus, such offense is not unknown, but Hindus are more forgiving and perhaps a little more at ease with disdain and ignorance than most. Largely due to an innate ethic of tolerance, Hindus can and do personally enjoy Homer's stupidity and narrow-mindedness toward their religion, and Apu's unctuous money grubbing. They've seen it before, and endured less good-hearted ridicule—probably daily if they live in Memphis or London."

Palaniswami stresses that humor can signal cultural receptivity: "Hindus in America don't yet understand that ridicule is actually part of the process of acceptance of minorities here, that once a minority has become prominent enough to attract ridicule in fictional pieces, be it cartoons, movies or TV shows, that is part of a process of education. It does seem strange, even cruel, but the creation of 'stock jokes' about a minority is part of letting them in, so to speak, welcoming them into the great melting pot.

"Still, Hindus will cringe knowing that *The Simpsons* is seen by millions of Americans who don't have a clue about the ancient and profound Hindu beliefs and customs. At least when characters go after a Christian or a Jew, most in the audience have a sense of the reality that writers are mining for humorous nuggets. They know about Christian beliefs and the people who follow Christianity, mainstream and fringe. When it comes to the Hindu references, the uninformed audience sees only the denigration, the inflated tale, the twisted view. They have met a dozen Indian spice-or-sari store owners, but probably have not been introduced to a single Indian neurosurgeon or high-tech CEO.

"Hindus will note the factual failings of the writers, who would do well to consult more with those who know. . . . Most Hindus will enjoy the fact that karma and reincarnation are subjects for today's films and cartoons, reflecting the fact that the West is intensely interested in and believes in these fundamental Hindu principles. They will smile to see Apu rejecting Lord Ganesha, then coming back, just as so many Indians abroad have done, coming to America the Beautiful, Land of Money, then later rediscovering their faith."

What would the editor of *Hinduism Today* have Homer Simpson understand about the "miscellaneous" Hindu faith?

"Tell Homer there are a billion Hindus in the world; one-sixth of the human family living on Earth today. Tell Homer that in Hinduism it's okay to be a heretic, an agnostic, a disbeliever. Tell him there is no eternal hell in Hinduism, and that all spiritual paths are honored and encouraged. Tell him Hindus believe every single soul will ultimately reach God, not just the saintly ones, not just the chosen believers of this Christian denomination or that Muslim sect. Tell him Hindus learn the value of nonviolence from childhood and have spread the principle to the far corners of the Earth. Tell him all that, and you might one day find Homer going back to India for good."

Twelve

Gay Marriage: Out of the Closet, Left at the Altar.

W
ell before the 2004–2005 season, there was informed speculation that one of *The Simpsons* characters would come out of the closet and reveal a homosexual orientation. Widespread conjecture—and no small amount of betting—ranged from candidates such as Waylon Smithers, sycophantic assistant to Mr. Burns, to Homer's colleagues at the nuclear power plant, Carl and Lenny (although at least one is or was apparently married to a woman). But it was not until a few weeks before the episode aired, in February 2005, that it became clear the show would focus on a gay wedding.

At the beginning of the episode, Bart and one of his friends manage to provoke a downtown depression—complete with boarded-up storefronts—by mistreating a visiting television correspondent. Desperate to revive tourism, Mayor Quimby calls a town meeting, opening the floor to "all crazy ideas that come to people's minds." Lisa raises her hand and suggests legalizing same-sex marriages, which would simultaneously attract a growing segment of the marriage market and "strike a blow for civil rights." In the real world, cities such as Fort Lauderdale have recognized the economic potential of gay tourism. During the annual Gay Days in Orlando in 2006, the Greater Fort Lauderdale Convention and Visitors Bureau rented a billboard, urging visitors to visit their city. "We rolled out what we call the rainbow carpet a couple of years ago, and we've had a lot of green success," Nicki Grossman, president of the organization, told Beth Kassab of the *Orlando Sentinel*. Springfield residents recognize the logic. Instead of objections and prejudice, the idea is equally popular among the townsfolk, with even Moe the bartender recognizing the lucrative possibilities for overpriced, exotic drinks. The mayor agrees they should legalize "gay money—I mean gay marriage," and the proposal passes by acclamation.

A national television advertising campaign is launched, featuring gay couples walking on the beach at sunset, skipping, and kissing. Even Chief Wiggum, in his police uniform, appears in the commercial, embracing a couple. A rainbow banner welcoming gays is stretched across Main Street, where cars from out of town are bumper to bumper. The couples get out of their cars and march en masse to the logical place for a wedding—Springfield Community Church. There the good feeling and the hustle end. Reverend Lovejoy is frantically nailing a large board across the front door, but he tries to put the best face on his actions. "While I have no opinion for or against your sinful lifestyles," he tells them, "I cannot marry two people of the same sex. . . . Now go back to working behind the scenes in every facet of entertainment." (This is a less categorical view than that of the leaders of the Southern Baptist Convention and the Assemblies of God, two denominations that urged a boycott of the Walt Disney Company in the late 1990s when the entertainment giant offered health benefits for partners in same-sex relationships.) As the disappointed visitors begin to scatter, Marge steps out of the crowd. Reverend, she says, "as long as two people love each other, I don't think God cares whether they have the same hoo-hoo or ha-ha." Lovejoy, his arms crossed, is unmoved. The Bible forbids same-sex relations, he says. Which book? she asks. Lovejoy doesn't know—the correct answer, some would say, is Leviticus—and he just repeats, "The Bible." Marge, the true believer, attempts to argue that scriptural scholars disagree on that point, but the minister rings the church bell to drown her out.

Mayor Quimby declares Lovejoy an idiot, not for his intolerance and closed-mindedness, but because he is passing up such an opportunity, in this case, weddings at two hundred dollars apiece. Here again, a serious point is being made. In city after city— including Orlando—decaying downtown areas and neighborhoods have been revived and gentrified after gays have moved into the areas. They often comprise upscale, two-income households, many without children, and rebuild homes and start businesses. The Springfield mayor's point attracts Homer's attention. Previously, he had been holding a sign outside the church reading, "Death before Gay Marriage." Now he sees the light; if Lovejoy won't conduct the weddings, someone else could. "I gotta get in on this. These people have rights," Homer says, as he tosses the placard into the trash can and speeds home to his computer. He soon finds the Web site for the "ePiscopal Church Internet Divinity School," an online diploma mill. "Now begins the long and spiritual journey to becoming an ordained minister," Homer says, and within seconds a clerical collar is coming off the printer. He cleans out the garage, transforming it into the "Li'l Chapel," which he advertises all over town with fliers.

Homer strikes gold. Couples are lined up around the block. Lisa, Bart, and even baby Maggie have been drafted to help with the weddings, as their father rakes in the money, marrying Adam and Steve and Madam and Eve and every gay couple in town. He says he loves love, but what he really loves is money. A sign goes up, advertising "The Church of Matri-Money," and his willingness to "marry anything to anything else. Diaper fee for chimp brides." This should sound familiar to those following the ongoing debate over gay marriage. As local TV anchorman Kent Brockman puts it on the news show *Smartline*, "Have we started down a slippery slope where marriage becomes so meaningless that anyone could marry anything?" In the real world, other demagogic opponents, including some Republican members of Congress, charge that gay marriage will lead to legalizing polygamy (which was permitted in the Bible; the patriarch Jacob married two sisters) and even bestiality. Homer has illustrated this disingenuous argument by marrying two of Springfield's resident yokels, Cletus and Brandine Delroy, whom he believes to be brother and sister. Homer debates the issue with Lovejoy on *Smartline* and seems to hold his own. Watching the show later at home with the family, Marge says she's proud of her husband. "You stood up for people's right to express love in its most perfect form: a binding legal contract." On this note of principle and good feeling, the doorbell rings.

It is Patty Bouvier, Marge's gravel-voiced sister. In the past, she and her other sister, Selma, have never disguised their loathing for Homer. Both sisters are single, and Marge is ecstatic to hear the news that Patty is going to be married and that she wants Homer to perform the ceremony. When Marge asks who the lucky man is, Patty replies, "Veronica." Perplexed, Patty explains as clearly as she can: "I'm marrying a woman. I'm, I'm gay." Seeing that her sister is taken aback by the declaration, Patty asks if Marge is disappointed. No, Marge replies, she is just surprised. But after her outspoken support for gay marriage—in the abstract—Marge is shaken. Patty marvels that her sister did not recognize the signs earlier. "You could see it from space," she says, asking again if Marge has a problem with it. Not at all, Marge says. Since she loves her sister and she loves gay marriage, she would be a super-hypocrite if she didn't love her sister's gay marriage.

To demonstrate that approval, the Simpsons dress up for a dinner at home for the couple. But like many parents placed in a similar situation, Marge is uncomfortable and to some degree evasive in explaining the party and guests to her children. Patty and her fiancée arrive, and Veronica is introduced as a professional golfer. No surprise there, Marge says, endorsing another stereotype. But when the couple kisses on the sofa, Marge instinctively covers baby Maggie's eyes. Asked one more time by her sister if she is okay with the situation, Marge comes unhinged, slipping into the notion that gay marriage represents a thread that leads inevitably to the unraveling of society. "Everyone should do whatever they want," she babbles. "Take a bear to church, read a book with your feet." This snaps it for Patty. "You get all liberal, but you can't handle it when your sister finds love in her own locker room. . . . Marge, if you can find it in your heart to accept me for who I am, I would love to see you at the ceremony."

Days later, the wedding is about to begin in Homer's garage chapel. Grampa Simpson is en route, until he learns there will be a cash bar, which prompts him to denounce the ceremony as "against nature." Upstairs, preparations are underway. In one room, the bride is being dressed by her twin sister, Selma, who has been married and divorced many times. Homer is donning clerical attire and praying: "Oh Lord, please help me say the right words as I consecrate another gay union that angers you so. Please let thy Holy Spirit open the heart of my wife." Not much luck there. Marge rationalizes her opposition by framing it as a matter of honesty: Patty hid her orientation until her wedding and now expects complete acceptance. Looking in the mirror, Homer gets carried away by his new power, imagining the possibility of marrying himself and somehow reproducing. Heading for the bathroom, Marge accidentally walks in on Veronica, who is standing in front of the toilet—with the seat up! She looks again and sees *him*, in a wedding dress, shaving his face while singing the Aerosmith song "Dude Looks Like a Lady." Marge laughs behind her hand and walks away singing the Wedding March.

Patty is delighted to see Marge arrive at the ceremony, giving her a thumbs-up sign as she takes her seat. Homer begins the proceedings with the words "Queerly beloved . . ." Patty's vow speaks of finding a soul mate who is truthful, honest, and hides nothing. Homer calls for objections, and Marge speaks up, enraging her sister. But Patty is stunned when Marge exposes Veronica as a man. He confesses that he pretended to be a woman to get on the LPGA tour and that he didn't reveal himself because he didn't want to lose her. Dropping to one knee, he asks her to marry him as a man. Patty rejects his second proposal: "Hell no, I like girls." The crowd in the chapel applauds, and Patty thanks Marge for at last accepting her for who she is. Marge says she has learned a lesson: "Just because you're a lesbian doesn't make you any less of a 'be-in,'" that is, a human being. They embrace, and Patty walks off into the sunset with her sister Selma. As they do, Homer greets the line of other couples waiting to be married: the Sea Captain and a ship's wooden figurehead, the Comic Book Guy and a cutout of the TV horror show host Elvira, and little, slow-witted Ralph Wiggum, with a live tiger.

By the end of the episode, which drew 10.5 million viewers, it was difficult to say what side of the issue *The Simpsons* writers were on—which was not unintentional. Both sides of the controversy had their say, voiced by various *Simpsons* characters, but there never was a gay marriage of anyone in the regular cast. "Gay people came out very much in favor of it and were very happy with the episode," writer-producer Mike Reiss told the Australian magazine *Encore* in August 2005. "But arch conservatives and right-wing Christians loved the episode, too, because they seemed to think we were making fun of gay people. We really had it both ways." The episode is one of the best examples of what the show's writers call a "take-back gag," in which a point is made with one joke and then immediately undercut by another that follows, or some transparently hypocritical act. In "Something about Marrying," the whole episode came off as a take-back gag. Even before it aired, the series show-runner Al Jean promised, "We'll offend you whether you're gay or straight."

Still, when Fox first announced that an episode of *The Simpsons* would deal with gay marriage, it stoked a debate that few issues and few television shows could. As author of the first edition of this book, I was interviewed on ABC's *World News Tonight*, CNN, and BBC radio, among others, before the episode aired. *The Advocate*, the national gay and lesbian newsmagazine, called it a "milestone." Robert Castillo, a gay activist with Equal Marriage Now, told the *Chicago Tribune* on February 21, 2005, that he thought it was "cool [that] the imaginary Springfield is tackling same-sex weddings." Another activist, Rick Garcia, of Equality Illinois, told the paper the show would have a positive impact on society: "It's just a cartoon, but it's an icon, and it does shape our attitudes as well as reflect our attitudes."

Marty Kaplan, associate dean of the University of Southern California's Annenberg School of Communication, told Sharon Waxman of the *New York Times*, "It's saying to those who demonize homosexuality, or what they call the homosexual agenda, anything from 'Lighten up' to 'Get out of town.'" Kaplan, also the host of a media show on the talk radio network Air America, told the *Times* there was a larger message: "It sounds as though they're saying that what the religious right calls 'the homosexualist agenda,' as if it were creeping Satanism, is: These people are your neighbors in the Springfield that is America."

Conservatives were not so sure. Peter LaBarbera, head of the Illinois Family Institute, told the *Tribune* he wasn't that upset about the episode. "Every TV show has to have the 'gay episode,'" he said. "I just think the 'all-gay-all-the-time' is generally wearing on people." L. Brent Bozell III, president of the Parents Television Council, was more put out. Without screening the episode, he told the *Times* that "at a time when the public mood is overwhelmingly against gay marriage, any show that promotes gay marriage is deliberately bucking the public mood." Despite the parental advisory that preceded the show, Bozell said he would have preferred that *The Simpsons* not tackle gay marriage. "You've got a show watched by millions of children. Do children need to have gay marriage thrust in their faces as an issue? Why can't we just entertain them?"

The show's advisory cautioned, "This episode contains discussions of same-sex marriage. Parental discretion is advised." By no stretch of interpretation was the show an endorsement of gay marriage, nor was it a condemnation of the same. Instead, it was a plea for human understanding—the standard *Simpsons* line—and it probably concluded in the same muddled middle where most Americans are on the issue.

Thirteen

The Creators: "Humor Is in Indirect Proportion to One's True Belief."

Over the lifetime of *The Simpsons*, hundreds of writers, producers, and animators have helped shape the show, beginning with creators Matt Groening, James L. Brooks, and Sam Simon. Others, including George Meyer, John Swartzwelder, John Vitti, Bill Oakley, Josh Weinstein, Mike Scully, Ian Maxtone-Graham, Al Jean, and Mike Reiss have left their mark on the series and scores of scripts. Through his attorney, Susan Grode, Groening told me that he wanted to encourage critical studies of the show like this book. However, Grode said that because Groening sees *The Simpsons* as a collaborative and sometimes collective effort, the show should speak for itself, and he declined further comment.

More than anyone else associated with the show, Groening has been the subject of innumerable interviews and feature stories, but he has rarely spoken about the role of religion in his own life and the show, apart from his comment to *Mother Jones* about the portrayal of God. He told one British journalist that he considers himself a "crusader against injustice in my own little way. Of course, I'm not advocating the religion of 'Simpsonism,' although judging by the fanatics it is almost religious in nature. We cater to obsessive fans."[1] In an interview with Groening about *The Simpsons* for the Web magazine A.V. Club on April 26, 2006, Nathan Rubin asked, "From the beginning, the show has dealt with faith more openly and extensively than anything else on television. Was that by design?" Matt replied, "We had the ability to do it, and because it's a cartoon, we can show all aspects of religiosity. It's not just the family saying grace, which would be dreadful in isolation, but we also show eternal hellfire, the Devil, and even God, who is

199

199

a 12-foot-high guy in a long white robe with five fingers and a big white beard. So that's fun. We haven't shown God's face, except once in a 'Treehouse of Horror' episode when Kang and Kodos used an accela-ray on a boring baseball game and ended up collapsing the universe. Generally, you don't see his face, but I always thought that we should show God's head with a long, white beard, with his face blurred out because of internal illumination, but the top of his head would have Homer's two little hairs."

At various times, Groening has said he patterned the character of Bart after himself, the cartoon strip character Dennis the Menace (but not the television version), and the character of Eddie Haskell in the television series *Leave It to Beaver*. Haskell, he told a television interviewer, "was the bad kid, and he got away with stuff, and I liked that. I thought, 'Eddie Haskell should have his own show and when I grow up, I'm going to do my own show and it's going to star Eddie Haskell or a version thereof.' Hence, Bart Simpson."[2] Springfield, he said, was named for the hometown in another early television show, *Father Knows Best*.

The cartoonist grew up in a middle-class home in Portland, Oregon, the son of Homer and Marge Groening and the brother of four siblings, including sisters named Lisa and Maggie. He told *My Generation* magazine in 2001 that his relationship with his father—who was himself a cartoonist, filmmaker, and advertising executive—was "contentious." Homer Groening was raised a Mennonite and spoke German until he attended school, his son told the magazine. Matt recalled in numerous interviews that his was by and large a happy childhood; he favored Dr. Seuss books and, as an aspiring eleven-year-old cartoonist, began imitating Batman comics. He did get into periodic scrapes in elementary school that landed him, like Bart, in the principal's office.

His career as a Boy Scout foundered on his refusal to cut his long hair and the trip on which he took the Gideon Bible from his motel room, thinking it was free. "The scoutmaster screamed, 'You stole this Bible on top of everything else?'" he recalled. "So I prayed to God and said, 'I know you'll forgive me for not believing in you.' . . . Basically I was a pagan." Groening made good grades in high school and was elected student body president. He also spent a lot of time in his room, listening to rock music and perusing magazines famous for their cartoons—*The New Yorker*, *Esquire*, and *Punch*—and read a book that impressed him, Walter Kaufmann's *Critique of Religion and Philosophy*. "I had a strong sense of bitterness and self-pity," he said in an interview with Richard von Busack in 1986, published in *MetroActive* magazine in 2000.

The teenager continued to do good deeds, even without the Boy Scout merit badges. For a time he worked in the kitchen of a convalescent home. But he was rejected when he applied to Harvard in the mid-1970s. Instead, he went to Evergreen State University in Olympia, an experimental, progressive college where he was editor and cartoonist for the campus daily, *The Cooper Point Journal*, and a friend of the artist and cartoonist Lynda Barry. He enjoyed his time at college and returned the favor by situating the Simpsons' household on Evergreen Terrace.

Early influences on his comic art were polar opposites: Charles Schulz, creator of *Peanuts*, and the ribald, 1960s undergound cartoonist R. Crumb. Groening moved to Los Angeles in the 1980s, recalling that he lived in "a seedy Hollywood apartment." He did a variety of odd jobs and hawked his original comics until he launched his alternative comic strip, "Life in Hell." One of his strips was entitled "What Not to Say During Moments of Intimacy" and included this one: "O My Lord in Heaven, forgive me for this vile sin I am about to commit." For nearly a decade, he worked on the strip in his garage, "lonely and socially backward," he told *TV Host* magazine in 1989.

In the late 1980s, award-winning film and television producer James L. Brooks, a fan of *Life in Hell*, tapped him to help develop cartoon vignettes—which would later become *The Simpsons*—for *The Tracey Ullman Show*. It was a good match. Brooks had also produced *The Mary Tyler Moore Show* and *Taxi* for television and made the Academy Award–winning *Terms of Endearment*, *Broadcast News*, and *Jerry Maguire* for the big screen. Brooks said in a broadcast interview that he believes that "television is probably one of the last stands for writer control. A writer can still control his work almost utterly on television."[3] At a meeting of the Television Critics tour in January 2007, Brooks reflected, "The thing I love most about the show is that you can do any form of comedy. You can do low comedy, high comedy, romantic comedy. You can take it any place."

Groening, who by some media accounts has had his ups and downs with Brooks since they began working together, gave much of the credit for the series' success to the producer. "It was his clout that allowed the show to be made without compromise," the cartoonist said.[4] Neither Brooks nor Groening nor anyone else present at the creation was prepared for the worldwide phenomenon *The Simpsons* became. Over the years since, Groening has played a diminishing role in the show's day-to-day production, telling interviewers he sticks his nose in the door every so often and keeps an eye on his characters. "Matt is good at keeping the writers honest," said Mike Scully. "If he thinks Homer is becoming too insane, he'll pull us back."

In 1999, Groening launched another animated comedy for Fox, *Futurama*, set in the year 3000, where one target of satire was the "Church of Robotology." Here again, Groening took a shot at Scientology, which is ironic in light of the fact that Nancy Cartwright, the voice of Bart Simpson, is an outspoken Scientologist. In a 1997 interview with National Public Radio, Cartwright said that once she started practicing the religion in 1989, her reaction was, "Oh, God. This is cool." She said that Scientology is different from other faiths: "not like a real religion . . . you don't pray." She said she found both a spiritual life and a husband when she discovered Scientology. The writing of Scientology founder L. Ron Hubbard "totally makes sense to me," she said, and in her autobiography, *My Life as a 10-Year-Old Boy*, she describes Hubbard as a "humanitarian," although she makes no other mention of Scientology in the book. One of the show's writers told me that producers vetoed an episode-length swat at Scientology in fear of the group's reputation for suing and harassing opponents. Other character voices part ways with the parts they play. Harry Shearer, the voice of Ned Flanders and Reverend Lovejoy, said in an interview with the online magazine *FilmForce* that these two parts no more reflected his personal spiritual and theological views "than doing the voice of Otto (the stoned school bus driver) has affected my choice of intoxicants."[5]

Groening's interview with *Mother Jones* was one of the most incisive and revealing of his moral moorings. In both *The Simpsons* and *Futurama*, he said, he has tried to use the guise of light entertainment to wake people up "to some of the ways we're being manipulated and exploited" by modern American culture. *The Simpsons'* message, in particular, is that "your moral authorities don't always have your best interest in mind. Teachers, principals, clergymen, politicians—for *The Simpsons*, they're all goofballs, and I think that's a great message for kids."[6] In a more recent interview with the Spanish language newspaper *La Opinion* in Los Angeles, he said that the show was "secretly educational, not for giving sermons or giving lectures about morality. *The Simpsons* is good for children because it's about learning how to tell a story."[7] Despite the series' underlying support for marriage, family, and values, Groening's wife, Deborah, told the *Seattle Times*, "Republicans and religious fanatics don't always get Matt's intentions. . . . [They] keep trying to convert Matt because they're worried he's going straight to hell—the real hell."[8] And, at one point, the burly, bearded father of two acknowledged that he did not permit his own elementary school age sons to watch *The Simpsons*.

Without live, aging actors and their egos to deal with, *The Simpsons* has evolved into a writers' medium. "As a writer," said Mike Scully, an executive producer who joined the show in 1993, "you really get spoiled on *The Simpsons*. I tell all our younger guys to enjoy this while it lasts, because you'll never have it this good again from a creative standpoint." Groening admitted that if he hadn't help create the series he probably wouldn't have been hired to write for it. "It's next to impossible to break into the inner circle unless you went to Harvard with one of those eggheads," he said, later referring to them as "Harvard-grad-brainiac-bastard-eggheads."[9] Richard Appel, a graduate of Harvard and Harvard Law School, left a job with the United States Attorney's office in Manhattan to write comedy in Los Angeles, where he joined other members of the Harvard *Lampoon* on *The Simpsons* in the 1990s. "It's like there's a conveyor belt now of people coming out here," he told the *New York Times* in 1997.

When I first approached *Simpsons* writers in 2000 to ask them about the frequently positive portrayal of faith in the series, they seemed extremely reticent to acknowledge this fact, even when presented with example after example. It didn't fit the show's edgy, antiauthoritarian image and reputation. Their fallback position— always offered on an off-the-record basis—was that the large role of religion in *The Simpsons* was merely "creative desperation." No one on the staff imagined the series would last as long as it has, and they simply began running out of situations for their situation comedy, especially one in which characters did not mature or fundamentally change. For a variety of cultural and economic reasons, religion had not been worn out by previous decades of network sitcoms. Thus, religion in *The Simpsons*. This may be true, at least in part, but I have my doubts. Writers, even the most cynical on the surface, tend to be thwarted idealists—disappointed or, as one observer suggested, "mugged by reality."

Typical of the writers who have shaped the series from the beginning is George Meyer, who started writing for the show in 1989 and wrote the episode "Homer the Heretic." Raised in Arizona, the oldest of eight children in a Catholic household, he was an A student in school, on the speech team, editor of the school paper, and an Eagle Scout. At Harvard, he was elected to head the *Lampoon*, the fabled humor magazine. After graduation, he was accepted to medical school but gravitated to comedy writing, working for David Letterman and *Saturday Night Live*. Scully called Meyer "the best comedy writer in Hollywood." The myriad of writers, producers, and consultants listed at the end of each *Simpsons* episode makes it nearly impossible for anyone outside the show to know (or recall) who was responsible for what joke or what plot twist. Much of the credit, most agree, goes to Meyer.

"I felt I was a happy kid," Meyer said in a 2000 *New Yorker* profile, which was written by David Owen, his Harvard roommate and longtime friend. But, as a Catholic, "I did feel that I was made to shoulder a lot of burdens that shouldn't have been mine—such as the frustrations of older women wearing nun costumes. People talk about how horrible it is to be brought up Catholic, and it's all true. The main thing was that there was no sense of proportion. I would chew a piece of gum at school, and the nun would say, 'Jesus is very angry with you about that,' and on the wall behind her would be a dying, bleeding guy on a cross. That's a horrifying image to throw at a little kid. You really could almost think that your talking in line, say, was on a par with killing Jesus. You weren't sure, and there was never a moderating voice."[10]

Another import from the Letterman show—and former *Lampoon* president—was Jeff Martin, who wrote for the series for three of the early seasons. Martin also came equipped with considerable knowledge of evangelical Protestantism. He is the son of William Martin, the author of *A Prophet with Honor: The Billy Graham Story* and *With God on Our Side: The Rise of the Religious Right in America*, and professor of the sociology of religion at Rice University. "We were active in church when the boys were growing up," said William Martin, a graduate of Harvard Divinity School. The family attended a Church of Christ in Massachusetts and, later, a moderate Southern Baptist Church in Houston, which he described as being "ecumenical, with evangelical roots." Family ties were also strong, William Martin said. "Nearly all of our relatives are actively religious, and Jeff saw a very positive representation of that tradition." His son "grew up recognizing that there were a lot of healthy and positive aspects to it, seeing the good sides of sincere, positive, true belief."

Martin admitted that he and his wife were skeptical about Jeff's move from the Letterman show to *The Simpsons*: "When he told us he was going to California to write an animated show about a loser working-class family, we thought, 'This is a bad career move.'" But at Rice, being the father of a writer for *The Simpsons* has turned out to carry considerable cachet, he said. "I get lots of mileage out of it." He never missed an episode and, early on, found himself providing informal script consultation to Jeff. "He would call about scripture or reference or phrase or a song—some technical point."

For his part, Jeff Martin said, "I knew I could always call my parents" for background information on religion, in addition to calling on his own memories. "My extended family contains many, many people who have an abiding faith that sustains them." Not surprisingly, he liked writing for the Flanders family. "Their religion obviously gives them a great deal of happiness and guidance, and the writing staff has respect for that. Ned is a truly nice man." But Jeff said he had a particular affinity for the two boys, Rod and Todd: "I'd have them singing songs I learned in vacation Bible school when I was a kid."

As an industry, comedy writing is dominated by Catholics, Jews, and atheists, which made Martin a valuable resource in creating episodes of *The Simpsons.* In the months-long process—which is at once cooperative and competitive—script ideas are proposed, outlined, written, rewritten, and polished, often by more than a dozen writers and producers on a single episode. "I was in a minority as a Protestant, but I wouldn't say anyone deferred to me. It wasn't a case of me being an expert, although I suppose I did have more hands-on experience with a Protestant service." Martin moved on from *The Simpsons* to become cocreator of another animated series about a family, *Baby Blues.*

Steve Tompkins, a veteran of three seasons with the series during the mid-1990s, was another writer who brought a Protestant perspective to *The Simpsons.* His insight is valuable because he is also a distinctive voice for religious values in Hollywood's high-powered world of animated comedies. Most of the writers on the show "were atheist Jews or atheist Christians, and only two of us were churchgoing Christians when I was there." Yet, when Tompkins and I first spoke, for a short article in *Christianity Today* magazine, he admitted to being wary of being identified as a Christian in print, in part because the label can be the kiss of death for a comedy writer. "The two are seen as antithetical," he said, sounding perplexed by the notion that a self-described class clown like himself should have to choose between the kingdom of heaven and a successful writing career. "I do believe that Jesus is the Son of God, that he was crucified, and that he rose again." Tompkins was raised an Episcopalian in an upscale Massachusetts town, where he attended the same church as the novelist John Updike. As a child, he recalled watching *Davey and Goliath*, an early animated show produced by the Lutheran Church that used biblical themes, before going to church on Sundays.

Tompkins drifted from faith in his twenties, like many young people. While writing for *The Simpsons*, he had what he called a "reconversion experience," one he emphasized was unrelated to his comedy writing. Because he had not fallen out of faith, Tompkins hesitated to call it a born-again experience: "A little slice of me made itself known again. When that happened it *informed* my life, but didn't *transform* my life."

In the fall of 2000, Tompkins showed clips from *Simpsons* episodes while speaking at Fuller Theological Seminary in Pasadena, California, on a program entitled "Does God Have a Sense of Humor?" as part of the school's "Reel Spirituality" series. He admitted that writing for Homer, Marge, Bart, and Lisa was a challenge. "There were some rabid atheists at *The Simpsons*," he said, yet it was not as much of a challenge as believers might think. "If you look at *The Simpsons*, no matter how twisted the story, no matter how profane the jokes, goodness wins, goodness prevails. No matter how much those writers pride themselves as being atheists, probably deep down, they're not. They have love for humanity, and they love those characters." (Like many Christians, Tompkins equates believing in God with loving humanity and assumes that not believing is the same thing as not loving humanity. Atheists, who sometimes prefer the term "humanist," say they act in a moral and humane way because it is the right thing to do, not because they are bound by some supernatural set of beliefs.)

Tompkins too is a graduate of Harvard University and the *Lampoon*, and so was well equipped for the vigorous cut-and-thrust of *The Simpsons'* writing regime. "You pride yourself on being able to pitch jokes on any subject, no matter how blasphemous or sacrilegious," said Tompkins, who has also written for comedies such as *In Living Color* and *Everybody Loves Raymond*. "Whatever your religious beliefs might be, the process doesn't injure your personal spirit at all." In fact, he said, being able to participate fully in this raucous "room" can inoculate writers from concerns that they are pushing a particular agenda.

"At *The Simpsons*, you are reined in," Tompkins said. "You can't stick your neck out and do anything that's overtly religious on its face. You must undercut it. There's a gag reflex in comedy writers to undercut any honest religious sentiment. It is easier to pass a camel through the eye of a needle than it is to make a comedy writer quote scripture with a straight face." The key, he said, is "respecting the faith of the characters because it's true to the characters. I think that's what's going on in the best moments of *The Simpsons*. Marge's faith is respected because that is a huge part of who she is as a character. Homer has no faith, so we use him to tromp over Marge's faith, or whatever needs to be done comedically." At times, the show does seem to engage in "blasphemy for blasphemy's sake, an omnidirectional assault on all that's sacred." It helps, he says, that "no one really takes its blasphemy seriously. The things that should be mocked are mocked, and the things that shouldn't be mocked are mocked."

Tompkins worked on several *Simpsons* episodes that dealt with religion, the church, and faith, including the one in which Ned, like the Bible's Job, has his faith tested. "There is a tremendous amount of affection for Ned" among the writers, he said. That episode, "Hurricane Neddy," used as its comedic premise a faithful Christian singled out for devastation, and "how a person behaves in times of crisis." Still, he insisted that, for the most part, he is a secular writer. "I had no ax to grind at *The Simpsons*. I believe the quality of humor is in indirect proportion to one's true belief. The more those beliefs are put in, the less funny it gets. The characters on *The Simpsons* do not represent the writers' faith." This is in contrast to *Touched by an Angel*, where, he said, "the stories those show-runners are creating really represent the way the world should be, could be." *Touched by an Angel* takes a more direct approach, using its content to communicate the message, Tompkins said, a conscious choice which works well for that show. "*The Simpsons* doesn't do that. The mark of good writing is letting the message be true to the characters, to honor their beliefs and keep them sacred to the character."

Ian Maxtone-Graham is an articulate representative of nonbelievers on *The Simpsons* staff, and he confirmed Tompkins's observation about the show's frenetic writing and rewriting process. This is especially true when it comes to the matter of credits for writers. "The titles don't mean much," he said. "Everyone's in the room and pretty much everyone moves up the ladder to 'co-executive producer.' Then there are the 'consulting producers' who—it's too complicated. We're all writers. The 'writer' of the episode wrote the first draft. It might be their story; might not. They might keep 80 percent of their jokes and lines. Most likely they'll keep way fewer. To my knowledge, no *Simpsons* writing credit has been disputed or arbitrated by the Writers' Guild. The first-draft guy or gal keeps the writing credit come hell or page one rewrite."

Maxtone-Graham, who has written many episodes, also confirmed Tompkins's description of the theological mix among writers: "There are many, many atheists in that room." A graduate of Brown University, *National Lampoon* magazine, and *Saturday Night Live*, Maxtone-Graham grew up in New York in an Episcopal family but never attended church. "I don't believe in God particularly," he told me, "although I always enjoyed Christmas carols. You don't need to believe in all the religious details to have it work. You don't have to believe in a higher power."

Music has been a path to spirituality of a sort for Maxtone-Graham. He helped write the popular "Hanukkah Song," cowritten and introduced by Adam Sandler on *Saturday Night Live*, as well as a Kwanzaa song for that show. In the early 1990s, Maxtone-Graham also wrote new lyrics for the classic "Silver Bells," which was sung by Glenn Close, who was hosting the holiday *SNL*, in her opening monologue. The Academy Award–winning actress was accompanied by about a dozen residents of her hometown in upstate New York.

"It was in the middle of a huge blizzard in New York," he recalled. "These poor guys—none of them performers—had come down to sing on national television. I had spent several hours teaching them the song, and I conducted them, quite inexpertly. Everyone was nervous, but they did a hell of a job, and the audience loved it. At the end of the song, they dropped artificial snow onto the stage, and the effect was just magical. A colleague came up to me and told me it had made her cry. It was a deeply moving experience, one of the greatest I have ever had as a writer.

It was a hugely emotional moment for me. And I'm sure that's what got me interested in writing 'religious' songs."

After joining *The Simpsons*, Maxtone-Graham made a study of Christian rock music. His nonbelief notwithstanding, Maxtone-Graham wrote the episode in which Maude Flanders dies, including the moving, contemporary Christian rock song that sets up the dramatic reconciliation between Ned and his faith. This preparation helped him understand the characters' religious life. "It seems like a natural, everyday thing that they go to church," he said, "but they are not slavishly devoted to organized religion. They like the routine of going to church. And that's probably the way most people feel. They all have their skeptical moments."

It was while writing for *The Simpsons* that the skeptical Maxtone-Graham developed his own serious interest in religion and in the Bible. He stumbled across the book *Gospel Truth: The New Image of Jesus Emerging from Science and History, and Why It Matters*, by the journalist Russell Shorto. In part, Maxtone-Graham said he liked the book, which relies on the scholarship of the Jesus Seminar, because the author does not come from "a religion-hating background." He was so impressed with the work that he loaned it and gave it as a gift to other *Simpsons* writers. Before long, he was reading *Jesus: A Life* and *Paul: The Mind of the Apostle*, both by A. N. Wilson. "I was fascinated by the truth behind the New Testament. It turned me into a Bible know-it-all, but it didn't make me more or less religious. I admire many of the things Jesus said, but I'm not religious. I never was."

In writing about religion for the series, he said, "there is an attempt to universalize things without losing the Middle American flavor of their church, to leave it open to many intelligent people who are atheists." Thus, in writing about Flanders's crisis of faith following Maude's death, the viewer can interpret Ned's return to the church as God's answer to his prayers, or, for skeptics, that Ned simply found the inner resources to cope with his loss. "It seemed to have a message that works for both sides," Maxtone-Graham said.

Mike Reiss is one of those "Jewish atheists" on the show's writing staff. "I know Jewish culture," he said. "I was bar mitzvahed, but I've never been a believer. It's a rich culture full of interesting quirks, yet sometimes I wish Jewish kids would go to karate class rather than Hebrew school." Reiss grew up and attended synagogue in a Connecticut city that was home to only fifty Jews out of a population of fifty thousand. He went to Harvard, where he roomed with future *Simpsons* writer Al Jean, who would become his longtime writing partner. Both worked on the *Lampoon*, where Reiss said Jewish and Irish students tended to congregate.

His atheism notwithstanding, Reiss said, "I don't know any show that covers religion like *The Simpsons* does. The very best episodes are the ones that take a big, big issue like religion and look at it, and turn it upside down and examine it from all angles. We know there's no one answer to these things. It's one of those really big topics we come back to a lot, and I'm glad we do." If *The Simpsons* seems to favor religion, he said, it's more of a case of "being nice by accident. . . . As writers for the series, we go to church partly for mockery and comic value, for its ripe comic potential. Homer is always punished for his sins, and always punished way out of proportion. But there has always been a basic humanity to the show, and sometimes that manifests itself religiously."

Not that there aren't limits, even for an atheist, he said. "Every writer has built-in boundaries, a taste level that they won't cross. I consider myself one of the most conservative guys. The name 'Jesus' comes in as a punch line every so often. The show has gotten more sacrilegious as time has gone on. There's much more leeway. The cartoon format provides a buffer against these hard issues. The best live action sitcom couldn't play with religion the way *The Simpsons* does. You can't beat the cuteness factor, it looks so innocuous." The show's writers have learned through experience that viewers are willing to accept jokes and situations if they are presented in an animated form. In a larger sense, humor does not touch the same nerve with the faithful as drama. *The Last Temptation of Christ*, a serious attempt at portraying the gospel, attracted far more Christian protests than the outrageously blasphemous *Monty Python's Life of Brian*.

In an interview with the Australian magazine *Encore* in August 2005, Reiss said, "We try really hard not to have a political message with *The Simpsons*. When we do an episode or cover a topic and we start to feel like we're preaching or pushing too far in the one direction we'll take a right turn and go in the opposite direction. I think it's one reason we're popular; any point of view watches our show and goes, 'Oh they support us.'" Being able to have it both ways, Reiss said, has its advantages. "It's a good lesson not only in entertainment but also in politics. That is, never say anything. Or say just enough to make people think you're on their side. You can generally see our bias come out. Another thing is that we make vicious fun of Republican conservatives on our show. We had an episode where we showed that Dracula was a member of the Springfield Republican Party and the guy who wrote that joke is an archconservative Republican. He wrote that joke because that's the funny joke to make about Republicans. You take a stand because that's where the comedy is." That may have been what the writers had in mind years later, when they had Homer, as a Puritan taking the wheel of the storm-tossed *Mayflower*, promise Marge he would stay alive long enough "for all you fundamentalist Christians to take over by the twenty-first century."

In 2000, Reiss wrote a children's book called *How Murray Saved Christmas*, in which a Jewish delicatessen owner fills in for Santa Claus. Although there were some obvious Jewish references in the manuscript, Reiss said that his editor, a gentile from North Dakota, kept pressing him to add more. It was the same dynamic he experienced when he and Al Jean wrote *Simpsons* episodes together. Everyone assumed that he was the source of any "Jewish" material, when, in fact, as often as not it came from his Catholic partner. "In the writing room, Jewish people are there to provide authenticity—and pronunciation," Reiss said. "It's the gentiles who get a real kick out of this stuff."

"I consider myself someone who believes in the teachings of Jesus Christ but who is not a huge fan of organized religion," said Al Jean, who returned to the job as *The Simpsons'* show-runner in 2001. "We respect everyone's belief." Jean began working on the show in 1989 and, with Reiss, is credited in over 200 episodes, which provides him with perspective on the way the presentation of religion in the series has evolved. "Often things on the show grow of their own accord," he said. "We didn't set out on the show with an agenda. But very early on we showed characters going to church, and we began exploring that venue, which was obviously very rich. So, for example, we looked at the Ten Commandments as source material. As writers, we are always looking for aspects of life that are undercovered or underrepresented on TV, and religion is definitely one of them." And the frequent inclusion of and favorable slant on faith? "It wasn't because of any conscious attempt at the beginning," he said. "We didn't want to take cheap shots. It was a subject that was not explored much in prime-time sitcoms. We're not perfect, but we definitely are very thoughtful and funny. The show is something a family can watch."

Jean acknowledged that there are some taboos in the religion area; crucifixion or resurrection jokes are generally off limits. "People are very sensitive to those things," he said. "Images of Christ on the cross, things like that can't avoid offending a huge group of people. We're pretty cautious about that." Crossing such lines, he said, "would erode all the goodwill the show generates and would undermine the show's moral messages."

While there are people on the staff who may now be irreligious, he said, religion plays a part in *The Simpsons* because the writers were raised in middle- or upper-middle-class homes where faith and observance were part of their lives. "We're just aiming to depict what we saw as reality. We just want you to believe these are real people. Without a doubt, religion has been accepted in the show because it is reflective of life, but we never forget that comedy is the real point of it all."

Particular care is taken not to single out one denomination or another for praise or pillory, Jean said. "I can't say one faith is right over another." Salvation by faith is eclipsed by salvation by works for a very simple reason. "As writers, we're always interested in dramatic actions. Works are more interesting to watch than grace."

Over the years, *The Simpsons* has made fun of Protestants, Catholics, Jews, and Hindus. Jean, a Catholic, admitted that Muslims have also been largely off limits. In one episode, however, Homer explains that Muslims once worshiped turtles and badgers.

Inverting history, he says, "Thank God we've come to our senses and worship a carpenter who lived two thousand years ago." Jean said, "One reason [for largely ignoring Muslims] is, I don't think we've had a writer who was Muslim," noting that there was a chill resulting from the Salman Rushdie affair. "It's a faith where you don't want to offend, because we're not Muslim, and we're not sure what might be offensive." In retrospect, it was a wise choice, given the worldwide outcry in 2006 over Danish cartoons—widely reprinted in Europe—that lampooned the Prophet Muhammad.

As early as October 2005, there were indications of the cultural pitfalls of integrating *The Simpsons'* brand of humor with Islamic sensibilities. Officials at an Arab cable network, MBC-TV, announced that they would be initiating broadcasts of *The Simpsons* in Arabic, just in time for the holy month of Ramadan. "I think *The Simpsons* will open new horizons for us to the future," Michel Costandi, the network's business-development vice president, told the *Wall Street Journal*. "We are opening up a new genre of programming in the Middle East." Of course, there would be some changes, in addition to prominent Egyptian actors such as Mohamed Heneidy voicing the roles. The family would be called "al Shamshoon," and Homer would be known as Omar. Bart would be Badr. In accordance with Qur'anic law, beer became soda and Moe's bar was gone. Also gone were Homer's beloved pork chops. Doughnuts became the Arab confection known called "khak." Barbecued Egyptian beef sausages replaced hot dogs. No mention was made of how Krusty, the Jewish clown, would appear.

Arabs on the street in Muslim countries and Arab American academics voiced skepticism that something so uniquely American could be translated into another culture, despite the fact that the show already airs in more than seventy countries worldwide. After watching a promo for the Arab version of the show, As'ad Abu Khalil, a professor at California State University, Stanislaus, denounced the cultural hybrid as "beyond the pale" on his "Angry Arab" blog. "It was just painful," the self-proclaimed "huge fan" of *The Simpsons* wrote. "The guy who played Homer was one of the most unfunny people I ever watched." Later, after watching a complete episode, Abu Khalil amplified his initial reaction, which was quoted in the *Wall Street Journal* story: "It was worse than what I had expected, but at least I knew what the problem was. . . . It became obvious while watching it that none of the people who either translated, or produced, or acted in the series had watched or understood the original *Simpsons*. The entire personality of Homer was missed. . . . It is just worse than being unfunny: it is painful to watch. You feel sorry for the original talents behind the real *Simpsons*, and you feel sorry for the Egyptian actors being part of a most unfunny show. And it is obvious that those who translated the show were not people who know idiomatic American English expressions and nuances. So much of the show was missed." Al Jean, *The Simpsons'* show-runner at the time, was equally doubtful about Homer's transformation. "Well," he said, "if he doesn't eat bacon and, you know, generally act like a pig, which I know is also against Islam, then I don't think it's Homer." In the end, Fox quietly killed the deal, citing provisions in the standard syndication agreement that require network approval for all script and content alterations.

Why do the writers and creators believe the role of religion in the show has gone unnoticed until the 1990s? "Two or three things can pigeonhole a show," Jean said in 2000. "Our pigeonhole was that we were the outrageous show that had no conscience. We got this bad boy image since the beginning, but over the past ten years it has evaporated. We're a little less outrageous compared to *South Park*. People are looking beyond the surface. There is a thoughtful core to the show. We believe in the little guy, the triumph of the family. Our characters are real; they want love and companionship in the end."

Fourteen

Conclusion: Cloaking the Sacred with the Profane?

I f you excise the jokes, *The Simpsons* is a tragedy of operatic proportions—repeated failures and frustrations, punctuated by the
occasional, wacky, life-affirming reprieve that returns everything
to the status quo. And, like any comedy aimed at a mass audience,
it is at its roots doggedly conservative. Leon Trotsky, one of the
fathers of Russia's Bolshevik uprising, used to characterize a political movement he opposed as being "left in form, right in essence,"
which is to say that his opponents were revolutionary in appearance but reactionary in nature. With *The Simpsons*, I think it may
be a similar case: cloaking the show's sacred essence in the guise
of profane storytelling, although there is no evidence that this is
a result of any conscious, consistent effort on the part of the show's
writers and producers. Longtime writer George Meyer argued
just the opposite in a *My Generation* magazine article. "It's like a
Trojan horse that gets past people's radar because it's superficially
conservative," he said. "The show's subtext, however, is completely subversive and wild."

Whether the series, once considered so antiauthoritarian, is
subversive or supportive of faith is largely in the eye of the beholder.
Some Christians remain resolutely unconvinced of its value. The
Reverend Francis Chan of the evangelical Cornerstone Community Church in Simi Valley, California, told the *Ventura County
Star* in 1999 that he once found the show funny, but gave it up. "It
portrays Christians as being out of touch with reality. It makes
anyone who follows God look like a fool."[1]

The Reverend Clark Whitten, former pastor of Calvary Assembly of God in Winter Park, Florida, one of the largest Pentecostal

churches in that area, tries not to miss a single Sunday night episode. "It's life, it's hilarious, and it's so insightful into the culture," he said. The Anglican Archbishop of Canterbury, Dr. Rowan Williams, called *The Simpsons* "a positive example to children" and a show with "a strong sense of family values." In June 2004, a spokesman for Williams told the BBC that the head of the Church of England would "look very seriously" at any invitation from the show's producers to appear as a character, as Prime Minister Tony Blair did.

In his study of religion in the television series, Jim Trammell of the University of Georgia arrived at a similar conclusion. "Despite the church's depicted irrelevance, despite the depicted wrath of God and the likeable character of the Devil, despite the disrespected devoted neighbors, despite the inadequate minister, despite even the insignificance of spirituality upon one's behaviors, the Simpson family, the show's heroes and representatives of the American family, remain committed to their religion."

Some atheists think *The Simpsons* is so proreligion that it's more like a Sunday school lesson than a sitcom. In a 1995 atheists' Internet discussion group, one member wrote, "The central message of the show, I've noticed, is that only the good people are religious and that those who are not are immoral. Some episodes really hammer the point home. And the true religious fanatics in that show are portrayed as the most moral, ethical people around. I stopped watching in disgust a long time ago." Like the Christians, even the atheists are split on the series. "It's a great show," said George H. Smith, author of *Why Atheism?* and *Atheism: The Case against God*. "I think there's a good balance" on religion, he said. "It's a remarkably well-done show."

This appraisal has not escaped the attention of a growing number of commentators who argue that the show is far more conservative and supportive of traditional faith and family values than you would think. "What I do appreciate about *The Simpsons* is that evil often—if not always—is punished with consequences," said Robert Knight, former director of cultural studies for the Washington, DC-based Family Research Council and author of *The Age of Consent: The Rise of Relativism and the Corruption of Popular Culture*. "*The Simpsons* function in a moral universe and, while the show seems to make fun of moral standards, it often upholds those same standards in a backhanded way."

"The show provides elements of continuity that make *The Simpsons* more traditional than may first appear," according to Paul A. Cantor, writing in the December 1999 issue of the journal *Political Theory.* "The show's creators have been generally even-handed over the years in making fun of both [political] parties, and of both the Right and the Left," providing something to both liberals and conservatives. In essence, Cantor argues that "*The Simpsons* seems to offer a kind of intellectual defense of the common man against intellectuals, which helps explain its popularity and broad appeal."[2]

Take, for example, the characters' hometown of Springfield. Cantor argued in his award-winning paper for the American Political Science Association that, while the show makes fun of small-town life, "it simultaneously celebrates the virtues of the traditional American small town. . . . *The Simpsons* is profoundly anachronistic in the way it harks back to an earlier age when Americans felt more in contact with their governing institutions and family life was solidly anchored in a larger but still local community."

In his essay, Cantor suggested that an even more telling analysis would focus on the family. "*The Simpsons* shows the family as part of a larger community and in effect affirms the kind of community that can sustain the family. . . . For all its slapstick nature and its mocking of certain aspects of family life, *The Simpsons* has an affirmative side and ends up celebrating the nuclear family as an institution. . . . Though it strikes many people as trying to subvert the American family or to undermine its authority, in fact, it reminds us that antiauthoritarianism is itself an American tradition and that family authority has always been problematic in democratic America. What makes *The Simpsons* so interesting is the way it combines traditionalism and antitraditionalism. It continually makes fun of the traditional American family. But it continually offers an enduring image of the nuclear family in the very act of satirizing it. Many of the traditional values of the American family survive this satire, above all the value of the nuclear family itself."

Jonah Goldberg reinforced Cantor's take on the series in an article in the *National Review.* Many conservatives share a negative view of *The Simpsons*, based on the controversies generated in the first few seasons, he wrote. "That's regrettable, because it's possibly the most intelligent, funny and even politically satisfying TV show ever." In contrast to previous sitcom hits, which he said were "invariably and predictably liberal," *The Simpsons* "is never predictable; and its satire spares nothing and no one. . . . This even-handedness is noteworthy. Against the backdrop of conventional sitcoms, it makes *The Simpsons* damn near reactionary; if 50 percent of the jokes are aimed leftward, that's 49.5 percent more than we usually get." Yes, Goldberg acknowledged, "Christian fundamentalism get[s] the full treatment," but the satire "is aimed at all of society's false pieties. . . . What should dismay liberals about this is that so many of today's pieties are constructs of the Left. . . . Some important pretensions are being punctured here—but not the usual ones."[3] Targets include liberal Democrats, environmentalism, gun control, and '60s radical sellouts.

Even *The Plain Truth*, a nondenominational magazine affiliated with the Worldwide Church of God, took favorable note of *The Simpsons* in a lengthy article by Barbara Curtis in the January/February 2001 issue of the evangelical magazine. Under the headline, "Are the Simpsons 'Okily Dokily'?" Curtis answered vigorously in the affirmative. The show was "long-forbidden fare in many Christian homes," she wrote, including her own. "Like most good Christians, I refused to give them the time of day." After giving the show a chance, however, "I was impressed with the grace abounding in the characters' relationships, as well as the intelligence and wit of the writing. . . . There is no other show in TV land that so acknowledges the immediacy of God and the effectiveness of prayer. Peel away the laughter, and you will find *The Simpsons* have a strong foundation in love and faithfulness."[4]

The show's potshots at Christians and their church did not offend Curtis. "When it comes to exposing human foibles, *The Simpsons* is an equal opportunity employer. . . . I'm glad I'm not alone in finding the Christian highlights hilarious. Our weaknesses are, after all, our weaknesses. We all know Neds and Maudes and Reverend Lovejoys—may even *be* them from time to time ourselves. Perhaps the greatest weakness of all is to take oneself too seriously."

If these conservative commentators are correct, how did this happen, and why? Televangelist and Christian Coalition founder Pat Robertson, who told me he much preferred *Touched by an Angel* to *The Simpsons*, suggested that the Great Man Theory of History might explain why the Fox show has turned so positive on faith. "I was somewhat appalled at what I saw of *The Simpsons* initially, and I am frankly not an aficionado of *The Simpsons*. I know Rupert Murdoch, and Rupert's a pretty good guy, and it may be that he has allowed some of these good things to come through in this cartoon. I am delighted if I could see any type of family values being shown in that show."

In fact, the opposite appears to be the case. Murdoch, an outspoken conservative and owner of Fox who bankrolls the *Weekly Standard* magazine and the Fox News Network, has taken a hands-off position with the show, which takes frequent potshots at him and his network. Characters on *The Simpsons* repeatedly call Fox's programming cheesy, while at the same time taking credit—accurately—for playing a critical role in its financial survival in the early years of the upstart network's existence. The autocratic media mogul has also endured personal criticism from *The Simpsons* on numerous occasions, and Murdoch's good grace has even included voicing dialogue for the unsympathetic caricature of himself on one episode. This self-parody is probably an example of what the Marxist philosopher Herbert Marcuse called "repressive tolerance." Since Fox and its parent company have fattened on worldwide syndication deals for *The Simpsons* and license fees on more than a billion dollars worth of series-related merchandise, it is literally a case of Murdoch laughing all the way to the bank. "As a commercial program," writes Jim Trammell of the University of Georgia, *The Simpsons* simply "follows an entertainment and capitalistic ideology."

There may be another incidental, economic reason for the show's conservative bent and the relatively prominent role played by religion in it: production costs. Harry Shearer, the gifted writer and actor who provides the voice of Ned Flanders, Reverend Lovejoy, and many other characters, offered this explanation. He told me that, in his opinion, "the richness of the religious universe of the show is, I think, a largely accidental byproduct of the fact that, because it's an animated show, the creators decided to fill

it with—for television—an unusual number of secondary characters. It's these characters—Ned, Lovejoy, Krusty—who would be
economically impossible in a live-action show, whose stories led
the writers into normally uncharted territory for sitcoms. So, yes,
I'm saying follow the money."

There are other ways to follow the money. In his preface to *A
Contribution to the Critique of Hegel's Philosophy of Right,* Karl Marx
wrote, "Religion is the sigh of the oppressed creature, the heart of
a heartless world, and the soul of soulless conditions. It is the
opium of the people." Most social scientists agree that if Marx
were writing today he would substitute the word "television" for
the word "religion." An article by Associated Press writer Todd
Lewan, "How the Talking Box Changed a Village," in the March
2001 issue of *Catholic Digest* examined the impact of television on
one of America's most remote communities. The Alaskan village
was home to ninety-six members of the Gwich'in people in 1980,
when television was introduced there. Until then, the native peoples lived as their ancestors had, their lives circumscribed by the
hunt for caribou and telling stories about their culture. Two
decades later, Lewan reported, every cabin had at least one television, consumerism had invaded the village, and storytelling was
nearly extinct: "Old legends told around campfires could not hold
[the children] when Bart Simpson was talking."

Television, what Homer calls his "teacher, mother, secret
lover," has transformed Homer's own family into a consumer unit.
"They're creatures of consumption and envy, laziness and opportunity, stubbornness and redemption," Matt Groening said in a
1998 talk at the Museum of Television and Radio University Satellite Seminar Series. "They're just like the rest of us. Only exaggerated." His television family is "utterly addicted to TV," and the
series is "about watching TV," he told the students. Or, as the
authors of *Watching What We Watch: Prime-Time Television through
the Lens of Faith* put it: "The message is that the great American
viewing public is now watching a show about *themselves,* in front
of their own television hearth."[5]

As Clay Steinman, professor of communication studies at
Macalester College, noted, most people watch television commercials along with any programs, though this can be defeated by

zapping or muting or buying or renting DVDs. Thus, the mean-
ings of the programs are intertwined with those of the commercials embedded within them. Indeed, this is what advertisers hope:
that the products advertised will gain value by their association
with elements of their adjoining programs. "Advertisers are aware
that men aged 18–49 make up 40 percent of the audience of *The
Simpsons*," writes William D. Romanowski, in *Eyes Wide Open:
Looking for GOD in Popular Culture*.

In *Consuming Environments: Television and Commercial Culture*,
Steinman and his coauthors, Mike Budd and Steve Craig, argue that
a telling way to analyze shows like *The Simpsons* is to look at the
advertisers and their target audiences. Using this criterion, could
any program that counted among its regular advertisers in the
2000–2001 season the U.S. Army, the Air Force, and Old Navy
clothing be considered subversive of traditional religious values?
"Except for certain shows intended for specific, smaller audiences,
'Don't offend' remains the slogan of the age as far as desired viewers are concerned," Steinman and his coauthors wrote. "That means
don't challenge any desirable sector of the audience, don't question
conventional wisdom, don't risk driving anyone you want away."[6]

In a backhanded way, Andrea Alstrup, corporate vice president
for advertising for Johnson & Johnson, which spends $600 mil-
lion a year in television commercials, confirmed Steinman's analysis in a June 1998 speech to three hundred advertising executives
at a luncheon meeting of the Advertising Women of New York.
"Do we really need to continue to support with our advertising a
constant barrage of media that appeals to the lowest common
denominator of values?" Alstrup asked, according to the March
2001 issue of *Brill's Content*.

Of course, strictly speaking, every episode of *The Simpsons* can be
seen as a twenty-two-minute commercial for the show's vast and
durable array of licensed merchandise. And the broadcasters don't
care how critical viewers are, as long as they continue to watch and
see the ads. Clearly, members of the Simpson family spend many
more hours worshiping together before the altar of their screen than
they do in the pews of their church. In that, they are like most people in the United States, and increasing numbers throughout the

world. "To the extent that people take *The Simpsons* as being about real people or being magical or godly," Steinman told me, "they are engaging in contemporary forms of idol—or idle—worship."

Politically, in *The Simpsons'* portrayal of nuclear plant owner Montgomery Burns and others of great wealth and power, "it would appear that the ultimate antagonist is really the competitive, materialistic nature of American capitalism," according to *Watching What We Watch*. Lenny and Carl, two stalwarts of the working class at the Springfield Nuclear Power Plant, have long been rumored to have been named for Lenin and Marx. The show articulates "a vision critical of the unjust distribution of power in America. . . . *The Simpsons* can continue to skewer the evils of society while not seeming too dangerous."[7] The key word here, I think, is "appear." *The Simpsons* only *seems* to question conventional wisdom and values. For me, the consistent message of *The Simpsons* is this: if you are part of the American working class, your family—and to a lesser extent your faith—are the only reliable defenses against the vagaries of modern life. (For some, "modern life" may mean carpooling, office politics, making ends meet, or anxieties about raising kids in a risky world; for others, it is a convenient euphemism for globalized capitalism.) Or, as the authors of *Watching What We Watch* put it, "The only thing that really matters in life is having a supportive family." As always, Homer says it best: "I guess I'll have to give up my hopes and dreams, and settle for being a decent husband and father."

In this context, religion serves as a palliative, comforting characters in their social futility. "*The Simpsons* represents both a model of and a model for contemporary American society, not only because it reveals contemporary attitudes about religious institutions, morality and spirituality, but also because it functions in the time-honored way of religious satirists," observed the authors of *God in the Details*.[8] "Traditionally, religions have employed humor and satire to bring people together and dissolve their differences," Joseph Bastien wrote in the *Encyclopedia of Religion*.[9]

The Simpsons' gospel is not the fighting faith of the Old Testament prophets or of the confrontational Jesus, both of which sought to rock the boat of unrighteous comfort. At the same time, *The Simpsons'* theology is not one that takes joy in acceptance. Marge,

Ned, Lovejoy, and other believers in the series are not like those collaborationist ministers of the early twentieth century who were accused by radicals of preaching "pie in the sky, bye and bye." Their faith is a bulwark, a highly meaningful and relevant refuge. And, as it is for many of us, faith is a last resort against the pressures of the ever faster pace and power of the global market, personal and natural disasters, or whatever significant stresses one might face.

"The question arises as to whether the satirical tenor of the show actually causes viewers to look critically at their culture and their own lives," according to *Watching What We Watch*. "Are audience members likely to agree with the overall message of the series about the importance of having a supportive—if 'dysfunctional'—family to shield individuals from the oppressive forces of society? If so, are we likely to react by trying to change alienating social institutions along more humane and egalitarian lines?"

John Heeren puts the question another way in *The Simpsons and Philosophy: The D'Oh! of Homer.* "Does *The Simpsons* use its humor to promote a moral agenda?" His conclusion is also different: "*The Simpsons* does not promote anything, because its humor works by putting forward positions in order to undercut them. Furthermore, this process of undercutting runs so deeply that we cannot regard the show as merely cynical; it manages to undercut its cynicism too."[10] Steve Tompkins, the former *Simpsons* writer, made that same point to me, explaining the tortuous and sometimes frustrating process by which positive messages regarding religion ultimately make it into the show.

Given the world we live in, and the economic system we live under, *The Simpsons* is about as trenchant, as life-affirming, as socially critical a prime-time situation comedy as we can reasonably expect on a major, commercial television network. So, what impact does television, in particular a show like *The Simpsons*, have on tens of millions of viewers? That question remains open. The Rev. Donald Wildmon, head of the ultra-conservative American Family Association, based in Tupelo, Miss., believes it is considerable. "You may think that Billy Graham is the leading evangelist in America, but he's not. The leading evangelists in America are those people who make the TV programs." Graham himself has written that "television is the most powerful communication ever devised by man." But communications scholar Quentin Schultze of Calvin College disagrees. "Research clearly documents the ineffectiveness of electronic media as agents of religious conversion, yet the popular mythology holds that spiritual battles can be won electronically."

Does the favorable portrayal of God, faith, and, to some extent, religion in *The Simpsons* have any lasting effect? What is the message the show's writers and producers—non-Christians and nonbelievers, in the main—want to convey? There is a clear contrast between *The Simpsons'* writers and producers and one of the best-known and intentional purveyors of moral values and religious faith in popular culture. The late Charles Schulz used his *Peanuts* characters to communicate his gentle, New Testament faith, along with a darker undercurrent of life's unfairness, from the Old Testament's book of Job. I asked Robert Short—author of the best-selling *The Gospel according to Peanuts* and a pioneer in the study of religion and popular culture—what he thought. In the lectures he gives around the country, often to church groups, he said, "*The Simpsons* always comes up. People seem very impressed with it, with what they find in *The Simpsons*. They look at it as the same kind of thing as *Peanuts*, in another medium. They know *The Simpsons*, and they are convinced it is on their side." The people he meets, Short said, believe that the show's writers are more fond of Christian faith and Christianity than they are critical. They feel that the writers seem to be saying that they have no quarrel with the basics of religion, that they "support it in a very subtle way and Christian viewers are appreciative of that, but not surprised." They sense "a genuine admiration and respect."

And what about viewers who don't come to Short's church lectures, namely, the legion of the unchurched? If, as some researchers and many observers have suggested, television can inure impressionable minds to violence through repetition, might not the same hold true for repeated and positive portrayals of faith in *The Simpsons*? Granted, it is just one show, but it is one with millions of devoted adolescent and teen fans who watch the episodes over and over. In this way, Short believes *The Simpsons* can have an impact in the postmodern world.

"It's amazing how God can speak in these out-of-the-way places," Short said. "He can be very deliberate in using a medium like *The Simpsons*. It's the shock of the surprise: The arts get under our skin far more effectively than direct discourse, far more effectively than a sermon. People don't even realize what has been said to them. They like what they hear and see. It makes a deep impression on them. It's a form of indirect communication. Even someone who is a hard case, an agnostic, is probably going to be impressed with the way Christianity is portrayed. It can be cool to find great values there."

The movie industry—television's older sibling—has always been fascinated by its younger rival for a mass audience and by TV's impact on society. One such examination, *The Truman Show*, posits a ratings hit "reality" series about a totally artificial environment in which everyone except the program's title character, played by Jim Carrey, is in on the conceit. The show's advertisements promise "No Scripts . . . No Cue Cards . . . It's Genuine . . . It's a life." At the film's conclusion, the unsuspecting Truman finally punctures his television-created environment. Just as Truman is poised to escape, the show's developer and director introduces himself: "I am the Creator," he explains, "of a television show that gives hope and joy and inspiration to millions."

Matt Groening probably wouldn't put it exactly that way. In its animated, absurdist form, *The Simpsons* is about as removed from "reality" television as one could imagine. "We try to put real human emotion into it," he told one interviewer. "Most other cartoons, except the Disney films, don't seem to do that. They are just about surface emotion. The [*Simpsons*] has a rubber-band reality. We stretch it way out into the far reaches of human folly, and it snaps back to relative sanity." So, in essence, while not at all dangerous or threatening to the status quo, it is a sweet, funny show about a family as "real" as the faith lives of many Americans. It is a show that does in fact give hope and joy and, yes, inspiration to millions. But mostly, as my wife reminds me, it's funny. And as Homer says, "it's funny 'cause it's true."

Afterword

Unintended Consequences: Through an Open Door

Futurama, King of the Hill, Family Guy,
American Dad, and, Yes, South Park

One of *The Simpsons'* great contributions to popular culture, albeit both unintended and unanticipated, has been to make it safe for other animated shows to deal with religion in a comic way. Shows such as *Futurama, Family Guy, King of the Hill, South Park,* and *American Dad* have all taken advantage of what *The Simpsons* has made acceptable. Most if not all of these other shows have taken a more harsh, less subtle, and largely unsympathetic approach to faith and organized religion, although there have been exceptions. But some treatments have been exceptionally insightful. One Christmas in the 1990s, for example, Robert Smigel did a short animated film for NBC's *Saturday Night Live* that featured a wordless but obviously disapproving Jesus turning televangelist Robert Schuller into a ballerina during a money-raising pitch, and transforming Pat Robertson into a rat midway through an antigay diatribe. On the positive side, the Evangelical Lutheran Church in America is attempting to revive *Davey and Goliath*, its 1960s, stop-action animation series with a message, from the creators of Gumby, through a documentary, a new Christmas special, and a witty Mountain Dew commercial. The *Davey and Goliath* revival, in turn, has sparked a dead-on parody version, *Moral Orel*, on Cartoon Network's late night Adult Swim. In one 2007 episode of the determinedly anti-Christian show, a Jewish surgeon, Dr. Chosenberg, is accidentally injured when Moral Orel's ceramic bobblehead Jesus hits him in the chest. Orel gets him to the hospital but refuses to allow him treatment, saying the holy laceration should be left untreated as an object of miraculous veneration. Some shows on the cable network are truly bizarre. The title character of *Assy McGee* sings "Ave Maria" out of his naked rear at a karaoke bar. In *The Squidbillies*, a family says grace, asking for a winning lottery number, but a squid Jesus rejects the prayer, suggesting they try Satan.

Inevitably, there is a downside to this increased portrayal of religion, and some blows are exceedingly low. Religion occasionally provides a tempting and convenient opportunity for creative lassitude—in the form of obvious cheap shots. Characters on Comedy Central's *Freak Show* display religious lapel pins or shout unforgiving Bible verses like Leviticus 20:13 (homosexuality) and Romans 1:32 (various evildoers); one character asks a jingoistic country singer named Toby Tritt Greenwood to sing his hit, "If Jesus Was a Gun." In *Freak Show's* very strange two-part season finale in 2006, Judaism—taken over by a corporate conglomerate—conjures up a giant messiah made of countless foreskins, who does battle with an equally large Jesus, who is actually a robot operated by televangelist Pat Robertson.

Another show that comes to mind is *Empire Square*, a pixilated British import, nominated for England's equivalent of the Oscar, which began airing on Fuse, the American music video channel, in March 2006. The show had its genesis in a series of animated shorts created by the drummer from the group Blur, Dave Rowntree, and a partner. In the premiere, a burn scar in the form of the Virgin Mary on the series' lead character is used in a money-making scam and later becomes the object of an erotic fantasy. In another episode, Jesus is referred to as "the gayest superhero ever." The reaction to this on the part of the usual suspects was predictable. "People tend to fall back on these things when they can't think of anything else. They think, 'How can I create attention? Oh, I know, let's make fun of Jesus,'" Kiera McCaffrey, communications director for the Catholic League for Religious and Civil Rights, told Catherine Holahan, of the *Record* of Hackensack, New Jersey, on April 27, 2006. "I think it's a cheap trick," she concluded.

In *Drawn Together,* another show from Comedy Central that recently devoted two episodes to a satire of the rapture and the *Left Behind* novels, a racist, religious character named Princess Clara mistakes another character for a Jew. "You are getting baptized right now," she says, pushing him into a backyard swimming pool. He struggles in the water and cries out for help. "You're a Christian now," Princess says "Jesus will be your life preserver." The scene cuts to a buff, sharply drawn Jesus sitting on the lifeguard stand. But he is not sympathetic. "That Hebe is pretending to drown," Jesus says. "Those Jews kill me." Both of the show's creators, incidentally, are Jewish. The show takes a typically nasty shot at the successful, Christian-oriented *VeggieTales* series, having the beloved Larry the Cucumber character go berserk, mowing down most of Comedy Central's main characters in a murderous rampage, shooting some in the head.

In the rest of this chapter we'll look at how five popular adult cartoon television shows have walked through the door opened by *The Simpsons.*

1. Futurama. Despite its creative DNA, there is relatively little religion in Matt Groening's *Futurama, The Simpsons'* most direct descendant. Set in the year 3000, it features a layabout young New Yorker named Fry who awakes after a thousand-year, cryogenic sleep and who goes to work with a space delivery system—a shoestring, galactic UPS. In the four seasons that original episodes appeared on Fox (later rerun on Cartoon Network, with new episodes commissioned in 2006), *Futurama* had only a few episodes focusing on religion, about one each season, with occasional lines and jokes tossed in. For example, wandering around a hotel lobby in search of food during his company's corporate meeting, Fry walks into a "Bot Mitzvah." The robot rabbi explains to him that Jews believe Jesus was a real and good robot, but not the Messiah.

Two episodes involve Bender, the loveable reprobate robot, who is Fry's best friend and coworker. In "Hell Is Other Robots," Bender becomes addicted to jolts of electricity after a concert by the Beastie Boys, who performed as cryogenically preserved heads.

(The episode's title is an allusion to Jean-Paul Sartre's play *No Exit*, in which one of the French existentialist's actors says, "Hell is other people.") Bender's addiction lands him in a skid row gutter, where he is accosted by Preacherbot, who speaks in the cadence and dialect of an inner-city, African American pastor. "Wretched sinner unit," the mechanized minister exhorts him, "the path to robot heaven lies here in the Good Book 3.0." But Bender is not receptive until days later, when his addiction brings him back to the neighborhood, to the roof of the Temple of Robotology, where he is siphoning more electricity from the congregation's fluorescent sign.

He stares down into the sanctuary, where Preacherbot—with purple vestments painted on—is in full voice: "I see a lot of fancy robots here today, made of real shiny metal. But that don't impress the robot devil, no sir!" A deacon standing nearby, in what is called the "Amen corner" in black congregations, supports the squat robot as he preaches. " 'Cause if you're a sinner, he's going to plug his infernal modem in the wall, belching smoke and flame, and he's going to download you straight to robot hell! So I ask you, who will stand up and be saved?" At this point, Bender falls through the skylight, landing on the floor in front of the pulpit. Taking the accident as divine intervention, Bender tells Preacherbot he wants to be saved.

The next morning, his life transformed by faith, Bender returns to work at the space delivery service singing and wearing a white bow tie. He has to convince the show's other main characters that his mood is not the result of being high again on excess electricity but rather that he is "whacked out on life." "My friend," he continues, "I've found religion!" What follows is typical of how the newly saved and freshly converted may first be perceived by their relatives, friends, and coworkers. Even Fry is at first wary. "Is this another scam to get free yarmulkes?" he wonders. But Leela, the voluptuous, one-eyed alien captain, wants to give their mechanical friend the benefit of the doubt. "If this helps Bender clean up his act, I think we should be supportive." In real life, those close to people who have found faith are often willing to trade off their skepticism of even outlandish theology if it appears to be an effective vehicle for personal transformation.

Also typical is Bender's response to his friends' support, which he takes as evidence that they, too, are potential converts. "Then you'll all come to my exceedingly long, unair-conditioned baptism ceremony?" At the service, the double-edged portrayal of religion—at least organized religion—continues. Beneath a sign that reads, "To sin is to go to hell," Preacherbot addresses the congregation: "We are gathered here today to deliver Brother Bender from the cold, steel grip of the robot devil to the cold, steel grip of our congregation." Worshipers jump up in the pews to shout, "Tell it, preacher!" The minister then addresses the robot: "Brother Bender, do you accept the principles of Robotology? On pain of eternal damnation in robot hell?" When Bender agrees, he is dipped in a drum of holy, highly viscous oil, and Preacherbot welds a sign of his new faith to the convert's chest.

At a dinner celebration with his friends after the ceremony, the freshly anointed Robotologist begins to demonstrate some of the less pleasant characteristics of the newly pious. First, he takes Leela's hand and assures her, "The old Bender's gone. He won't trouble you again." Then, without consulting his friends, he shreds the wine list, telling the waiter, "No poison for us." As those around the table begin to eat, the robot stops them, in order to say grace, which can be a touchy moment when people of different faiths—and different degrees of faith—eat together in public. Bender begins the grace, "In the name of all that is good and logical, we give thanks for the chemical energy we are about to absorb," and drones on with hours of scripture quotations. Bender makes the group even more uncomfortable when he suggests hugs to "tear down some emotional walls."

At work, Bender's pushy faith continues to grate on his friends, as he tries to impose his beliefs on them. For example, he affixes a fish sign, enclosing the word "Robot," to the rear of their ship. When Leela, the vessel's captain, asks what he is doing, Bender replies, "I'm sanctifying it. That ought to convert a few tailgaters." The robot's coworkers have had just about enough. "Bender's stupid religion is driving me nuts," Fry says, to which Leela adds, "Amen!" The Professor, Fry's descendant and the owner of the shipping company, laments, "If only he joined a mainstream religion—like Oprah-ism, or voodoo." So, as sometimes happens in real life, Bender's friends conspire to draw him back to his old life, because his new one is making everyone around him miserable. Initially Bender resists, pleading, "Stop tempting me. For once in my life I have inner peace." Fry is having none of it: "That's for losers. Come on, sin your heart out."

Bender quickly reverts to his true nature, succumbing to drinking, smoking, gambling, and cavorting with naughty female robot dancers. Later that night, his hot tub reverie with three fembots is interrupted by a summons from a glowing red trident that draws him to robot hell, where he is greeted by the robot devil, Beelzebot. Carried in a coal car down a long mine shaft, Bender tries to plead his case, without success. "You agreed to this when you joined our religion," the devil replies, in logic any Southern Baptist would recognize. "You sin, you go to robot hell—for all eternity." Punishments in the mechanical underworld echo the levels and rationale of Dante's Inferno. They know of Bender's sins, the devil tells him, and "we have prepared agonizing and ironic punishment" for each one of them.

Leela and Fry come to their friend's rescue, discovering an entrance to hell at an abandoned New Jersey theme park, through a defunct ride called "The Inferno." As Bender is tormented with irritating, up-tempo singing, his friends try to invoke the "Fairness in Hell Act," apparently drawn up by country recording artist Charlie Daniels in his hit "The Devil Went Down to Georgia," in which anyone who can outplay the devil on a gold fiddle can escape hell. Instead, Leela simply bops the devil with the instrument and the three escape, borne by Bender on improvised wings. The lesson, he concludes, is that "I'll never be too good or too evil. From now on, I'll just be me." Of course, that would seem to contradict the book of Revelation's admonition not to be lukewarm in faith. According to at least one fan Web site, Groening and series codeveloper David X. Cohen consider "Hell Is Other Robots" to be among *Futurama's* four best episodes. Its opening credits contain the disclaimer "Condemned by the space pope."

The robot devil returned to *Futurama* later in the run, in a gloss on the opera *Faust*. Fry, his love for Leela unrequited, tries to learn the futuristic instrument called a holophoner to woo her. But his efforts are fruitless until he goes back to robot hell, where he trades his hands for the devil's. With them, he is not only able to play the honophoner but also to compose an opera based on Leela's life. The devil wants his hands back, and the whole affair dissolves into chaos, although Leela assures Fry that "the beauty was in your heart, not your hands." In an April 26, 2006, interview with Nathan Rabin for the *Onion* online magazine's A.V. Club, Matt Groening was asked about religion on *Futurama*. "Robot Devil has appeared a number of times," Rabin observed. "Is there a Robot God to go along with him?" Groening replied, "That's one of the things we're probably going to explore in one of the *Futurama* movies," one of four planned direct-to-DVD features. "In one of our best episodes, we had a conversation between Bender and what apparently was God, and I think we're going to explore what was really going on in that conversation." The episode Groening was referring to was "Godfellas," which aired in the show's third season and won a Writer's Guild award.

As "Godfellas" opens, Bender, asleep in the torpedo tube of his intergalactic delivery ship, is mistakenly launched into space when he and his coworkers come under attack by pirates. The robot ends up adrift, hopelessly out of reach of his friends, when two tiny communities, each living on an asteroid, smash into his chest and his butt. Because of his size, both mistake him for God. The group on his front side does everything it can to please him, including brewing a beer they call "Lordweiser." Yet everything Bender does to help those who worship him ends in disaster, climaxing in a nuclear exchange between the two colonies, wiping out every one. "Who would have known playing God can have such terrible consequences?" he asks. The answer—of a sort—comes when the robot encounters a swirling cosmic presence, with blinking multicolored lights. A deep voice from the mass speaks to Bender, who asks if it is a computer. "I *am* user-friendly," comes the reply. The robot, being a robot, asks the disembodied voice who built it. "I have always been," the voice says, cryptically. Asked if it is God, the voice answers, "Possible. I do feel compassion for all living things." Still, Bender wonders if he is speaking with the remains of a space probe that collided with God. "That seems probable," the voice acknowledges.

At this point, the dialogue between the robot and the voice takes a much deeper and more theological turn, first on the matter of predestination. It is one of those moments (more frequent in *The Simpsons*) when the viewer needs to be reminded that this is a cartoon and not a divinity school class. Bender asks if the voice knows what the robot is going to do before he does it. When the voice says yes, Bender asks, "What if I do something different?" In that case, the voice replies blandly, "Then I don't know that." The robot begins a different, equally fundamental line of inquiry: prayer. "I bet a lot of people pray to you," he says. Wearily, the voice replies that they do, "but there are so many, asking so much, after a while you just sort of tune it out." Bender commiserates on that point, recalling the demise of the tiny colonies and prompting the voice to reassure him, "You were doing well until everyone died."

For Bender, playing God was a disaster. "It was awful. I tried helping them. But in the end, I couldn't do them any good. Do you think what I did was wrong?" Here the dialogue takes yet another profound turn, toward the nature of salvation: through grace, good works, or some combination? The voice goes for works. "'Right' and 'wrong' are just words," it says. "What matters is what you do." Bender isn't satisfied. As in a number of human-divine colloquies in the Bible, he wants more from the voice. "Being God isn't easy," the voice explains. "If you do too much, people get dependent on you. And if you do nothing, they lose hope. You have to use a light touch, like a safecracker or a pickpocket." So, back to humor.

The show's writers understand that there is only so much time in a cartoon comedy for profound musings. So Bender picks up on the metaphor. "Or a guy who burns down a bar for the insurance money." Yes, the voice says, "if you make it look like an electrical thing. When you do things right, people won't be sure you've done anything at all." Thinking he is out of earshot, Bender says that if he prayed to the voice, he would ask to be sent back to earth and to his friends.

On earth, the robot's friends are enlisting religion to help locate Bender. Fry consults the spiritual leader of the First Amalgamated Church, apparently a consolidation of all of the world's faiths in the third millennium. Fry asks, "Is there anything religion can do to help me find my friend?" Well, the pastor says, "we could join together in prayer." Right, Fry says, "but is there anything *useful* we can do?" No, the pastor replies. So Fry and Leela trek to the Monastery of Teshuvah (which, no one explains, is Hebrew for "repentance") in the high Himalayas, where apparently Buddhist monks are searching for God using a giant radio telescope. When the monks refuse to shift their cosmic search to locate Bender, Fry and Leela lock them up in a laundry room and send their message to Bender themselves. By coincidence, it is the voice in space that hears the message and flings the sleeping Bender earthward. He lands, still glowing from his reentry, in the snow near where his dejected friends are trudging down the mountain. They're overjoyed, but they show no inclination to climb back to the monastery to unlock the forgotten monks. Fry says, "I'm sure their God will let them out." But Bender, for all his venality, has not forgotten his conversation with the voice. "You can't count on God for jack," he says. "He pretty much told me that himself. If we don't save those monks, no one will." Looking down from the cosmos, the voice chuckles, and repeats, "When you do things right, people won't be sure you've done anything at all."

2. King of the Hill. I am not a big fan of Fox's *King of the Hill*, but that may be because it is so brilliant at what it does: conveying the sad and depressing reality for many who live in the Sunbelt suburbs. Cocreator Mike Judge, a native of Garland, Texas, was also responsible for the much less sophisticated 1990s MTV staple *Beavis and Butt-head*. In *King of the Hill* we meet the Hill family, occupants of a tract house in Arlen, Texas: Hank and Peggy, their adolescent son Bobby, and their troubled and sometimes wayward niece Luanne, whose mother is in prison. Hank, who wears thick, square, black glasses, works for a propane supplier; Peggy is a substitute Spanish teacher. Like the Simpsons— and much of middle-class America—the Hills struggle with mixed success just to keep even. Emotionally repressed, their faces are usually pinched and pained, their lips often pursed. Much of Hank's spare time is taken with drinking beer in the alley with three of his neighborhood buddies, who are lovable losers in one way or another. Infidelity, divorce, and thwarted dreams are distressingly common in their circle.

The Simpsons portrays Southerners through the stereotypical character Cletus Delray, the slack-jawed yokel, and his slatternly, inbred clan, in much the same way as other cartoon comedies written from a New York or Los Angeles perspective. By contrast, *King of the Hill* does not indulge in such gratuitous cracker-bashing; it is sympathetic and knowing of its culture. The humor is "insider," much like Comedy Central's *Blue Collar Comedy*, or Brad Stine's sly, evangelical rants. "If Hank Hill votes Republican," Matt Bai wrote in the June 26, 2005, *New York Times Magazine*, "it's because, as a voter who cares about religious and rural values, he probably doesn't see much choice. But Hank and his neighbors resemble many independent voters, open to proposals that challenge their assumptions about the world, as long as those ideas don't come from someone who seems to disrespect what they believe." One fan is North Carolina's Democratic governor Mike Easley, according to Bai, who said *King of the Hill* was only the second television comedy "that doesn't make fun of the South," after the *Andy Griffith Show*.

The Hills attend Arlen First Methodist Church, a small congregation with one service on Sundays. Hank's main concerns regarding worship are not arriving so late that he has to park in the unpaved lot, and getting out in time to watch sports events on television. There are references to religion in *King of the Hill*, mostly reflecting the characters' imperfect understanding of Christianity, but not nearly as many episodes built around it as in *The Simpsons*. For instance, on the road (back) to respectability, Luanne joins a Bible study and a "second virginity" program.

Son Bobby, in one episode, is so impressed by a magician that he decides to do his Sunday school report on Jesus, to his teacher's pleasure. With all the parents on hand, Bobby comes out in a cape, for a performance—complete with biblical citations—that innocently confuses magic with miracles. "Good morning, ladies and gentlemen. I am the Amazing Jesus, son of God and master of prestidigitation! Has this ever happened to you? Your followers want a glass of wine, but all you have is water. Well, if you're the Amazing Jesus, no problem! Water into wine! It's a miracle! John 2:11. Thank you. Now you're going to need something to go with all this wine—maybe some bread. But how are you going to feed all these hungry people with just one slice? No problem, if you're the Amazing Jesus! Amen! It's a miracle, ladies and gentlemen! Mark 6:44. Thank you! Now for my next miracle, I'll need a large wooden cross and a couple of volunteers." At this point, the presentation ends before blasphemy can be uttered, as Hank and Peggy scream, "No!" Hank is more agreeable when Luanne asks him to play God in her Christian puppet show, "Manger Babies."

Like the Sunbelt as a whole, the Hills' neighborhood and its ethnic and religious landscape is changing. One neighbor family, the Khans, are immigrants from Laos and nominal Buddhists. They are quick to assimilate many aspects of American culture, including prejudice: the father refers to Hank and his friends as hillbillies. In one episode, monks move into the Khans' house and believe Bobby Hill is the reincarnation of a lama. The boy becomes interested in the discipline and begins to meditate, to his father's chagrin. "You can call putting paint on your head anything you want," Hank tells him, "but we're Christians and we don't do that kind of stuff. Why do you think we go to church every Sunday—for fun?" Hank's knowledge of Judaism is also slight. "Suffering is a part of every religion," he observes. "The Jews have suffered for thousands of years and I don't hear them complaining about it."

Those episodes that do center on religion are typically astute, touching familiar bases for evangelicals and people of other faiths, although there is little or no evidence of the supernatural (except in dreams). Take the issue of women in the pulpit. Female senior pastors can be a very tough sell in the Sunbelt suburbs, even in a mainline denomination like the United Methodist Church. The congregation at Arlen First Methodist, a small, white, wooden church with lots of stained glass windows, is shocked one Sunday morning when Reverend Thomasson announces at the end of a typically short, anecdotal sermon (about being stopped by a state trooper) that he is retiring from the pulpit. Peggy wonders why he would want to retire, since he only works half a day a week. Hank likes the short sermons, which get members home in time to watch major sporting events, like NASCAR races. But Thomasson is not leaving because he has run out of faith or evangelical fervor. He tells them that, after much reflection and soul searching, "I've decided that the future of God is on the Internet." He plans to use his new Web site, CyberRev.com, "to spread the gospel to every online soul in the world."

Before the people in the pews can regain their composure, the minister invites everyone to a church basement potluck the following Saturday night, which he will host, to welcome the new pastor. Hank leans over to Peggy and confides that "the new guy better like sports," just as Thomasson announces the name of the new minister—the Reverend Karen Stroup. "A woman?" Hank blurts. Later, in the alley with his buddies, who are also members of the church, the men can talk about nothing but the new pastor. Hank's friend Dale suggests that the congregation is "the latest victim of the secret lab in the basement of the Harvard Divinity School, where they ordain women surgically." Hank's concern is whether he will get home in time to watch the Pebble Beach Pro-Am Golf Tournament the next Sunday. "If this gal's sermon runs late, . . ." he worries. "You know how women like to talk."

In the church basement that Saturday evening, Peggy does her best to make the young, single pastor welcome, and urges her son Bobby to do the same. With Hank standing nearby, his wife says (no doubt thinking of herself as well), "Some people cannot accept women in positions of real authority." Peggy, like several other members, has brought Frito pie to the potluck. Stroup (voiced by Mary Tyler Moore) has prepared her own specialty, lutefisk, the odoriferous Scandinavian fish dish made famous by public radio's Garrison Keillor, host of *A Prairie Home Companion* and, like the pastor, a Minnesotan. Stroup does her best to put Hank's mind at ease about sports—especially the next day's golf tournament—and confides that she is a big fan of football: "Between God and the Vikings, Sunday's not my day of rest." Hank replies, "You might be all right." With the ice broken, Stroup confides to the Hills that she was worried when she learned she was being assigned to Texas. "A lot of female ministers don't last too long down here," she says. Oblivious to what she is saying, Hank responds, "Yeah. It gets pretty hot in the summer." Peggy and Stroup just look at the clueless man.

While this discussion has been going on, Bobby has taken the dish with the lutefisk under one of the tables and, concealed by the edges of a tablecloth, has consumed the whole thing. Guilt-stricken, he drops the fish-shaped dish into the trash can. Stroup is anxious for Hank to try her delicacy and is crushed to find it has disappeared. When the dish is found, she assumes someone who opposes her appointment has trashed it. She is still angry the next morning when she takes the pulpit. Using a tentatively concilia-tory "y'all," she tells the congregation she is certain they are good, decent people and that she "won't judge the whole town on the sins of one lost soul"—the person who destroyed her lutefisk. As a gesture of reconciliation, Stroup suggests a Minnesota tradition, that people rise and hug someone near them—another tough sell in some Sunbelt congregations. Hank's loud-mouthed, archcon-servative father, Cotton, chooses this inopportune moment to arrive, already incensed at the idea of a woman pastor. Stroup tries to embrace Cotton, but he angrily rejects her, quoting from Corinthians verses traditionally used against women in Chris-tianity. "Women should remain silent in the churches," he snaps. "They are not allowed to speak, but must be in submission." She tries to protest, but Cotton brushes her aside with the (uninten-tionally ironic) examples of Billy Graham—whose daughter Anne Graham Lotz is a well-known Bible teacher, despite ill treatment at the hands of fellow Southern Baptists—and Jimmy Swaggart, of all people.

In his seat, Bobby has been feeling the burden of unconfessed sin and, more than that, the digestive upheaval of the previous night's gluttony, exacerbated when Stroup cites Mark 6:41, from the story of the feeding of the five thousand. The boy flees to the restroom to purge himself in a stall. Cotton follows but is nearly overcome by the resulting foul odor, which he does not realize has been produced by his own grandson. The older man tries without success to neutralize the smell by burning several matches but gives up in frustration. Bobby panics when someone else tries to enter, and he tosses a burnt match into the trash can as he slips out the window. The match is not out, however, and the fire spreads from the trash can to the church, burning it to the ground. Lingering outside to watch in horror, Hank prays that one of his propane tanks was not the cause of the conflagration. The answer comes when officials tell the congregation they suspect arson. Based on the lutefisk incident and Cotton's outburst, Stroup jumps to the conclusion that the fire was a hate crime. "Someone did this because they don't want a woman minister," she declares. "To him I say, 'You can burn down our church, but you cannot burn down our faith.'" Peggy concludes that the motive was to kill Reverend Stroup, and soon an ecumenical prayer service is convened on the site of the smoldering ruins.

Investigators find a wet matchbook from a Houston strip club, turning suspicion to Cotton, who declared at the end of his confrontation with Stroup in the sanctuary that he was heading for the only room in the building where she wasn't welcome. At first, Cotton denies responsibility, because he is in fact innocent. But later, when Bobby confesses to his parents and grandfather, Cotton takes public responsibility for causing the accident. Stroup forgives him and, as his only penance, orders him to hug everyone in the congregation.

Another example of the show's perfect pitch with its cultural and religious environment is an episode from 2003 called "Reborn to Be Wild," which deals with what some call "Extreme Christianity." As the cliché goes, it could easily have been "ripped from the headlines"—of some of my own *Orlando Sentinel* stories. I have reported on segments of evangelical Christianity that have taken a dramatic turn toward appropriating and adapting youth culture to their own purpose: rock music, skateboards, tattoos, wild hair, piercing, ripped clothes, and a certain way of talking and style of worship. I have written about locally based ministries as well as national figures, like Luis Palau, who have made this approach their trademark. For them, only the content—which is invariably very conservative theology—is what counts, not the packaging.

While traditional (and, yes, older) Christians see this approach as an act of desperation, in the Sunbelt suburbs it has a constituency. The issue for younger, more innovative evangelicals is how to capitalize on and channel youthful rebellion and alienation. Teens and twentysomethings often feel persecuted and yearn for some way to push back, either individually or with peers. Or, in the extreme, they may turn to a gang to provide unconditional acceptance, as a substitute for a family.

In *King of the Hill*, the dilemma is illustrated when Hank finds Bobby in his room, where the boy keeps a Bart Simpson doll on the shelf, playing air guitar to heavy metal music while wearing a fake goatee and a dreadlocks wig. Despairing that Bobby is heading in the wrong direction, he takes the boy to see their pastor. She first suggests an "awesome video" to the boy, who snaps back with an obvious reference to *VeggieTales*, the witty and popular series of Christian-oriented videos for younger children. "If it's the one about Esau the Eggplant and the Prodigal Cucumber," he says, "I've seen it about a thousand times." (*VeggieTales* went into Saturday morning syndication on NBC and Telemundo in the fall of 2006, with much of the religious content edited out.)

The minister instantly recognizes that Bobby is on the other side of adolescence and recommends an after-school youth group at the Arlen Community Center. Naturally the boy resists, as his father drives him up to the center. "I can't believe you're making me do this," Bobby protests. "It is so *uncool!*" Hank replies, "You know what is not cool? Hell!" Dressed in a suit and tie, and carrying his Bible, the youngster glumly approaches the front door, where he is in for a surprise.

After some initial skepticism, he is welcomed by a group of very cool looking teens with skateboards, long hair, piercings, and tattoos. Is this the Christian youth group? he asks. Bobby is welcomed to the flock by the extreme Pastor K, a somewhat older version of the others, and later he tells his father how excited he is about the group. He asks if he can invite the teens back to his house and, when Hank agrees, his son says, "Thanks for making me go, Dad." Hank marvels to his alley friends that his son "just thanked me for making him come to church." Later, a racket in the alley brings Hank running, to what he assumes is a bunch of rowdy youths using his trash can to elevate a makeshift skateboard ramp. Before he can run them off, Bobby introduces them. "These are my friends from the youth group," he proudly tells his father. "They're cool and they're *totally* Christian." One is wearing a tee-shirt that reads, "I broke a rule. I prayed in school."

Hank is conflicted. He is glad that his son likes the group, but he doesn't like their attitude. His wife, Peggy, is less troubled. "I'd rather Bobby be in a Christian gang than in one of those murdering gangs." However, as Bobby throws himself into this flavor of Christianity, his father becomes even more upset. The boy dresses and talks in a way that doesn't seem particularly religious to his father, exemplified with a tee-shirt that reads "Satan sucks." Yet Bobby asks to say grace at dinner. "I wanna give a shout-out to the man who makes it all happen," the boy prays. "Props to you for this most bountiful meal that sits before us. Okay, check it, God, you've got the skillz. You represent in these vegetables and in this napkin and in the dirt that grows the grain that makes the garlic breadsticks that are on this table, yes-shizz." Hank tries to be supportive, but his patience is wearing then. "Okay, Bobby, God appreciates your support, but I'm sure he wouldn't want the pot roast to get cold. Now let's wrap it up." His son agrees: "Sure thing. Thanks, J-Man. Peace."

At an informal prayer meeting at the park, Pastor K outlines his theology after one of the boys reads a New Testament verse. "To be tight with the Lord, you gotta take your faith to the limit," he says. "Test all things to find the good." When Bobby asks him what is good, the minister replies, "Whatever sticks to your spirit, man, whatever God tattoos on your soul. We're all searching for that eternal ink." As weird as he may sound to the uninitiated (and unsaved), Pastor K might easily have been based on a minister like Steve Bensinger, who presides over the Come as You Are Church in Kalamazoo, Michigan. Known as "Pastor Freak," Bensinger also heads the Christian Tattoo Association, and he has his own personal body art that includes Jesus on the cross and an angel killing a demon. Pastor K, who also has plenty of tattoos, also has an airbrushed painting of the resurrection on the back of his SUV.

Soon Bobby is so committed to his variety of faith he is preaching to his cousin Luanne from the "Extreme Team Bible," which he has gotten from the youth group. His version of Genesis goes like this: "And then Cain was all like, 'I ain't s'posed to be lookin' out for my bro, yo.'" Bobby tells his cousin that Pastor K has written a twenty-two-minute rock song based on the disciples for an upcoming gathering called "Messiahfest," and that he has asked the boy to back him up. But he is certain that it will take a miracle for Hank to let him go to the festival. And the father is also furious when his son shows him a sketch with his idea for a tattoo featuring Jesus. "Dad," he explains to the incredulous Hank, "it's just my way of giving mad respect to the Lord." Hank decides to go to the park and confront Pastor K directly, demanding that the young minister stop "this garbage you're teaching my boy" and stay away from his son. The message is not well received. "Dude, you don't have to act or dress a certain way for God," Pastor K says. "You can hang with him any way, anywhere. Don't you think Jesus is here in this half-pipe? . . . What's more important," Pastor K replies, "that Bobby's a Christian—or that he has a proper haircut?"

Things accelerate. In his room, Bobby—now sporting a black-knit, seaman's watch cap with the letters "WWJD"—is playing a biblical video game with his mother, based on the exodus. Hank storms in and, brushing his wife aside, declares that from now on, Bobby is "going to go to church in a suit and tie like we've always done." He can forget about Pastor K. Again, Peggy tries to reason with her husband. "You are overreacting," she argues. "These are good Christian kids having good Christian fun." Then why does the boy look like a burglar, Hank retorts. Then he notices that Bobby has had his ear pierced for a cross earring, which he confiscates. Then he grounds the boy. "You just don't understand how I feel about Jesus!" Bobby shouts. Despite his actions, Hank is still perplexed, as he confesses to his friends while scraping off the "Believer" bumper sticker the boy has put on his father's pickup. In the old days, he recalls, they went to rock concerts on Saturday nights and asked forgiveness at church on Sundays. "Now it's all mixed together."

Although forbidden by Hank to attend Messiahfest, Bobby goes anyway, pursued by his father. The man is more than a little bewildered by the scene he finds: his son onstage, wearing a tank top reading "Rejoice," leading a call-and-response chant with the crowd: "Holy! Ghost! Holy! Ghost!" With this, Hank boils over, voicing his antipathy for the music, which is shared by many in real life. "Can't you see you're not making Christianity better?" he tells Pastor K. "You're just making rock 'n' roll worse." This is too much for the minister. "You people are all alike. You look at us and think we're freaks." It's left to a member of a real contemporary Christian band, Sum 41, voicing the role of Pastor K's father, to caution the minister to remember the Fifth Commandment and never to come between a boy and his dad.

After the concert, Bobby is still resentful. "When I turn 18," he tells Hank, "I'm going to do whatever I want for the Lord: tattoos, piercings, you name it." As gently as he can, the father shows the son a box in his bedroom containing all of his discarded fads and enthusiasms, from beanbag animals to a photo of him in a Ninja Turtle costume. Hank says he just doesn't want Bobby to burn out on his religious enthusiasm. "I know you think stuff you're doing now is cool, but in a few years you're going to think it's lame. And I don't want the Lord to end up in this box."

Pastor Jim Poorman helps run a downtown ministry in Orlando called H2O Church in a converted country-and-western bar and music hall, geared to the "next generation." A handsome, rugged ice hockey fanatic, he acknowledges his age without apology: "I'm 39, which makes my shin pads older than some of the 20-year-olds on my hockey team." More amiable than edgy, Poorman welcomes the tattooed and pierced to his congregation, and he doesn't condemn members for quaffing an occasional beer. I asked him to screen the episode and let me know what he thought. "It was really funny," he said, "and pretty well written too. I thought it was cool that Bobby's dad really just wanted him to have a faith that would last. That last scene with the box was well done. Also, I gotta admit I know a guy that reminds me of Pastor K, and he drives me nuts. I can't have a sentence of communication without him calling me 'dude,' 'bro,' or 'chief' or something—the guy is really annoying. Whenever I try to have a decent conversation with him it's like I'm talking to a fourteen-year-old with all the jargon, and I just laugh to myself. It's really quite funny.

"I thought the show did a good job of showing how some of these kids are really just exchanging one subculture for another. True, maybe it's not as dangerous, but it does miss the point. I have had quite a few conversations with some overzealous college converts on how to communicate with their parents about their faith and how to honor them in light of their newfound excitement. Some have done a great job of telling their parents and living their faith quietly and humbly in front of their folks—not being weird. And in some cases their parents actually have come to faith as a result of their kids' influence—now that's pretty wild. I remember one conversation I had with a parent who said, 'I'm really glad my kid has been hanging out with you. It's funny, though, he tells me the stuff that you share with him and I think, 'Man, I've been telling him that for years, and yet he thinks you're a genius and I'm an idiot.' We laughed about that."

There is a lot of truth in the episode, Poorman said, although some things were exaggerated for the sake of humor. "Young people need to fall in love with God," he said, "not fall in love with a new subculture. Each of these tends to produce two very different things. It's helpful to meet young people where they're at and try to speak their language—even Jesus did that by using fishing analogies with his fisherman disciples to try to help them understand spiritual concepts. But we need to be who we are too. Authenticity is key, and most kids nowadays are sharp enough to pick up on the goofiness of an adult not being who they are. The cover of a recent issue of the magazine *Group*, which deals with the youth ministry industry, was titled 'Busting the "Cool Leader" Myth.' The 'extreme' concept has been so overused that most of us can't take it anymore. What kids need are just authentic, godly examples to follow and interact with—and that's 'extreme' enough." Poorman admits, "Some youth pastors may have gone overboard in trying to speak the language of their kids. A little balance might help, because, in reality, living a faithful life unto Christ in today's culture might not look all that cool or appealing. We need to be careful that it's not about being cool and living this hyperlife but at times it's rather mundane and downright difficult. That, I think, will help kids to not burn out and have a more realistic expectation of what it means to live for Christ. The goal is to approach our relationship with God like a marathon, not a sprint, and hopefully not a one-night stand. I do think it's helpful that kids are aware that you don't have to become a nerd to be a Christ follower. At the same time, they need to see that there's no need for them to be 'cool' either. Both are missing the point of the gospel: it's becoming a new person that desires to honor God—and that may not be all that 'hip' at times."

Congregational membership is one of the few broadly based, purely voluntary associations in America: You don't have to go, and you don't have to stay. It is a tricky, sometimes volatile mixture of autonomy, affinity, and affection. And sometimes there is also antipathy, up to and including seething resentment—over everything from theology to music to finances to governance. In the suburbs at least, smaller, denominational congregations seem to be losing ground to independent megachurches, just as small retail stores have lost market share to big box and warehouse outlets. Critics say the megachurches are winning the battle because they offer low-impact services that emphasize entertainment at the expense of worship, or that they offer a service model, complete with scores of niche ministries. All of these weighty issues figure in the *King of the Hill* episode entitled "Church Hopping," which, along with its corollary, "church shopping," have become common terms for religious mobility among academics and consultants. The people who wrote this show have clearly spent some time in Sunbelt megachurches.

The Hill family is put out when, after arriving late to Sunday services at Arlen First Methodist Church, they find a new family sitting in "their" spot in "their" pew, where they have been worshiping for twelve years. The interloping family, which includes a baby, declines to move, so the Hills move to the back pew, where Hank cannot find a comfortable sitting position and where the sunlight reflects off the altar cross and directly into his eyes. He is

still upset the next day when talking to his buddies about the dis-
placement. "I know God's up there, and he knows I'm smack dab
in the middle of the second pew." Hank is further miffed that the
minister "acted like that new family owned the place." Inside the
house, Hank tells Peggy, "I'm having trouble letting this pew situation go. Maybe I'm being too petty." His wife assures him he
is not; the pew incident is the last straw for her. She has made
numerous suggestions for Reverend Stroup to add some pizzazz
to the staid, mainline services, all of which the female pastor has
rejected. The pastor, Peggy says, has "lost touch with the little
things that matter."

Hank visits the pastor in her study, to plead his case. But Stroup
refuses to intervene, telling Hank she wouldn't do what he is asking, even if she could. "This is God's house, not mine, not yours.
Hank, let it go." In this situation, Stroup is handicapped less by
her harsh Midwestern accent than by her tin ear for Southern sensibilities. Where Peggy wants to go is to a new, five-thousand-
member megachurch nearby, the Church of the Rising Son,
whose charismatic African American pastor is a former college
football quarterback. Members there, she tells Hank, have a whole
array of amenities to pamper them—a coffee shop, mini-mart,
florist, even a dry cleaner. But Hank, who is still not sure he wants
to leave his old church, is put off by the scale of the megachurch,
said to be the ninth largest in Texas. "If I wanted to go that route,
I could just walk around the mall and think about Jesus." Instead,
at work the next day, Hank casually mentions to his friends that
he is thinking about attending a new church. In the Sunbelt,
where the evangelical spirit runs high, this is enough to send his
coworkers into a feeding frenzy: all want him to try *their* church.
So, in the weeks that follow, they do. In a sequence that spans a
good chunk of the Christian spectrum, they attend a shouting,
arm-waving Pentecostal service in a tent, a Spanish-language
Catholic mass, and a contemporary service whose bland music
repels them before they get through the front door.

"I just want a decent, normal church," Hank says at the dinner
table, with his trademark sigh. "Is that too much to ask?" This provides Peggy the opportunity to renew her case for the megachurch,

which she insists is their only choice. When he tries to resist, she invokes what in the Sunbelt is the nuclear option. "Fine," she snaps. "We won't go to any church. You and I and our son will live the empty, barren lives of secular humanism." Hank succumbs, and the next Sunday they are in line at the coffee shop on the campus of the megachurch, where they see Reverend Stroup getting coffee and a cruller—free to local clergy. Despite their best efforts, the Hills cannot avoid meeting the minister, and Hank and Peggy admit that they have been "trying out" other churches. Stroup is incredulous. "Is this over the seats? You've got to be kidding!" But Peggy is not embarrassed. The minister even rejected her suggestions for an "open mic" sermon on Sunday. "You reap what you sow," Peggy huffs. The minister is still shaken. "You can't seriously be thinking of worshiping at this behemoth?" Hank declares that they are leaving Arlen First Methodist and they aren't coming back. Miffed, Stroup informs them that the new family never seems to miss a Sunday, and they actually sing during worship.

But when the intercom announces that the tram from the parking lot to the sanctuary is about to depart, Hank's misgivings surface again. "What have I gotten us into?" he wonders. The mall-like interior of the sanctuary lobby—which is a close approximation of numerous megachurches I have attended—intensifies Hank's doubts. The family is instantly pegged for newcomers by one of the congregation's official greeters. The man almost overwhelms them with enthusiastic hospitality. While simultaneously filling out a customer satisfaction survey—there are only two choices, "satisfied" and "extremely satisfied"—the greeter volunteers (in too much detail) how the church saved him and his wife from a life of depravity. The situation is rescued when the senior pastor, Rev. Nealey (voiced by rapper Big Boi), rolls up in a golf cart and takes over. Hank explains that they are there because of problems over pew seating at their previous church. Nealey says he understands and starts to show them around, beginning with the sanctuary. Bobby spots three huge, high-definition television screens hanging from the ceiling—not uncommon in large Sunbelt congregations. The minister confides to the boy that the screens are used for services, but during the NFL season they are left on for Dallas Cowboy games, instantly winning him over. Encouraged, Hank says he wants to hurry to get a good seat. When the pastor tells him all seats are assigned, the deal is done. "I think we've found a new home," Hank says, as a heavenly chorus is heard in the background. This, of course, is fantasy. Few if any houses of worship assign seats any more, except perhaps some Jewish temples and synagogues at the High Holidays.

A honeymoon period ensues between the Hill family and the Church of the Rising Son. In the alley, Hank tells his buddies, "I admit I was skeptical at first, but that church really understands the concept of customer service." Yet it soon becomes apparent that there is a price to be paid for congregational involvement. A megachurch—despite its large staff—has to depend heavily on volunteers to provide the many services it does. Hank is issued a device used by many suburban restaurants, one that hums and lights up when your table is ready. "It's like being paged by God," one of Hank's alley friends observes. Before long, it seems as if the pager is going off and the phone is ringing nonstop. If it's not a satisfaction survey about last week's sermon, it's an invitation to join one of the activities on the church's apparently 24/7 schedule. Weeknights offer Christian woodworking classes, and afternoons are for men's rope football, where the team kneels in prayer before calling each play. One Saturday, the Hills spend sixteen hours on the campus, capped by a midnight showing of Mel Gibson's *The Passion of the Christ.*

Peggy has volunteered to become Nealey's secretary and immediately takes charge, organizing the office. At first she is such a success, demanding the same price for Communion wafers that the supplier gives to the Baptists, that the pastor dubs her "a gift straight from heaven." However, over time Peggy's overbearing and insensitive enthusiasm begins to drive Pastor Nealey crazy. The last straw is when she takes the microphone with a personal message before his sermon. While Peggy is fulfilled, Hank—like Reverend Nealey—has had enough. The propane salesman misses his home and his friends. So one Sunday, he drops his wife and son off for services, and, on the pretext of needing rest, flees to his house. There he sees Luanne's hyperrelaxed boyfriend,

Lucky, who has declared earlier that he does his praying wherever he is, whatever he is doing. Hank once dismissed this notion as asinine, but now he is not so sure. "I'm fed up with church," he tells Lucky. "My old one didn't pay enough attention to me and my new one won't leave me alone."

The boyfriend makes a point nearly identical to that made in 2006 by the Christian pollster George Barna. "You need to get in touch with God, not church," Lucky advises. "I find that sometimes church just gets in the way." The pair heads to a bar to drink beer and watch football. Hours later, Hank returns home, loaded and unrepentant, declaring he is "done with church. Period." The megachurch "just keeps coming at you." Luanne denounces him as an apostate, someone who has abandoned his faith. Peggy treats him as if he has been possessed, enlisting Reverend Nealey for an "intervention." However, the minister admits that a small church may be where both Hills belong. In the end, he suggests that Hank pray on the matter. That night, tossing and turning, Hank is distraught. Then a solution comes to him and, with a relieved, beatific smile on his face, he says, "Thank you, God."

Back at First Methodist, Stroup has felt the market pressure of the Hills' defection and has responded on several fronts. In a nod to customer service, she has designated the last two pews in the sanctuary as a smoking section. On the church sign, the message reads, "No assigned seats in heaven." Still, she is in a conciliatory mood when Hank comes to visit her in her study before services on Sunday morning. "It seems God thinks I should be here," he tells her. Relieved, she is magnanimous in victory. "God knows best," she says. "That's why he's God, and he would want me to forgive you and welcome you back." But Hank is not finished. Gesturing toward the second pew, where the rest of his family is, he adds, "That's where God wants me to sit." How could that be? she wants to know. Where is that nice young family? Hank replies that after he informed them of the many amenities offered at the megachurch, including daycare and Bible bingo, they decided to go there. "That place is really good for them," Hank tells the pastor, "but we like it here." Back in "his" pew, Hank looks heavenward and declares, "Good to see you again, Lord."

Although neatly resolved, this episode raises a serious point, albeit subtly, about the pressures on mainline Christianity, whose numbers are declining, while the average age of members bumps fifty. It would only be natural for the pastor of a small, Methodist church, seeing a new, young family in the congregation, to be pleased. But the dilemma for such endangered congregations has always been: How do you expand your base to new, younger members (customers?) without at the same time eroding your older, established base, the faithfully attending members who do the bulk of the volunteering and giving? Most often, this issue manifests itself over the issue of worship style or music rather than seating.

Few megachurch pastors have as sure a feel for what worshipers are looking for as Joel C. Hunter, minister of Northland Church in Longwood, Florida, a thriving congregation of eight thousand that met for many years in a converted roller skating rink. An author and a radio broadcaster, Hunter, who preaches half a dozen times a weekend, is part of a generation of younger evangelical leaders who are conservative but not captives of the Republican Party on every social issue, especially the environment. When I first screened this episode of *King of the Hill*, I immediately thought of him and asked him to view it. As I suspected, he did not find it threatening or demeaning.

"This *King of the Hill* episode rightly portrays that the challenge of American religious institutions is not merely mobility but consumerism," he said. "I once was talking with a rabbi about the fears that religious leaders have about their members being converted to another faith. He quipped, 'My main competition is not Christianity; my competition is the mall!' Amen. The Hills are looking for the church that offers them the best deal. Maybe the smaller church gives them more fellowship and less pressure; maybe the larger church gives them more program choices and places to get involved. But where does spiritual growth in their relationship with God figure into the picture? The churches are being evaluated, the attendees are being recruited, but God is a third party in the interchange. Both pastors are trying to do their best, but their church worlds, like shops in a mall, offer different experiences that must be useful to the religious consumer but not too intrusive. The voluntary church in America is largely thriving while the government-supported ones in Europe are dying, yet are the people who attend becoming more selfless servants like Jesus?"

3. Family Guy. By a wide margin, *Family Guy* is one of the meanest and coarsest animated comedies on network television (even for Fox), which is why I am baffled that it has become a favorite of my daughter Liza—who is neither of those things— and her teenage friends. Still, it is undeniably clever and often extremely funny, and, despite my objections to its cruelty and viciousness, I find myself laughing when I watch it. Although structured like *The Simpsons*, it has few if any of its predecessor's redeeming qualities. *Family Guy* aired on Fox for three seasons, beginning in 1999, before it was cancelled in 2002. But strong ratings for reruns on Cartoon Network's Adult Swim, coupled with the sale of millions of DVDs, brought it back to Fox in 2005 with all new episodes. Like the other animated shows, it makes occasional use of religion for story lines. In a 2007 episode, Pat Robertson and Jerry Falwell are mysteriously left behind in the rapture. Since they recall hating all the right people, they are puzzled and frustrated, which leads to a heated make-out session between the men—verifying a number of suspicions about homophobia in the religious right that predate the Ted Haggard revelations.

The title character, Peter Griffin, is the grossly fat, buffoonish father, who comes from a working-class, Irish Catholic background. He works factory and fishing jobs in and around his hometown of Quahog, Rhode Island, when he is not unemployed. His wife, Lois, the daughter of wealthy, Protestant parents, is a piano teacher, sweet but with a libidinous past. Their lower-middle-class household—they can afford only one car—includes a doltish adolescent son, Chris; a precocious but insecure teenage daughter, Meg; an infant named Stewie who speaks with a mannered English accent; and a sophisticated talking dog named Brian, who is an alcoholic. The show's structure includes flashbacks and asides that have nothing to do with the main plot of the episode. In an August 17, 2004, interview with the Web site IGN, series creator Seth MacFarlane was asked if there were any scenes cut from the show he wouldn't ever want to see restored. "Yeah, there was one," Mac-Farlane said. "Actually, I wonder if we should put that into a current script. It was 'The Last Supper,' and it's Jesus saying, 'Drink this, all of you, for this is my blood . . .' and the Apostles all do this huge spit take. That sequence was cut." Some of the show's Catholic comedy that survived the censors is particularly savage—blasphemy by any definition. In one episode, Peter mocks Holy Communion at the altar rail, suggesting to the priests that Jesus was drunk at the time of crucifixion, since his blood was now wine. One reason the show has not attracted criticism may have to do with the clergy sex abuse scandals, McFarlane surmised. "Since the Catholic Church has been having the troubles it's had, I've been hearing that they've been a little less quick to open their mouths to criticize. Because it's just a little hypocritical."

Jesus appears in other episode flashbacks, as an adolescent who can't get along with Joseph, and, later, performing a seaside singing act for his followers. In yet another, he is an adult appearing in the back of a pickup truck in a compromising position with a farmer's wife, whereupon the husband confronts him with a shotgun. This image of Jesus—usually a young, bearded white man—is not entirely consistent. When baby Stewie is sucked through the television by poltergeists, he returns from the other side to report that he has seen Jesus, who turns out to be Chinese. His last name is Hong, rather than Christ. A sequence cut from another broadcast has Jesus playing golf in a foursome. When he misses a putt, which would have been his third birdie, the ball backs up into the cup, miraculously. He also appears as a disco dancer and a cheering sports fan with a large foam hand, as well as a passenger on a spaceship with aliens when an accidental nuclear exchange devastates the earth. Once, Lois imagines what Jesus would have been like—a dissolute, ill-tempered father of a poor family—if he had given up on his dream. In a modern version of the second coming, a diminutive Jesus has to explain to a crowd in a park that people were much smaller in biblical times.

And Jesus is not alone in heaven. When Peter thanks him for bestowing an act of good fortune, Jesus starts to explain that credit should actually go to Vishnu, but the blue-skinned, four-armed Hindu deity shushes him.

The Bible also figures in plots. Peter acknowledges that he is unfamiliar with the scriptures, because they take "way too long to read." He is always ready to step forward at a funeral and misrepresent Jesus' biblical message. Pressed by his devout father to name his favorite book of the Bible, Peter says, "That one where Jesus swallows the puzzle piece and the man in the big yellow hat has to take him to the hospital," a reference to the children's book *Curious George*. Peter is not alone in his fractured understanding of Christianity. One young, Republican character proclaims, "Jesus created this country to destroy nonbelievers and brown people."

God the Father is not exempt from gratuitous gibes, including those of a rude and sexual nature. In one episode, a white-bearded, white-robed Creator sets off the universe's Big Bang creation with flatulence. In other episodes, God, sometime accompanied by Jesus in a Cadillac Escalade, uses his supernatural powers to pick up women at the bar and the bowling alley. In heaven, God is shown being forced to use a condom in bed by a woman he is with—despite pleas that it is his birthday. In the garden of Eden, God cautions Adam and Eve not to eat from the tree of knowledge. When Adam asks if they can at least sit under it, God looks over his shoulder at a pile of *Playboy* and *Penthouse* magazines at the tree's base and says that wouldn't be such a good idea.

Occasionally, God plays a more traditional role in the series. Peter pretends his son Chris is dying in order to get an organization like the Make-a-Wish Foundation to put a favorite television show back on the air. Then, to extricate himself from the situation, Peter pretends he has the power of miraculous healing, which in turn leads people to worship him as a god. For violating the First Commandment, the real God smites the Griffin household with biblical plagues until Peter begs for forgiveness. An angel informs God, who is sitting at his desk in heaven, that the message has been received, and the plagues are called off. Peter also provokes God's wrath for relatively minor infractions, in one case for thinking a wind-blown shopping bag is more marvelous than the human circulatory system. Peter prays for God to let his son win a Youth Scout soap box derby, with the opposite result. Baby Stewie prays to God—to stay out of Brian's way as he begins an army basic training obstacle course. Stumbling into success with the New England Patriots, Peter looks into the TV camera and thanks God for his success, but also for the Devil, for giving God something to do—an interesting theological point. He even blames the Trix rabbit for trying to "steal Easter from Jesus." In several other episodes, Death, complete with black robe and scythe, plays a central role. Hitler, Al Capone, and John Wilkes Booth play cards in hell, along with Superman, who got there for killing a hooker in a fit of rage.

Current controversies also pop up, as when parent protests drive Lois from the sex education class she has volunteered to teach at James Woods High, the public school her children attend. Lois is replaced with a hip-talking youth pastor from First Evangelical Church, who pushes his "abstinence only" line by glibly giving the kids patently false and misleading information. He tells them that condoms have a "one hundred percent failure rate," and that sex is "bad, immoral, and wrong." Taking aim at another religious target, Peter rips Christian recording artist Amy Grant's NBC-TV reality show, *Three Wishes*, for being exploitative of a terminally ill child.

Religious differences between Peter and Lois are at the center of two episodes, each occasioned by visits from Peter's bigoted father, Francis. In the first, the elder Griffin set the tone of his relationship with Lois at the young couple's wedding when he added to the bumper sticker reading "Just Married" the words "to a Protestant Whore." After sixty years working at the Pawtucket Mill, Francis is forced to retire, a psychologically crippling experience for a man who lived to work, even at the expense of his relationship with his family and especially with his son. Still, Peter feels obligated to drag his family to Francis's retirement dinner, since Peter's mother is on what he calls a "mission trip" to Las Vegas. The children wonder why Francis never visits them, and Lois explains, "Your grandfather has never been comfortable with the fact that I'm not Catholic." Francis's religion, like his work, has been a big part of the man's life. After being presented with a gold watch by his boss, the retiree tells his coworkers that at mass earlier that morning it occurred to him that he might not be seeing any of their faces again. "I just want to say that Jesus loves you. But in my eyes, you're a bunch of sinners and slackers who force a hard-working old man to retire. So you can take this shiny watch and shove it."

Driving home from the dinner, Peter tells his father, who is sitting next to him in the front seat, that he wants the old man to stay with them. Francis says he doesn't want to be a bother, but immediately makes plain how difficult the arrangement is going to be. He tells Peter that it's a pity that he couldn't have found himself a nice Catholic girl. Lois pipes up from the back seat that her father-in-law must be embarrassed, forgetting that she is in the back seat—but he is clearly not. The best Francis can do is to acknowledge that, her religious failing notwithstanding, Lois is a good woman. "Perhaps you won't burn in hell after all. Maybe you'll just go to purgatory with all the unbaptized babies." Instead of coming to his wife's defense at the insult, Peter tries to be a peacemaker, or perhaps an enabler. "There you go, Lois," he says. "You love kids."

At the Griffin home, Francis makes his presence—and his religious views—felt. The old man's idea of an appropriate bedtime story for Stewie concludes, "So God cast the pagans and sinners into the fiery bowels of hell, where their flesh burned in agony forever and ever. The end." As Francis explains to Peter and Lois, "Children love a bedtime story from the Bible." Next he drags the whole family to 5 a.m. mass, which Lois gamely notes afterward was a lovely service. That is only the beginning. When Chris goes to the bathroom, Francis falsely accuses him of masturbating and tells him never to do it again. The boy misunderstands him and takes the admonition to be against future bowel movements. Francis calls Meg a "harlot" when she tells him she held hands with the boy next door—who has an Irish name, at that—and predicts that God will give her leprosy, causing the offending hand to fall off. Not even innocuous television viewing is exempt from the old man's wrath. He switches off an old *Dick Van Dyke Show*, telling family members how the episode ends: "Laura burns the roast and God kills her for parading her buns around in those pants."

Peter makes another desperate attempt to reconnect with his father, this time with a baseball game at Boston's Fenway Park, but the evening goes awry. With nothing working, Peter fantasizes going into business with his father manufacturing Virgin Mary shrines out of old bathtubs. A tour of the toy factory where Peter works presents a more realistic opportunity, and Peter asks his boss to hire Francis despite his age. The best argument Peter can make is that his father always put work ahead of everything—his wife, his health, even his own son. "Especially his own son," Francis chimes in for wounding emphasis. While the boss is thinking it over, the old man does so much work on the assembly line that he makes Francis the foreman. Peter is overjoyed at the prospect of working side by side with his father, after all the years of neglect. And to top it off, Francis is even grateful to Peter, and says so. "This is truly a miracle," he says, also giving thanks to Jesus for giving him a purpose in life again. Then he reverts to his mean-spirited personality, ordering his son and his friends immediately back to work.

As at the Griffin home, Francis's work ethic and religiosity soon take their toll at the factory. The new foreman turns the break room into a chapel, declaring both breaks and lunch to be sins. A coworker complains that, even while working triple shifts, he was not named Employee of the Week since his competition for the honor is Jesus, shown in an illuminated shrine. But Peter insists to Lois that he and his father have never been closer.

Coworkers at the factory see things differently. They ask Peter to go to his father with their complaint that work is no longer fun. When he does, Francis dismisses their concerns. "That's Satan talk! You're a failure as a worker and as a father!" Finally losing his temper at the insult, Peter says that, while he may not be perfect, "At least I love my kids enough not to spend every minute of the day working! I'm a damn good father, and that's more than I can say about you!" Francis is stunned, but not too stunned to fire his son on the spot. At home, Lois tells her father-in-law he needs to sort things out with Peter. But Francis insists that Peter needs to go to confession "to beg forgiveness for all his failings!" While Peter is crushed, a long-shot opportunity presents itself in the form of a visit to Boston by the pope.

The pontiff, looking more like John XXIII than John Paul II, arrives aboard Blessed Virgin Airlines. Without success, Peter tries to get an audience with the pope by dressing up as a bellboy. Then he lucks into an opportunity to drive the Popemobile and drives off with the pontiff to his home in Rhode Island. Peter wants the pope, arguably the only human his father respects— "God's go-to guy"—to intervene in their relationship. The pope meets Peter's family and assures Peter that he appears to be a good father, but suggests that the son needs to speak with Francis directly to resolve the matter. Still insecure, Peter says he needs the pope to come to the factory with him for backup. Francis is in the midst of denouncing the workers as "slothful sinners" when the visitors arrive. He kneels and crosses himself before the bishop of Rome. The pope pays Francis a compliment, calling him worthy because he has raised a fine son. Peter's "zest for life is an affirmation of God's great love within us all," the pontiff tells the old man. Cantankerous as ever, Francis accuses the pope of going soft. "Even a tambourine-shaking Baptist could tell this boy's no good!" he snaps. Thinking the man is calling him a liar, the pope threatens to excommunicate him, before Peter separates the two strong-willed men. "I have never met such an infuriating man!" the pontiff tells Peter. "You must have the patience of a saint." Peter, ever needy, doesn't see it that way. "Well, he's my dad. And I just want him to love me." Now it is Francis's turn to be stunned. He loves his son with all his heart, he explains—he just doesn't like him or anything about him.

For many, that is probably a distinction without a difference, yet for Peter, desperate for any crumb of affection from his father, it is something. He too admits he doesn't really like his father. The pope puts his imprimatur on the resolution. God says you must honor your father, the pontiff says. "He never said anything about liking him." Peter is liberated. "Well, in that case, Dad, I'm gonna eat meat on Fridays, play golf on Sundays, laugh at Jewish comedians, and yes, sleep with my Protestant wife," he says, adding that neither he nor Lois will enjoy it. Francis rehires Peter and takes a job as a hostile roadie with the pope's tour. Danny White, the episode's writer, was raised Catholic and, on the DVD commentary, notes that he doesn't think the episode was ever seen by his relatives or by "a series of nuns who battered me senseless."

Judaism is squarely in the sights of an episode called "When You Wish Upon a Weinstein." At the Drunken Clam bar, Peter complains to his neighbors that Lois thinks he is bad with money. Most recently, he has just been conned out of two hundred dollars—her emergency fund—by a fast-talking door-to-door salesman who hustled him for volcano insurance. His pals think Lois may be right. Friends Cleveland and Quagmire have had much better luck with money, thanks to a Jewish accountant and a Jewish stockbroker, respectively. Peter concludes, "I need a Jewish guy to handle my money," later that night launching into a production number entitled "When You Wish Upon a Jew." Peter sings that he needs a Jew "to teach me how to whine and do my taxes." The song has a slightly different melody, but it is a clear take on "When You Wish Upon a Star," from Walt Disney's *Pinocchio*, in both words and images. Like the Italian woodcarver Geppetto, Peter kneels by his window, hands folded, and looks skyward. The stars form appropriate constellations: a Star of David and a menorah. As he sings, Peter is ferried across the sky by an extraterrestrial vehicle in the shape of a dreidel. He is awakened the next morning by a knock at the door. A stranger named Max Weinstein tells him his car has broken down in front of the house and he needs to use the phone. Peter's prayer has been answered.

The first order of business is for Peter to get Max, who turns out to be an accountant, to help him get his volcano insurance money back. Max tries to flee, but his host chases him down, and the accountant successfully recovers the money—and balances the Griffins' checkbook. In return, Max is invited to have dinner with the family. He takes one look at Lois's marshmallow and fish casserole and begs off, allowing Lois to assume it is because he observes Jewish dietary laws. When Max offers to help Chris with his homework, Peter marvels at his skill and generosity: "My God! Is there nothing you people can't do? I mean, other than manual labor." Lois chides her husband for the last remark, calling it a ridiculous stereotype and, for proof, noting that the Jews built the pyramids.

Asked to join the Griffins for a board game, Max begs off because it is Friday night and he wants to go to temple for services. Soon they are all seen entering the synagogue, as Lois thanks the accountant for inviting them. "Your husband's got a good heart, but his views on Judaism are a little misguided," Max confides. At first, Peter worries that, as a product of Catholic schools, he shouldn't be attending a Jewish service. (Instantly, as he enters the sanctuary, an alarm goes off at the secret headquarters of an international order of nuns dedicated to corralling wayward Catholics.) Peter is impressed with the people in the congregation he recognizes: the principal of Meg's school; Bill Nye, the Science Guy; and half of singer Lenny Kravitz, who is half Jewish. Despite an understandable faux pas or two, the evening is a success. "That was so nice," Lois says. "A good sermon and such beautiful songs." Typically, Peter confuses the service with a performance of *Fiddler on the Roof* he once attended, starring William Shatner. Max thanks Peter for his hospitality and tells him he has faith that his son Chris "will grow up to be a real mensch," a Yiddish term for a well-mannered person.

Peter is inspired by his personal encounter with Jews and Judaism. (This is a little odd, since a regular character in the show, Mort the druggist, is Jewish.) Peter tells Lois he has hit on a plan to make Chris smart: make him a Jew. His wife tries to point out the fallacy of this approach, to no avail. Off go father and son to the synagogue to discuss conversion with the rabbi, who quickly disabuses them. "I appreciate your interest," the clergyman tells them, "but Judaism takes a serious commitment." The rabbi points to a boy nearby studying for his bar mitzvah the coming Saturday. Peter wants a bar mitzvah for Chris and asks the rabbi how much it would cost to buy one, since his son is clearly unable to study for it. The rabbi disappears, so Peter heads for Las Vegas, the only place in America he can think of "where you can take a solemn, ritual ceremony that begins a lifetime commitment and blow through it in about twenty minutes." They drive to the Vegas strip where, next to wedding chapels, they find a quickie bar mitzvah chapel. While waiting their turn in the pews as Rabbi Copperfield, a magician, runs through the ceremonies, Peter tells Chris, "In a few minutes, you'll become a smart, successful Jewish man." Somehow the boy has received some training, because soon Chris is chanting the Hebrew blessing over the Torah scroll—accurately—when Lois arrives. She interrupts the ceremony, calling it a travesty, because her son is doing it for the wrong reasons. The family flees the chapel, jumping into a passing bus, where Peter apologizes to his wife for the fiasco. Lois tells him Chris will do just fine without a conversion or a bar mitzvah. "I have faith in him, the way I have faith in you," she tells her husband. "Besides, a person's religion is no guarantee of success." Chris agrees, chiming in, in Yiddish, "Zoh zine mit glick"—everything will be okay.

In a DVD commentary, series creator Seth MacFarlane says the episode grew out of his experience as a gentile in the entertainment business whose many Jewish friends would not let him shop without their assistance. He decided to take this habit to absurdity, thinking it would be "funny to take that to the insane level where Peter just feels that somehow his life will be improved if he has a Jewish guy with him at all times." This innocuous genesis did not save the episode from being banned from broadcast by Fox, whose executives cited its problematic content. Yet after the series' initial cancellation, the episode was subsequently broadcast twice on cable, on Cartoon Network's Adult Swim segment, without generating significant controversy. The cast performed the same episode live on July 23 and 24, 2004, at the Just for Laughs comedy festival in Montreal, also without incident. Finally, on December 10, 2004, Fox aired the episode as part of its holiday package, with one change. In the original version of the song "I Need a Jew," Peter sings, "Even though they killed our Lord." In the edited version, the line becomes "I don't think they killed our Lord."

When the season three DVD was released, before the airings on Cartoon Network, the writers and producers, as well as MacFarlane, were still angry about the Fox decision. In their commentary, they agreed it was an "abomination" that the episode was censored and that certain Fox executives were cowards. Nothing similar happened on the many occasions when the show bashed Catholics, they noted. "This thing got me so angry, and it is so disgusting," says the writer of the episode, Ricky Blitt, who is Jewish. MacFarlane chimes in that special care was taken with the script by the show's writers, about 70 percent of whom are Jewish. Far more offensive gags that crossed the line were cut, and the final script was sent for review to two rabbis, whom MacFarlane does not identify. One wrote back to say, "Peter learns the right lesson in the end. It's fine. We don't have any problem with it."

4. American Dad. If *Family Guy*, as many have charged, is a blatant *Simpsons* ripoff, then *American Dad* is a copy of a copy. From the creator of *Family Guy*, Seth MacFarlane, *American Dad* is the story of Stan Smith, a pompous, blustery Central Intelligence Agency officer with a Jay Leno jaw, living in the Northern Virginia suburb of Langley with his family, which includes his ditzy, wearily devoted wife Francine; loose and liberal teenage daughter Hayley; nerdy, adolescent son Steve; a German-speaking goldfish; and a talking alien, Roger.

From the pilot episode, which aired after the Super Bowl in January 2005, religion has popped up on *American Dad*. When Stan mistakenly shoots a mangy, flea-bitten dog he brings home for a pet, the family conducts a funeral service and burial on the lawn, at which the father prays that God will take the animal to heaven. Also in the episode, God makes a personal appearance. The Smith family watches the *CBS Evening News* as Bob Schieffer announces an extraordinary development: God has placed a call to George W. Bush in the Oval Office. Bearded and seated on a throne among the clouds, God asks the president for a "big favor." Isn't there some way Bush could "play down our relationship a little more in your public addresses?" he asks. The chief executive, characteristically, is a little befuddled, asking what God means. Oh, the Lord says, like claiming he was the divine choice to be president. "That would be an example of something to keep to yourself, just to distance yourself from me a little more," God says. Bush is in the process of acceding when another call comes in on God's phone. Because it is Dick Cheney, the Lord has to break off with Bush, greeting the vice president with a deferential, "Yes, sir."

On the DVD commentary, one of the writers recalled that some of the dialogue between Bush and God had to be trimmed to get it past the network, but the concern was the anti-Bush tone, rather than any concern with blasphemy. In a recent season, after Stan is transferred to the Middle East, God also appears to young Steve as the boy wanders lost in the desert. God leads him to an oasis, assuming the form of the actress Angelina Jolie. God explains that she has taken this form since it was most likely to appeal to the delirious boy. The two-episode story line has Stan becoming a Muslim and taking a second wife, providing an opportunity for some jabs at the way women are treated under Islam, at least as it is practiced in Saudi Arabia. In another episode, Stan opposes his son's learning about sex education from "God-killing tree huggers" at public school. Instead, he instructs Steve to avoid premarital sex or "angels will kill you." Stan then launches a crusade to cleanse the television of sexuality in the role of a bearded, Christian TV folksinger.

Traditionally and historically, the CIA has had a strong WASP overlay. The first agents and analysts were typically Yale-educated white males who were members of the Episcopal Church. Thus, it is totally in character when Stan's competition with a neighbor escalates from a race to a shady parking place in the church parking lot to a contest to become deacon. (In a direct lift from *The Simpsons*, the sign in front of the First Episcopal Church provides an opportunity for a number of gags throughout the episode: "Restrooms for Christians Only" and "The Bible: The *Real* Powerbook.") Initially, Stan is so anxious to leave for church that he carries Francine from the bedroom, not giving her time to put on her bra. When she protests, he tells her to keep her arms crossed, so "Jesus won't see 'em."

After losing the parking space to the neighbor, Chuck White, and his perfect family, Stan listens grumpily to the weary priest's sermon. The text is Galatians 5:14: "Love thy neighbor as thyself." This is nothing less than "the most important lesson God wants you to learn," the priest tells the congregation. Suddenly the minister cuts short the sermon when his fishing buddies pull up to the front door of the church. Condensing his message as he dons his fishing gear in the pulpit, the priest says, "God is, uh, good. Devil's bad." On the way out, he asks the deacon to wrap up the service, whereupon the lay leader chokes to death on a Communion wafer—as the congregation watches helpessly. This delays the priest from his outing, causing him to complain that now the congregation needs a new deacon. Stan scoffs, "Long hours, no pay, whiny churchgoers—you'd have to be an idiot to volunteer for that position." Yet as soon as neighbor Chuck volunteers, so does Stan, requiring an election the following Sunday.

When the Smiths return home, the alien Roger asks how church was. Daughter Hayley replies, "Waste of time." Son Steve, still unspoiled (and enamored with Chuck White's daughter), says, "Love has a face." Stan begins planning his campaign for deacon, but his motive is naked envy, the opposite of the sermon's text to love your neighbor. The contest is important because Chuck White, he explains in a blithely hurtful way to Francine, has a better house, a bigger paycheck, and a nicer wife and family. Since the Whites have offered their home for the previous deacon's postfuneral potluck, the Smiths must arrive with the perfect dish—Francine's potato salad.

A particularly bizarre series of plot twists follow. Roger, who is a hermaphrodite and in the middle of an asexual reproductive cycle, eats all the potato salad and has to make a late-night substitute. Without mayonnaise, he resorts to his alien breast milk, without informing the Smiths. The adulterated potato salad is a huge hit among the parishioners, and Stan's prospects soar. But the congregation members crave more, so Roger has to be force-fed and milked to provide enough of the secret ingredient. Exhausted, the alien passes out in the Smith living room and has to be resuscitated by young Steve, who has just learned CPR. But in giving the creature mouth-to-mouth, he ingests an alien egg and becomes pregnant. Stan has another problem besides his pregnant son: he is afraid someone will learn the secret of the potato salad. So he calls on White House advisor Karl Rove, who arrives at the home in the form of the Angel of Death, although Hayley recognizes him as "the amoral puppet master behind George Bush."

The next Sunday, election day at church, the priest is recounting in his sermon a miracle he experienced personally: God turned around an NFL game he had bet on, enabling him to beat the spread in the closing minutes and buy a new car. Stan wins the election, declaring himself "the chosen one" and mooning his rival in the adjoining pew. However, his triumph is short-lived. First, Stan drives Steve to Mexico ("God's blind spot") for an abortion but then changes his mind and decides to support his son's desire to have the child. Knowing his choice will ruin him at church, the following Sunday he renounces his deacon's position before the congregation, claiming he is possessed by the devil. Steve's pregnancy is inadvertently transferred to Chuck White's gymnast daughter when she, in turn, kisses the boy. As nonsensical as the plot is, it still drew criticism from the conservative organization Parents Television Council, which named it the "Worst TV Show of the Week" on its Web site. Reviewer Caroline Schulenburg called it sacrilegious, adding, "'Deacon Stan, Jesus Man' attempted to satirize church politics and conservative views on abortion but failed." (In another episode, in the finest Fox News tradition, Stan does battle against secular nonbelievers in the bogus "War against Christmas.")

For all its scrutiny, the watchdog group overlooked a potentially more controversial undertone, namely, the strong gay subtext running through this episode. Like some other mainline Protestant denominations, the Episcopal Church is tearing itself apart over the issue of homosexuality: whether the venerable denomination should allow the ordination of noncelibate gay clergy and the consecration of openly gay bishops, and whether to bless same-sex unions. These issues are not directly addressed in this episode of *American Dad*, but they are certainly alluded to. The deacon who chokes to death is obviously gay, with a partner who mourns him, if churlishly. At the postfuneral potluck at the Whites' home, Chuck approaches another gay couple in his living room and suggestively tells the men that he would do *anything* to be elected deacon, as they look at each other quizzically. (In another episode, Log Cabin Republicans sing that it is possible to be gay and still have "good, old-fashioned Christian morals," as they kneel around a life-sized crucifix.

5. South Park. Much like my encounters with *The Simpsons,* Disney's animated features, and *Family Guy,* I discovered *South Park* in the early 2000s through my children. Now teenagers, they have considerably more latitude in choosing their weekend and vacation television viewing than when I began the first edition of this book. But what I gave up in parental control I made up for in walk-by derogatory commentary on their choices—like *South Park.* Passing through our living room, hearing bad language coming from the television voiced by crudely animated children, I would regularly disparage the cartoon show. Finally, my son Asher suggested I slow down and take another look. The show, he insisted, contained a good deal of religion and, yes, morality. I took his advice and learned, as happens from time to time, that he was right.

No animated show has dashed through the door to religion opened by *The Simpsons* with more gusto, or to greater effect and controversy, than Comedy Central's long-running hit. With the help of a full-length movie in 1999 that grossed more than $52 million at the U.S. box office, *South Park* is firmly ensconced in American popular culture, although with a far smaller audience than *The Simpsons.* New episodes of *South Park,* one of Comedy Central's highest-rated programs, continue to draw nearly 3.5 million viewers per week, most of them teenage boys and young men. *South Park*'s characters and creators have landed on magazine covers and are the subject of hundreds of Web sites. While it can be distasteful in the extreme, the show is especially popular with the 18–34 demographic coveted by advertisers. In 2005, the show extended its reach beyond cable, to syndication on broadcast stations, reaching an estimated 85 percent of the country, including forty-eight of the nation's top fifty markets. However, some of the episodes based on religion were considered so offensive to believers that they could not be edited for broadcast.

Before each episode, producers give fair, if absurd, warning: a disclaimer cautions that, due to offensive language and content, the show "should not be viewed by anyone." Pint-sized and potty-mouthed, *South Park*'s main characters are four fast-talking children in the third and fourth grade in the fictional Rocky Mountain town of South Park. Visually, Stan, Kyle, Eric, and Kenny are reminiscent of Charles Schulz's *Peanuts* gang, with round, oversized heads and short bodies. (In one of their Christmas specials, *South Park* characters recite from the Gospel of Luke, just as Charlie Brown does in the *Peanuts* annual holiday television special.) But for the most part, the *South Park* quartet is nasty, naughty, and nihilistic. In one episode of *The Simpsons*, Marge finds Bart and his friends watching *South Park* but makes them turn it off because the Comedy Central show is not "life affirming." Sometimes the dialogue that emerges from the *South Park* quartet's vile little bodies is almost impossible to listen to. And often the imagery is worse. There is a creepy—if age appropriate—preoccupation with feces. And nothing is off limits for humor, from cancer to children with severe physical and mental disabilities.

For more than a decade, creators Trey Parker and Matt Stone have simultaneously embraced and pummeled religion. While still in college in Colorado, the pair's first effort involved a short film in which Jesus used his halo to decapitate Frosty the Snowman, who was a serial killer. Today, *South Park* is one of the most cosmological shows on the small screen, where the philosophical nature of the universe is examined and a place where occasionally scatology meets eschatology. Religion appears in the show in many manifestations, some predictable and some unlikely. When characters—even the most unsympathetic—are in desperate need, they cry out to God for help or go to Jesus for advice (although not as frequently as they do to their school's cafeteria chef). When South Park residents begin to spontaneously combust, their first reaction is, "God must be angry with us." Infrequently, but occasionally, characters believe they have visions from God. Eric Cartman is the meanest of the crew and their foil, a misanthropic anti-Semite being raised by his sweet, promiscuous, single mother (in a home where crucifixes are prominently displayed). He believes he has a revelation that God wants him to form a boy band and earn ten million dollars.

Woven through the narratives are fundamental questions about faith, often going deeper and far beyond *The Simpsons*. Like its Fox predecessor, *South Park* has dealt with the nature and purpose of God, the role of prayer, salvation, hell, Jewish identity, cults, euthanasia, and the Christian missionary experience. But the Comedy Central show has also taken on religious broadcasting, Mormonism, the Roman Catholic Church's sex abuse scandal, anti-Semitism, spiritualism, and contemporary Christian music. An episode about teaching evolution at South Park Elementary despite the protests of religious parents features the biologist Richard Dawkins, author of *The God Delusion,* who argues his case for atheism. Another episode has Saddam Hussein in hell, taking the devil as his lover. There is also ecumenical syncretism in *South Park*: Moses, Muhammad, Krishna, Buddha, Lao Tzu, and the Mormon prophet Joseph Smith are all Jesus' friends and allies in combating evil. God their father, who says he is a Buddhist, appears as a cat with the head of a hippopotamus. "Every religion has their own version of God, and none of them makes sense," Stone explained in one DVD commentary. In a 1998 interview with the *Jewish Exponent* weekly newspaper, Stone, a self-described "agnostic Jew," offered a simple rationale for including so much theology in *South Park*: "Religion is funny."

During a lengthy telephone interview from the show's Los Angeles office, Stone told me that, at first, he and his partner were surprised to be asked about the show's religious content. "We never really thought about it until someone pointed it out," he says. "The real question is, 'Why is there so *little* religion everywhere else on television?' I don't know why. *South Park* carved out a niche there. Because we're on cable, and we already have a reputation for being outrageous, we can do stuff you can't do on shows like *Friends.* We're allowed to go places with religion that a lot of network shows are not. They think they're going to offend people. The only interest the shows that do deal with religion have is to slam it or rob its symbols, to pillage it."

South Park's writing staff took a different view. "Matt and Trey's approach is to go where nobody else will go, to areas that people are afraid to touch," said Anne Garefino, the show's executive producer, a product of Catholic schools and still a regular Sunday mass goer. "In writers' meetings, we spend 50–75 percent of our time talking about religious themes. You can't poke fun at something unless you have a serious understanding of what it is," she told me in an interview. This fascination with faith has not escaped the attention of perceptive fans and cultural critics. The show is "perhaps the most striking example of the peculiar places in which the media-consuming public is offered a chance to meet God," according to Gerry Bowler, a religion researcher and historian who was among the first to write about religious content in *The Simpsons.* In an essay for the Canadian Web journal ChristianWeek.org, he wrote, "Surprisingly, it is the foul-mouthed *South Park* where the theology is impeccable—a treacherous devil, an unconquerable Jesus, a fickle and greedy public, quick to desert God."

Other academic literature supports this view. In her 2002 honors thesis at the University of South Africa in Pretoria, based on the show's first five seasons, Janet Pantland found that *South Park's* approach to religion is roughly similar to that described earlier in this book to *The Simpsons*:

> Religion in South Park is about economy: the people give and believe only as long as they are on the winning side and therefore guaranteed of getting something back. . . . It simply allows religion (or aspects of religion) to be critically evaluated in the same way that other facets of society are evaluated.
>
> *South Park* does not teach us about or promote religions, nor does it try to destroy religion. In *South Park*, the poke is always at religious institutions and our expectations of religion, not at the spiritual heart of religion itself. Both God and Jesus are portrayed as loving and wise. . . . It is religious expectations and institutions—rather than genuine religious experiences—that bear the brunt of *South Park's* scathing satire.

Jesus. Jesus is not just a resident of South Park; he is a character who appears frequently. His most famous segment was a boxing match with Satan, prompted by a playground spat with the Prince of Darkness's son, Damien, and televised as a pay-per-view event. (Jesus is so overmatched that he triumphs only because the devil takes a dive, having bet against himself. The match has spawned popular tee-shirts and even action figures.) As host of a local, public access talk show, the Nazarene is portrayed as more of a flawed superhero than a savior. But there he is, flying around in the opening credits and taking center stage in more than a dozen episodes. Jesus came to live in South Park almost as an afterthought, Stone told me. Originally, the town's agents of supernatural intervention were to be aliens from outer space. But the *X Files* had become popular, and Stone and Parker did not want it to seem like their show was a satire of the live-action hit. Jesus of South Park often admits that he doesn't have all the answers, and sometimes he simply declines to intervene in the world, as when the local elementary school's football team was being shut out by a rival. And, like his biblical counterpart, he can be short-tempered.

Parker and Stone's college film led to a brief promotional video that in turn led to the series. In the college film, which the pair turned into a video Christmas card, Jesus gets into a swearing, kung fu fight with Santa Claus in a mall over the true meaning of Christmas (correct answer: presents). Another Christmas episode in the series called "Red Sleigh Down" features Jesus shooting his way into Baghdad to rescue Santa, who was kidnapped by Saddam Hussein. In the attack, Jesus takes an apparently fatal bullet in order to save Santa, who later tells the assembled South Park citizens that, in the future, Christmas will commemorate "a brave man named Jesus" who died for them. The cable TV phone-in show on South Park's public access channel is called *Jesus and Pals*—the house band is called "The Disciples"—and the host's unique abilities enable him to know callers' names before they identify themselves. When one caller asks "how the hell" he already knew his name, Jesus snaps, "Well, maybe it's because I'm the Son of God, brainiac!" Yet Jesus' powers are sometimes limited. When South Park is threatened with destruction by a monstrous, mechanical Barbra Streisand on the rampage, and one resident cries out for God's help, it is Robert Smith of the rock group the Cure who comes to the town's rescue. Even Jesus hails him as "our savior." "Jesus is open season," Stone told a meeting of a television critics association in Hollywood in July 2006.

This portrayal has set some Christians on edge. "As Christians, when they take the character of Christ and make him into a cartoon character and have him do and say things that are totally out of his character, that's a very flippant attitude to take toward a person millions of Americans believe to be the Son of God," said Donald Wildmon, president of the American Family Association (AFA), based in Tupelo, Mississippi. "They depend on humor being degenerate." His group has crusaded against *South Park*, taking credit for driving off advertisers Geico, Best Buy, Footlocker, and Finish Line, as well as for convincing JC Penney to stop carrying the show's merchandise. "I wish they would lose *all* their sponsors," Wildmon told me in an interview. "That show does not deserve to be sponsored by reputable companies." In the past, Wildmon and his organization denounced the show as "crude," "sacrilegious" and "despicable." And that was before yet another Christmas episode that featured a warm, woodland tableau of cuddly creatures surrounding a creche, all paying homage to a baby antichrist.

Over the years, Wildmon has had plenty of company. Conservative media pundit L. Brent Bozell III called *South Park* a "curdled, malodorous black hole of Comedy Central vomit" in a column posted on the Parents Television Council Web site. The movie version, *South Park: Bigger, Longer, and Uncut,* was denounced as coming "straight from the smoking pits of hell" by Thomas A. Carder, on the Web site of the Childcare Action Project. "This extraordinarily vulgar, vile, and repugnant movie [is] sinematic [*sic*] cyanide," designed "to promote licentious belittlement of wholesome life," Carter wrote. "Some of the scenes in *South Park* reminded me so much of the image of demons screeching and dancing around a boiling cauldron as Satan gleefully looks on from the background, as the demons pitch soul after soul into the boiling cauldron."

Many fans were not dissuaded by such attacks. Jesus is often put in situations that are "wrong and funny at the same time," said Teddy Dover of Longwood, Florida. "I can't think of any other show on television that uses religion so consistently and so blatantly." In *South Park,* Jesus' advice is occasionally categorical: "Cheating is lying and lying is wrong, no matter what the circumstance." Yet he refuses to take a stand on some thorny issues, such as homosexuality or assisted suicide, which he says he wouldn't touch "with a sixty-foot pole." Alone one Christmas, he sits before a cake with candles, singing, "Happy birthday to me." Jesus, who addresses God as "Dad," also has his lighter moments. While singing in a local nightclub, he twirls his halo on his finger. Perhaps because it is so over-the-top in its mocking of religion, like *Monty Python's Life of Brian, South Park* has largely escaped criticism from evangelicals, apart from Wildmon's group and a few Christian Web sites.

Parker, a Monty Python fan, is not surprised that Jesus' portrayal has not provoked a backlash from Christians. In *South Park,* he explained at a television critics' press conference in Pasadena in January 1998, "Jesus is a great guy." Stone acknowledged that the two writers bring a "humanistic approach to Jesus. He's a regular guy. But he's a very good regular guy." In several episodes, Parker added, "he's the hero and he tries to have other people follow him, so I don't know what they have to protest about."

Louis Giovino, a spokesman for the conservative, New York–based Catholic League for Religious and Civil Rights, has some suggestions. Giovino told National Public Radio that *South Park* made *Life of Brian* "look like a playground." The animated series "is very vicious in its satire toward most religions." Other Catholic observers disagreed. "In the midst of all this gross-out, puerile humor are flashes of insight into the religious condition," said Father James Martin, associate editor and culture critic of *America* magazine, the national Catholic weekly, and author of *My Life with the Saints.* "In a way it's very subversive because it leads people through one door—humor—and leads them out another," to a serious consideration of faith and theology.

As Martin suggests, Jesus also makes some profound theological points in the show. People in South Park are concerned that the world might end at the turn of the millennium, so they pray for revelation and assurance from God the Father, who doesn't respond immediately. "God can't answer every prayer and suddenly give you everything you want," Jesus explains to the waiting, restive crowd. "That takes all the living out of life. . . . If God answered all our prayers, there'd be nothing left for us to do ourselves. Life is about problems and overcoming those problems and growing and learning from obstacles. If God just fixed everything for us, there'd be no point in our existence. . . . Yea! Believe in me and ye shall find peace." Alas, that is not what the crowd has come to hear. "We've heard that crap for about two thousand years now!" a character shouts. "We wanna hear something new."

Sometimes what they hear is troubling. Kenny McCormick, the smallest of the *South Park* quartet, is a poor, forlorn boy whose dialogue is largely unintelligible, since he is usually muffled inside a hooded red parka. And in most episodes Kenny is killed—often horribly—only to reappear (resurrected?) without explanation the next week. Kenny's regular comings and goings provided an opportunity for *South Park* to deal with the controversial case of Terri Schiavo. In the episode, Kenny, like the Florida woman, is in a persistent vegetative state, being fed through a tube, with the last page of his living will missing. The doctor tells his parents, "Kenny is the same as he ever was. It's just that now he's more like a tomato." The boy's fate turns into a national media circus. Two angels insist that "God intended Kenny to die" and not to be "kept alive artificially," but only because the boy's spirit (and video game skills) are needed to help defend heaven from an invasion from hell. For the same reason, Satan needs Kenny kept alive—to keep him out of the cosmic fray. One of the Prince of Darkness's minions recommends that, in times like this, the devil should "do what we always do—use the Republicans." So the hellish emissary does just that, whispering into the ear of a posturing GOP congressman ("Removing the feeding tube is murder") on the steps of the Capitol. Kenny is finally permitted to expire when the last page of his will is found. In it he has written, "If I should ever be in a vegetative state and kept alive on life support, please for the love of God don't ever show me in that condition on national television." In an interview with the *New York Times*, Stone said, "There's kind of nothing funny about the Terri Schiavo thing—so that's why we did it." Like everyone else, he added, the show's creators "found the whole thing fascinating. That show, and humor in general, is how we work it out."

On other occasions, what South Park residents and viewers get is a very jaundiced, if not heretical, view of God. In an episode

dealing with the life-saving uses of stem cells, Stan asks the lovable cafeteria chef, Jerome McElroy, voiced by soul singer Isaac
Hayes, why God would let Kenny die. "Why?" Stan says. "Kenny's
my friend. Why can't God take someone else's friend?" As soothing piano music plays, Chef replies, in an equally soothing voice:
"Stan, sometimes God takes those closest to us because it
makes him feel better about himself. He is a very vengeful God,
Stan. He's all pissed off about something we did thousands of years
ago. He just can't get over it, so he doesn't care who he takes. Children, puppies, it don't matter to him, so long as it makes us sad.
Do you understand?" Stan is puzzled. If that is true, he asks, "Why
does God give us anything to start with?" Well, Chef explains,
"look at it this way. If you want to make a baby cry, first you give
it a lollipop. Then you take it away. If you never give it a lollipop
to begin with, then you would have nothin' to cry about. That's
like God, who gives us life and love and help just so that he can
tear it all away and make us cry, so he can drink the sweet milk of
our tears. You see, it's our tears, Stan, that give God his great
power."

Catholics. Apparently, with the exception of a small Jewish
community and the occasional Mormon family, everyone in South
Park is Catholic and attends one, unnamed church. That congregation is led by a priest, Father Maxi (probably a play on Maxi
Priest, the reggae singer), with the assistance of a sensitive nun, Sister Anne, whose order is called the Bleeding Eyes of Jesus. After
nine people are mowed down by an elderly driver at South Park's
farmers' market, the priest presides over a community memorial
service at the site of the tragedy. "It is sometimes hard in times like
these to understand God's way," he tells the crowd. "Why would
he allow nine innocent people to be run down in the prime of their
lives by a senior citizen who perhaps shouldn't be driving? It is then
that we must understand God's sense of humor is very different
from our own. . . . God needs complex irony, subtle farcical twists
that seem macabre to you and me. All that we can hope for is that
God got his good laugh and a tragedy such as this will never happen again"—which, of course, it immediately does.

Maxi is a narrow-minded theologian who denounces Halloween and preaches eternal damnation for a boy with cerebral palsy because he is unable to intelligibly confess his sins. (If the latter seems far-fetched, it isn't. In 2004, the first Holy Communion of eight-year-old Haley Waldman was revoked by the Catholic Diocese of Trenton, New Jersey. Bishop John Smith, citing a Vatican precedent set by Cardinal Joseph Ratzinger, said it was improper for the girl, who suffers from a rare digestive disorder that makes her allergic to wheat, to be served a rice wafer.) Maxi also condemns anyone who does not accept Jesus and profess Christian faith through Catholic doctrine, like the boys' friend Kyle Broflovski, who is Jewish. "The Jews crucified our Savior!" the priest says. "I mean, if you don't go to hell for crucifying the Savior, then what the hell do you go to hell for?" Sister Anne disagrees, at least with regard to the Jews, and phones the pope for support—without success.

But even the venal Father Maxi—who secretly bets on Satan in his fight with Jesus—has his limits. In an episode devoted entirely to the Catholic Church's sexual abuse scandal, he condemns his fellow priests and bishops for not repenting and for steadfastly refusing to renounce their sinful actions. Maxi carries his case to the Vatican, where his luck is no better. "You forgot what being a Catholic is all about," he tells the Curia and assembled cardinals and bishops in a televised address. "People are losing faith because they don't see how what you've turned religion into applies to them. . . . Look, I'm proud to be a Catholic, but I'm a Catholic in the real world. It's time for you all to do that too. It's time for change." Stone said there was a good deal of anger involved in writing this episode, that everyone on the staff was appalled by the sex scandal and the church's response to it. (That anger has not abated. In 2006, church leaders were shown in one episode dancing with naked boys at Satan's Halloween party in Los Angeles.) Father Martin, of *America* magazine, who had not seen this particular episode, said some material in the series "is extremely hostile and I find it offensive, but that goes with the nature of satire. It's not surprising that they take pot shots at the Catholics—everyone else has."

The Catholic League's founder, William Donohue, did not agree, and predictably tried to spin his criticism of the episode in a way that supported his view of the scandal. He wrote, "The way Stone and Parker have decided to approach the subject shows cowardice, not courage. . . . The scandal in the Church is not about priests having sex with prepubescent boys. It is about priests having sex with post-pubescent young men. . . . If Stone and Parker really had guts, they would do a show on gay priests. But of course, like so many intellectually dishonest elites in our society, they will go to any lengths to protect homosexuals."

While the Catholic League failed in its effort to keep Comedy Central from airing the clergy pedophile episode again in reruns and in syndication, the group had better luck in December 2005 when Parker and Stone made a more direct and less evenhanded attack on the church. On December 7, the day before the Feast of the Immaculate Conception, *South Park* aired a season finale called "Bloody Mary." In it, a statue of the Virgin in a town near South Park is reported to be bleeding from the rectum, to miraculous, healing effect to those who are anointed. At first a cardinal verifies the miracle, and Stan's father, Randy, is cured of alcoholism when a priest makes the sign of the cross on his forehead in the blood. But later, the new pope, Benedict XVI, arrives to inspect the statue and determines that the statue is menstruating and thus is not miraculous. (A parallel, interwoven plot denigrates the Alcoholics Anonymous organization's reliance on a "higher power.")

This time, the outrage was explosive. Donohue and other representatives were all over the media with their condemnations. "I don't mind some fun being poked at the Catholic Church," Donohue told *Rolling Stone* magazine, somewhat disingenuously, in light of his previous attacks on the show. "But this was simply vulgar." Another League spokesperson, Keira McCaffrey, told the *Boston Herald*, "We realize appealing to Comedy Central on a moral basis isn't going to get us anywhere." Nonetheless, the League demanded an apology, and the episode was removed from rebroadcast and any future DVDs. The League also called on former secretary of Health, Education, and Welfare Joseph Califano Jr., a member of the board of Viacom, which owns Comedy Central, to condemn the episode. A practicing Catholic himself, Califano screened the episode and then released a statement that called it an "appalling and disgusting portrayal of the Virgin Mary. It is particularly troubling to me as a Roman Catholic that the segment has run on the eve and day of the Feast of the Immaculate Conception, a holy day for Roman Catholics."

Why did *South Park* persist in its attacks on the Catholic Church? "People think that they can get away with it because Christians don't protest violently," McCaffrey told the *Hackensack (New Jersey) Record*. "We are not taking to the streets with violent signs; we are simply speaking up against disgusting things and making people aware of them and what the media is putting out there." She acknowledged that the League's previous letter-writing campaigns had limited impact. But this time the controversy lasted a month and spread halfway around the world. "On the face of it, it is a scurrilous attempt to lampoon Mary the mother of Jesus," Lyndsay Freer, communications director for New Zealand's Catholic diocese, told the *New Zealand Herald*. "It is completely unacceptable that any broadcaster can claim the right to lampoon one who is so deeply loved and esteemed," Freer said, explaining the diocese's demand that the episode not be aired and that advertisers boycott the network. The network aired the episode anyway, reaching an audience six times its normal size, but later apologized, thereby having it both ways. In the United States, Comedy Central announced that it would pull the episode from its second scheduled December 28 airing, but only because of the holiday season. Explaining its actions in an e-mail, Comedy Central wrote, "As satirists, we believe that it is our First Amendment right to poke fun at any and all people, groups, organizations and religions, and we will continue to defend that right."

The Catholic League did not get much help from Protestants over the "Bloody Mary" episode. Hall Poe, a professor of faith and culture at Union University, a Christian university in Tennessee, explained to the Hackensack *Record* that many Protestants are less offended by such images of the Virgin. "It is a normal thing for people to be insensitive to others," Poe told the paper. "It is normal but it is not good . . . [since] Mary has not done anything to deserve that kind of abuse." Still, he added, "if you are coming at it from a perspective purely of faith, then you know God will take care of these things."

Pentecostals and evangelicals also have taken some lumps of their own in the show. Cynically, Eric decides to form a Christian rock group just to cash in on a trend: "All we have to do is sing songs about how much we love Jesus, and all the Christians will buy our crap." Pat Robertson and his 700 Club and sanctimonious missionaries in Africa are ripped to shreds in one episode. They do a dead-on impression of Robertson, in particular his avuncular and never-ending begging on what they call the CBC's *600 Club.* The South Park kids and their starving Ethiopian friend return from an alien planet and report that it is the ideal destination to relocate his tribe. A white missionary asks, "Have people on the planet heard the word of Christ?" "No," Eric answers, "It's perfect."

In another episode, Eric reacts to the discovery of Father Maxi having sex with a married woman in the confessional by starting his own church for South Park's kids. As his equally outraged friend Stan says of the priest, "If this guy is going to hell, who's going to save us?" Eric's first vision is to build a glass-walled megachurch, virtually identical to Robert Schuller's Crystal Cathedral in Garden Grove, California. Then, watching religious television while working on his sermon, the boy is inspired to become a faith healer. His preaching is a direct lift from crusades conducted by evangelists like Benny Hinn, including domino-like smack downs of those in need of healing. His antics draw everyone away from the Catholic church to his swinging and swaying congregation. Ultimately, Eric is exposed as a money-grubbing fraud—by his friends and by Sister Anne, with a lot of help from Jesus himself. Before banishing him to Mexico for his sins, Jesus explains, "God doesn't want you to spend all your time being afraid of hell, or praising his name. God wants you to spend your time helping others and living a good, happy life. *That's* how you live for *him.*"

Yet for all his cynicism and venality, Eric, too, is a believer—at least in desperation. When his friends decide that he is such a pain they will totally ignore him, Eric believes he has died and become a living ghost. "How could my own God forsake me?" he asks. He concludes that his spirit is trapped on earth, blocked from going to heaven because of some unforgiven sins. In his eyes, this is a gross injustice. God forgave the Jews, Eric reasons, so why not him? This is important because of what Eric believes awaits him in heaven: "eternal bliss, divine rest, and ten thousand dollars." He breaks into a musical number, crooning, "Jesus wants me to have a clean slate." Roping in his gullible, insecure friend Butters to help him, Eric goes to everyone he has offended in life to ask their forgiveness and to atone for his sins. Instead of going to heaven, Eric learns he has been duped by his friends. Of course, he is more in character when he misuses his faith. As a power-mad school hall monitor, he tells bullied offenders to "go with Christ" to mend their ways.

Mormons. Growing up in Colorado, both Stone and Parker developed a strong interest in Mormons and the religion's charismatic prophet, Joseph Smith. "My first three girlfriends were Mormons," Parker told *USA Today* on January 20, 1998. "I was always sort of infatuated with their religion." Stone told me much the same thing in our telephone interview. In a DVD commentary, Stone notes that his best friend in sixth grade was a Canadian Mormon, and one summer he spent a week at camp with the boy's family at a Mormon retreat at Lake Powell in Utah. "That's where I learned everything about Mormons," Stone says. This interest and infatuation was not on display in 1998 when Parker directed and costarred in the live-action comedy *Orgazmo*, screened at the Sundance Festival, which spoofed the porn industry. In the million-dollar production, Parker plays a naive Mormon missionary in Hollywood who stumbles into the leading role in a porn movie in an effort to raise money for his upcoming wedding. In one scene, as the title character, the missionary declares, "I'm not a superhero—I'm a latter-day saint."

But in *South Park*, in the years that followed, the show included Joseph Smith in its episode about "Super Best Friends," putting the Mormon founder on a par with Jesus, Moses, and Buddha. When South Park residents build a ladder to heaven and are given a look, the only people there are Mormons. "Boy, did we guess wrong!" one of the visitors exclaims. And from time to time, Mormon missionaries pop up in various episodes. But in the show's seventh season, Parker and Stone turned their full attention to the faith in an episode entitled "All about Mormons." In it, a Mormon family named Harrison moves to South Park from Utah, and their young son, Gary (voiced by one of the show's writers, Kyle McCulloch, himself a Mormon), wants to be friends with Stan. What unfolds is a remarkable portrait of the history and modern practice of Mormonism, a mixture of a lot of ridicule and a modicum of grudging respect. The historical sections are punctuated by an off-camera chorus, which sings, either "dum, dum, dum, dum," or, more likely, "dumb, dumb, dumb, dumb." Gary's family is unfailingly positive, supportive, and happy, especially during the weekly "Family Home Evenings," when the television is turned off and Mormons sing, talk, pray, and play games. This kind of experience leaves Stan ambivalent: first he is hostile, then admiring, and finally skeptical.

The Harrisons are so sincerely loving that Stan's father, Randy—initially outraged by his son's interest in what he believes is a cult—decides the whole Marsh family should become Mormons, even though the Harrisons do not push their faith on their neighbors. "They're real nice people" who love each other, Randy explains to his wife, "so there must be something to their religion." Stan ultimately rebels at the conversion. He maintains that to accept Mormon theology is to choose faith over logic: "If you're gonna say things that have been proven wrong, like that the first man and woman lived in Missouri and that the Native Americans came from Jerusalem, then you'd better have something to back it up." Likewise the Book of Mormon's account of sacred writings Smith found on gold plates buried in Upstate New York: "All you've got are a bunch of stories about some [expletive] who read plates nobody ever saw out of a hat and then couldn't do it again when the translations were hidden!" Even Stan's denunciation does not offend the cheerful and unshakably positive Harrisons, who say it's fine if Stan doesn't share their beliefs. "Oh, stop it!" Stan shouts in frustration. "That's another thing! Why do you have to be so freakin' nice all the time? It isn't normal! You just weasel people into your way of thinking by acting like the happiest family in the world and being so nice to everyone that you just blindside dumb people like my dad!"

The episode concludes not with the traditional "lesson" voiced by Stan or Kyle, but with a clear-eyed plea for tolerance from Gary, who is cruelly rejected by the other kids. "Maybe us Mormons do believe in crazy stories that make absolutely no sense, and maybe Joseph Smith made it all up," Gary says. "But I have a great life and a great family and I have the Book of Mormon to thank for that." The faith's history and theology are irrelevant, he says, and he doesn't care. "What the church teaches *now* is loving your family, being nice, and helping people." Adding a very vivid insult, Eric—Gary's chief tormentor—declares him cool.

Interestingly, at the time it was broadcast this episode drew no significant official criticism from the Church of Jesus Christ of Latter-Day Saints. As the "All about Mormons" article on the Wikipedia Web site points out, Parker and Stone avoided the cheapest shot of all: there is no mention of polygamy, a discarded Mormon practice that has dogged the faith for more than a century. Years after the episode aired, it was still an object of interest to thoughtful and image-conscious Mormons. In August 2006 I was part of a panel on religion and popular culture in Salt Lake City sponsored by the liberal Sunstone Foundation. About 150 people watched the complete episode and listened to an academic presentation on the subject by Dennis Potter, assistant professor of religious studies and Mormon studies coordinator at the Center for the Study of Ethics at Utah Valley State College. Reading from a paper entitled "The Americanization of Mormonism Reflected in *South Park*," Potter asserted, "In telling the story of the founding of the religion, the *South Park* authors make it clear that the theology is rather unbelievable," in that they neglect the ways in which it mirrors the miraculous theology of Christianity. At the same time, he told the symposium, "it is clear that the authors embrace the Mormon lifestyle as an idealization of the perfect American lifestyle. The authors are not making fun of the perfection of the Mormons and so it is not anti-Mormon by being a mockery of Mormon life. They embrace the perfection of this lifestyle. However, the authors think that the theology is crazy."

Parker and Stone defend their portrayal of Mormonism in the episode's DVD commentary. "There were a lot of Mormons in Colorado—I guess because it's so close to Utah—where I grew up," Parker says. "My ex-girlfriend in high school was Mormon, and I had to go to her family's house for Family Home Evening a few times. . . . I'd always sort of said basically every Mormon I know is a really good person and really nice. And I can't really rip on them because it's obviously working because they're good people and nice people. . . . The hardest thing about this episode was that we were doing stuff and saying, 'Here's what Mormons think and here is the Mormon religion,' but everyone thought we were just making stuff up to be funny. But we're not. We're not making stuff up in this show."

Matt agreed. "A lot of people, especially like the younger audience, they never loved the more political or religious shows much. . . . The younger audience is like, well, that wasn't that funny, you know. Because they just didn't get it. But the people who thought this episode was really funny were Mormons, because they knew all this stuff and were told this stuff from the time they were little. And seeing this stuff animated just helped kind of showing them how dumb all this stuff is."

Jews. Kyle, who is Jewish, is frequently ambivalent about his faith and is often the target of crude, anti-Semitic taunts from Eric. When a whiny, complaining cousin from Connecticut comes to stay with him, Kyle is so embarrassed by the boy's stereotypical behavior that he feels he is in danger of becoming a self-hating Jew. Yet in another episode, Kyle enters a Hasidic yeshiva in New York—"The Jewleeard School"—to please his grandmother's spirit. He flees home with his brother Ike to save the adopted toddler from his scheduled circumcision, which he confuses with more drastic surgery. In another episode, confused when Father Maxi tells him that, as a Jew, he is doomed to an afterlife in the lake of fire, the boy is set straight by his parents. First, his mother tells him that Jews don't share the Catholic view of hell. Their faith, his father, Gerald, a lawyer, explains, "is all about being a good person now. You see, Christians use hell as a way of scaring people into believing what they believe. But to believe in something just because you're scared of the consequences if you don't is no reason to believe in something."

In another episode, Kyle brings Kenny, a Christian, to a "Jew Scouts" camp in the woods, for a celebration called "Jewbilee." Coached by Kyle's family on the drive, Kenny has to pretend to be Jewish, but is discovered and expelled from the camp. The convoluted plot involves a meeting of Jewish elders in one of the cabins—likely a reference to the anti-Semitic canard *The Protocols of the Elders of Zion*— a scene in the show in which fractured Hebrew is spoken. Later, the elders and the scouts sit around the fire, worshiping Moses and conjuring up his image. "All debts forgiven and all slaves freed," Moses intones, as everyone else sings "Kumbaya." In the end, Kenny foils a plot to destroy the world's Jews. "You know," says Kyle, "it's fine to have your own beliefs and your own traditions. But as soon as you start excluding people from your ways, only because of their race, you become a separatist," which he denigrates in a typically rude way. Kyle even questions the existence of God, to the point of renouncing his faith, when his tormenter Eric inherits a million dollars from his grandmother while Kyle gets a hemorrhoid. His parents' account of the book of Job, at his bedside, only exacerbates his feelings.

In August 2004, *South Park* released a DVD featuring three recent episodes dealing with faith, including their satire of *The Passion of the Christ*, mischievously timed to coincide with the DVD release of Mel Gibson's controversial blockbuster. An accompanying press release boasted that *South Park* "is one of the few shows to explore different religious themes in an intelligent and boldly irreverent way." Talk about understatement. *The Passion* episode, which originally aired while the film was still in theaters, was irresistible to the Gibson movie's critics. "Combining pop culture with that religiosity—there's great comedy there," Stone told the *Los Angeles Times*. Much of the episode, called "The Passion of the Jew," deals with the film's impact, stoking Eric's anti-Semitism and Kyle's Jewish guilt. After seeing the movie, Eric is inspired to organize a Nazi-like pogrom against the town's Jews, and Kyle demands that his congregation apologize for deicide. The episode also portrays Gibson as certifiably insane, less absurd in light of his 2006 drunk driving arrest and diatribe. In one scene he is shown playing the banjo in his underpants, singing "Jesus, How I Love You." However, the conclusion of the episode was anything but absurd. Stan says, "If you want to be Christian, that's cool, but you should follow what Jesus taught instead of how he got killed. Focusing on how he got killed is what people did in the Dark Ages, and it ends up with really bad results." People in the crowd agree. "We shouldn't focus our faith on the torture and execution of Christ," says one. "We shouldn't rely on violence to inspire faith," another agrees.

The South Park *Gospel.* The sermonette at the end of *The Passion* parody is typical of prime-time cartoon convention. For about twenty-six minutes on most *South Park* episodes, every subject on earth is fair game for ruthless lampooning. Then just before the final credits comes a two- or three-sentence moral lesson, usually voiced directly to the audience by Stan or Kyle, the voices of Christian and Jewish reason, respectively. These messages seem almost out of context and character, preceded by the words, "I think the lesson here is . . . ," or, "You know, I learned something today." They range from sincere to saccharine, although they are sometimes undercut with irony, what resentful comedy writers call "the take-back." After rejecting his baby brother Ike because he is both adopted and Canadian, Kyle observes, "Having a little brother is a special thing." In the episode dealing with Ike's belated circumcision, Kyle says, "Family isn't about whose blood you have. It's about who you care about." Or the mad scientist whose cloning experiment has gone hideously and hilariously awry concludes, "Perhaps we shouldn't be toying with God's creations. Perhaps we should leave nature alone." Some contemporary animators resent this convention. Stone told me he and Parker based these sometimes-didactic closing messages on early animated films for children. The lesson, he insists, is "not preachy, but it deals with ethics and morals, because that's where comedy comes from. It gives the show coherence."

In the end, the *South Park* gospel is simple, the watered-down antithesis of evangelical Protestant belief in salvation through grace, rather than through works: be a good person, be nice to others, try your best, and don't worry too much about the hereafter. As Butters puts it when Stan makes a fruitless effort in a good cause, "You gave it your best shot, and that's all Jesus asks of you." Or as Randy, Stan's dad, says in another episode, "The only heaven we can hope for is one here on earth, now. We should stop waiting to get into heaven, and start trying to create it." When the kids fail to build their own ladder to heaven, Stan says, "We think heaven is not a place you get to. Maybe heaven is just an idea, a frame of mind. . . . Maybe heaven is this moment right now."

At times, however, *South Park* characters can sound like angry, Old Testament prophets. One perceptive young girl, Wendy Testaburger, observes that "lewdness and shallowness are being exalted" by the celebrity culture. In a tirade worthy of the prophet Jeremiah, her father shouts, "Women are being marketed to by corrupt, moralless corporations." Fathers and mothers are allowing their preteen daughters to be sexualized by a stupid, superficial celebrity like Paris Hilton and her pop diva contemporaries, he says. Even the series degenerate, Mr. Slave, is outraged: "Parents, if you don't teach your children that people like Paris Hilton are to be despised, where are they going to learn it? You have to be the ones to make sure your daughters aren't looking up to the wrong people." No one was more surprised to hear this pulpit-worthy denunciation than Donald Wildmon, of the American Family Association, when I read it to him. "Preaching by *South Park?*" he said. "That doesn't sound right. That's strange."

But it is not so strange, in light of Janet Pantland's academic paper for the University of South Africa on *South Park*'s first five seasons. The show, she wrote, essentially

> tears down our pre-programmed answers and reactions, forcing us to re-evaluate religious issues. For many people religion has become habit. We have the right answers to the

right questions, we know what to do and when to do it, but we do not actually live religion. *South Park* questions our pat answers. It does not say they are wrong, it just forces us to actually think about them while we are reciting them. It takes away our religious crutches, forcing a radical examination of our own religious lives. If your own religious faith and moral principles are firm, it can be refreshingly unlimited, revealing and perceptive.

Scientology and Tom Cruise. Two high-profile controversies in the 2005–2006 season involving religion returned the show to the headlines. *South Park*'s reputation has always been that of an equal opportunity offender. The producers "pretty much go after every religion—Christians, Jews, Mormons," said one fan, Jeremy Smith, of Winter Park, Florida. "It's typical comedy; they don't care about offending anybody." In the fall of 2005, the show took on Scientology and its most visible proponent, Tom Cruise. When they did, the show's writers and its creators went into overdrive. Stan Marsh is mistaken by Scientologists for the reincarnation of the religion's founder, the science fiction writer L. Ron Hubbard, and the boy is given a behind-the-scenes look at the spiritual path made famous by Hollywood celebrities. For the next twenty minutes, the religion is described as a "global scam" and ripped to shreds. Objects of ridicule include Scientology's complex, cosmic cartoon origins involving an evil, alien lord in a galaxy far away, and disembodied, wandering souls frozen and dropped into volcanoes, according to the *South Park* montage. Another target is the religion's money-grubbing levels of enlightenment. Not a single redeeming aspect of the faith—whose adherents include Cruise, John Travolta, Kirstie Alley, and Nancy Cartwright (Bart Simpson's voice)—was presented. For a time, the words "This is what Scientologists actually believe" appeared on screen. Cruise is presented as being made so insecure by Stan's comment that he is a mediocre actor that he takes refuge in the boy's closet and refuses to come out. Thus, the refrain throughout the remainder of the episode is, "Tom Cruise, come out of the closet," clearly a reference to speculation about Cruise's sexual orientation. The last lines of the episode, repeated three times, are a challenge from Stan to Cruise and the Scientologists: "I'm not scared of you. Sue me!"

Initially, the episode was "no problem at all" for Comedy Central or its attorneys, according to Stone, who recounted the history at a July 13, 2006, press conference with television critics in Hollywood. "We were actually really surprised. We kind of avoided it for a long time because of Scientology's reputation for taking you to court. And when we ran the idea past Comedy Central, the lawyers, at least, they said, 'Yeah, that's cool.' So getting it on the air wasn't really a big deal." But Stone acknowledged that its helter-skelter production schedule, turning an episode around in a week, worked in their favor. "If the show sat on the shelf, so to speak, for a couple of months before it went on the air, I don't think it would ever have made it to the air."

When the episode was broadcast, it turned out to be a very big deal for Cruise. The reaction of the notoriously thin-skinned actor and his notoriously litigious religion was predictable—if largely delayed. Initially, they succeeded in blocking the episode from being aired in England. Then, in early 2006, the week it was set to rerun in the United States, longtime cast member Isaac Hayes, who plays the wise if lascivious cafeteria chef (with a taste for group sex), resigned from the cast. "There is a place in this world for satire, but there is a time when satire ends and intolerance and bigotry towards religious beliefs of others begins," said Hayes, who was raised as a Baptist but is a practicing and outspoken Scientologist. "Religious beliefs are sacred to people, and at all times should be respected and honored." Parker and Stone, no shrinking violets, shot back. "In ten years and over 150 episodes of *South Park*, Isaac never had a problem with the show making fun of Christians, Muslims, Mormons or Jews," Stone said in a statement issued by Comedy Central. "He got a sudden case of religious sensitivity when it was his religion featured on the show." Still, Stone added, "of course we will release Isaac from his contract, and we wish him well." Later Stone told the Associated Press that he and Parker "never heard a peep out of Isaac in any way until we did Scientology. He wants a different standard for religions other than his own, and to me that is where intolerance and bigotry begin. . . . This is 100 percent having to do with his faith of Scientology. . . . He has no problem—and he's cashed plenty of checks—with our show making fun of Christians."

Parker told the Web site ContactMusic.com that for years he and Stone avoided the subject of Scientology to avoid offending Hayes. "To be honest," he said in the interview, "what kept us from doing it before was Isaac Hayes. We knew he was a Scientologist and he's an awesome guy. We're like, 'Let's just avoid that for now.'" Ultimately, Parker said, "we just had to tell Isaac, 'Dude, we totally love working with you, and this is nothing personal, it's just we're *South Park*, and if we don't do this, we're belittling everything else we've ripped on.'" At the July critics' press conference in Hollywood, Stone added that Hayes came to them after the episode aired in November, for a two-hour meeting: "He asked us to pull the episode off the air, to go to the network and pull the episode off the air, don't ever have it made into DVDs." Parker, at the same press conference, said, "We knew what might happen when we made the episode. But we didn't want to be hypocrites. We always say, 'Hey, it's all okay to make fun of, or none of it is. Everything has got to be okay."

To be fair, no other religion sniped at previously on *South Park* received the unrelenting negative treatment meted out to Scientology in the episode. And in fact, Parker's comments notwithstanding, this was actually the second time *South Park* had taken a shot at the religion. The precursor came in a July 4, 2001, episode called "Super Best Friends," in which the boys' fascination with the magician David Blaine draws them into a cult—"Blainetology"—based on the celebrity and his best-selling book. In the end, the spell is broken, and Stan declares that cults are bad: "They promise you hope, happiness, and maybe even an afterlife, but in return they demand you pay money. Any religion that requires you to pay money to move up and learn its tenets is wrong." Does that sound familiar?

Regardless, the 2006 battle escalated, as some with longtime grievances against *South Park* joined in. "I'm glad Mr. Hayes is finally recognizing *South Park*'s bigotry and intolerance toward religion, and hope it is not just because his own beliefs were attacked on the show. Christians have been outraged with the show's handling of their faith, especially Trey Parker's portrayal of Jesus Christ, since day one," said Focus on the Family's Bob Waliszewski. "However, comments by Matt Stone raise an important question. Why has it become acceptable in Hollywood to completely skewer the Christian faith, but many other religions are considered taboo? Hayes's current opinion of the show as out of bounds is entirely accurate, and he should be commended for seeing it as such, despite the amount of time it took for him to come to this conclusion. Hopefully, this decision will go a long way to getting this trash pulled from the tube once and for all."

On March 15, 2006, the night of the scheduled rerun, the Scientology episode did not air. Without explanation, another episode was run, this one showcasing the libidinous side of Chef's character, as well as some scatological material. Speculation about that decision, in newspapers on both sides of the Atlantic and widely on the Internet, shone a spotlight on the corporate media culture. Cruise, it was alleged, threatened to withhold publicity support for *Mission: Impossible 3,* for which Paramount Studios had high hopes for the summer. Comedy Central's parent, Viacom, is also the corporate parent of Paramount. Cruise, Paramount, and Viacom all refuted these conspiracy theories. (Viacom severed its relationship with Cruise in August 2006.) At first, Comedy Central spokesmen said that Parker and Stone would have no further comment on the controversy. Of course, the PR people were dreaming. Employing the jargon of Scientology, Parker and Stone issued a statement to the entertainment newspaper *Daily Variety:* "So, Scientology, you may have won THIS battle, but the million-year war for earth has just begun! Temporarily anozinizing our episode will NOT stop us from keeping Thetans forever trapped in your pitiful man-bodies. Curses and drat! You have obstructed us for now, but your feeble bid to save humanity will fail! Hail Xenu." citing the evil galactic figure in Scientology. The *South Park* creators signed the statement "Trey Parker and Matt Stone, servants to the dark lord Xenu."

In the end, it's difficult to say how much of this was a Tom Cruise issue and how much was a Scientology issue. However, this much is clear. What the *South Park* gang failed to realize is that America's unassailable religion is corporatism and its unholy son, synergy. The commandment that is inviolable is: Thou shalt not jeopardize the commercial prospects of another business unit. As Stan Marsh might say, "I think the lesson here is that a minor profit center, like a single cable series, is no match for a major profit center like a movie studio with a potential summer block-buster." But if this skirmish was lost, the war between the *South Park* boys and Scientology—not to mention Comedy Central censors and the religious community at large—was just getting into gear. After making their blustering threat, Stone told *Rolling Stone*, they were in a corner. "Now we have to answer in some way," he said. "We just haven't figured out how." It didn't take long. "We were like, 'Okay, game on,'" Parker told the Holly-wood press conference. As Parker, Stone, and their creative crew readied the next salvo, one could easily imagine the conversation between the show's creators, on the one hand, and the lawyers and standards and practices people from Comedy Central, on the other: *Are you guys going to use the word "Scientology" in the episode? No. Are you going to mention Tom Cruise or any other celebrity? No. Okay boys, then do your worst.*

Their worst turned out to be exquisite revenge. The follow-ing week's episode, using previously recorded and reedited dia-logue from Hayes, had Chef brainwashed by a group called the "Super Adventure Club," clearly a stand-in for Scientology. The "adventurers" lionize their founder, a deceased author; use a mind-numbing device that obviously represents the Scientolo-gists' infamous E-meter; and adhere to a weird cosmic theory that justifies their central tenet: child molestation. During the explanation of their theology, words appear on the screen, explain-ing, "This is actually what the Super Adventure Club believes," just as they did in the original Scientology episode. Under the spell of this cult of predatory pedophiles, Chef makes a series of grotesque, explicit propositions and invitations to his beloved but bewildered young friends at school. In vain, the *South Park* kids try to extricate their friend from the "fruity little club" that has stolen him away. In the end, the Hayes character is struck by lightning, set afire, dropped down a ravine, impaled on a tree branch, and ripped apart by wild animals. Later, members of the club reanimate him into a child-molesting version of Darth Vader.

Islam. Perversely, Parker and Stone seemed miffed when in February 2006 a dozen cartoons in a Danish newspaper making fun of the Muslim prophet Muhammad, which were widely reprinted in Europe, set off worldwide riots in the Islamic world and Europe. Seeing the demonstrations while channel surfing, Stone leaped to an obvious—if incorrect—conclusion. He told *Rolling Stone* magazine, "I was like, 'Oh, [expletive], look what we did! We have to get on the phone to a lawyer!'" Years earlier, the Prophet appeared for the first time in a *South Park* episode called "Super Best Friends," a wacky paean to ecumenism. Together with Moses, Buddha, Lao Tzu, and Joseph Smith, Muhammad had superpowers—in his case the ability to shoot fire from his hands, incinerating cultists, and to turn himself into a badger. The Prophet explained that the religious figures were joined by "the desire to fight for justice." The reaction at the time from the Muslim world? Nothing. The episode is rotated through the normal syndication schedule and appeared on a subsequent DVD, without protest or controversy. "We had an animated Muhammad five years ago," Parker told *Time* magazine on March 13, 2006. "But people say, 'Oh, yeah, that's just *South Park*.'" A key difference, of course, was that the Danish cartoons were critical of Muhammad, while the portrayal in *South Park* was benign, if not positive. It still rankled, Stone told *Rolling Stone*. "I was like, 'Danish cartoons? That's our competition? The [expletive] Danish?'"

Perhaps emboldened by a recent Peabody Award, Parker and Stone proceeded to pick their biggest fight to date, making up for lost time on the subject of Islam. In a two-part story line, *South Park* presented the controversy over Muhammad's image in the form of a show-within-a-show. In this case, it was centered on an episode of Fox's *Family Guy*, a series that the Eric character—like Stone, Parker, and other animators around Hollywood—apparently loathes. ("The day that episode aired," Parker told television critics in Hollywood in July 2006, "we got flowers from *The Simpsons*. . . .

We got calls from *King of the Hill* saying we were doing God's work.") In the *South Park* episode, a rumor circulates that *Family Guy* is about to broadcast a show that includes the image of Muhammad, which South Park residents are convinced will result in a Muslim attack on their town. In a sensitivity session on Islam the next day, Mr. Garrison, the boys' teacher, explains that the reasons Muslim men hate Americans is that they live in sand and are sexually deprived by their religion. Kyle is not convinced that the threat is realistic. "Come on, people," he says. "Do you really think anybody is going to be that pissed off about a cartoon?"

Nonetheless, rather than defending free speech and expression, town residents resolve to avoid any retribution by literally burying their heads in the sand, albeit with snorkels, to demonstrate their sensitivity. While there is a reprieve when Fox blocks out the controversial image in the first *Family Guy* episode-within-the-episode, the network president then announces that he is powerless to prevent *Family Guy*'s writers from allowing the Prophet's image to appear in the second episode. Kyle goes to Hollywood, where, with the assistance of a crudely drawn Bart Simpson, he persuades the network to allow the image to appear. When it comes to satire, Kyle says, "if you don't show Muhammad, then you've made a distinction between what is OK to poke fun at and what isn't. Either it's all OK, or none of it is. Do the right thing." While in the fictional *South Park* episode Fox executives are ultimately persuaded to show the image, Comedy Central's real counterparts were not. Instead, the night of the broadcast the screen went black with the words, "Comedy Central has refused to broadcast an image of Muhammad on their network." Without elaboration, Comedy Central released a statement that said, "In light of recent world events, we feel we made the right decision."

Despite the recent battle over Scientology, and the worldwide demonstrations against publication of the Danish cartoons, Stone told the TV critics, "I was absolutely sure, I was a hundred percent sure that Comedy Central would have let us do that because of our track record, because of all the other things we had done, because of the way we were going to do it. . . . Comedy Central was going to be our teammate on this." As in the case of the Scientology controversy, Parker and Stone had more to say on the subject in a subsequent episode. In response to *Family Guy's* broadcast of Muhammad's image, Osama bin Laden's second-in-command, Ayman al-Zawahiri, retaliates with his own blasphemous cartoon, one in which Jesus defecates on George W. Bush and the American flag. What hits the president and the flag quickly hit the fan among *South Park* viewers. With obvious sarcasm, William Donohue of the Catholic League demanded that *South Park's* creators resign out of principle for being censored, according to the Associated Press. "The ultimate hypocrite is not Comedy Central. That's their decision not to show the image of Muhammad or not. It's Parker and Stone," Donohue said. "Like little whores, they'll sit there and grab the bucks. They'll sit there and they'll whine and they'll take their shot at Jesus. That's their stock in trade." On CNN, he added, "They take a cheap shot at Christ during Holy Week, and they think that we're going to sit around and smile about it. . . . Matt Stone and Trey Parker are whores. They are prostitutes. . . . They're cowards. . . . If they're men of principle, they should resign immediately and say, 'Listen, this is out of character. We're not going to put up with this.'" Stone and Parker, discussing the issue months later with the television critics, did not disagree. "That's the point," Stone said, of the network's hypocrisy. "It's open season on Jesus." Parker agreed: "You can do anything you want to Jesus." The lesson, Parker said, is that "if the Catholics don't want us ripping Jesus anymore, they should just threaten you with violence, and they'll get their way. That's why it is such a slippery slope and such a dangerous path to go down."

Religious Censorship. Parker and Stone had the last word (to date) on the censorship issue, according to the July 13, 2006, *Daily Variety.* The pair refused to discuss future projects with Comedy Central unless they agreed to show the original Tom Cruise episode, which the network did on July 19. To drive home their point, the duo made the episode, "Trapped in the Closet," the series' only submission for an Emmy nomination—which it received. (*The Simpsons* won in the best animated series category, prompting show-runner Al Jean to quip, "I guess this is what happens when you don't mock Scientology.") "It's true we are not as big as Tom Cruise, but we've done two movies for Viacom and 10 years of *South Park* episodes, and this has been our home," Stone told *Variety.* "If they hadn't put this episode back on the air, we'd have had serious issues, and we wouldn't be doing anything else with them. . . . We've been through a trifecta of annoyances. The 'Bloody Mary' episode angered Catholics. And we had a big fight when we wanted to show Muhammad." Stone repeated his belief that Cruise and Paramount were behind the earlier decision to yank the Scientology episode: "I only know what we were told, that people involved with 'MI3' wanted the episode off the air and that is why Comedy Central had to do it. I don't know why else it would have been pulled." The fight over the Muhammad episodes was still on their minds. "The mantra has always been everything is fair game," Stone said, but he believed that the Comedy Central chief who insisted the images of the Prophet be blacked out was mistaken. "I love Doug Herzog, but I think he's dead wrong and made a totally cowardly decision," Stone said. "*Harper's* recently published the Danish cartoons, and nobody got blown up. The magazine asked us for our uncensored image of Muhammad, and Comedy Central refused." The network declined comment, *Variety* reported.

Part of the "anything else" the partners threatened not to do with their corporate parent involved an appearance of Parker with Comedy Central executives at the Television Critics Association visit to Hollywood later that same day, July 13, at the Ritz-Carlton Hotel. The purpose was to promote the show's upcoming tenth season and a special DVD release. On stage with Stone and Parker were Doug Herzog and Comedy Central spokesman Tom Fox. Stone kicked off the question-and-answer session deadpanning, "First of all, we can't take any questions about Tom Cruise or Scientology or *South Park*." And then they proceeded to talk a good deal about Cruise, Scientology, Muhammad—and corporate censorship. Stone said that he and Parker had not been prepared to quit over the Cruise controversy. They had some leverage with the parent company. "We have a couple of movies with Viacom, and it's tough to go to work for people you think may be holding one of your episodes hostage. But that's sort of water under the bridge now because it's going back on the air." Parker said he was not surprised that the episode had been nominated for an Emmy. "You can't pick anything where people are more on your side. This entire city—except Scientology—were like 'Yeah! Go get 'em!'" Stone said they had struck a rich vein with Scientology. "It's like a field of flowers to run in, for comedians. There's a lot of funny stuff that is there to be made fun of that some people just won't go to. For us, it's material."

Comedy Central representatives alternated between appearing lame and game at the press conference, explaining why they pulled the rerun of the Scientology episode and then why they permitted it to air. Fox, a spokesman for the cable network, said the episode was pulled so they could choose another one as a tribute to Hayes. "That's our story and we're sticking with it," he said. "This episode just happens to be rotating back in." Nicely done, Stone piped up. After the session, Herzog told Lisa de Moraes of the *Washington Post*, "We reserve the right to air them when and where we see fit."

"So there's two things we can't do on Comedy Central," Parker said, "show Muhammad and Tom Cruise." Stone was more concerned about Muhammad. "We have this really strong political and philosophical position on the Muhammad controversy, and no one wants to talk about that. Everyone just wants to talk about Tom Cruise." Their original decision, he said, was innocuous. "We wanted to make Muhammad's image just standing there, totally harmless," and he and Parker were "one hundred percent sure" Comedy Central would back them. Instead, said Parker, "a new taboo was created out of nothing." Herzog said the decision to block the image was a "judgment made on behalf of a big media company," and, in a perfect world, he would have liked to air the episode with the image. He admitted that it was possible that "history might show we overreacted—and we're willing to live with that. . . . The ramifications are Matt and Trey are pissed off at you and Matt calling you a coward in *Daily Variety*." Stone corrected the executive, slightly, saying he called the decision cowardly.

Then Herzog joked that the Muslim prophet's image was still there, "underneath the black screen," adding, "We're looking forward to the day when we can uncover it."

When I visit churches to talk about *The Simpsons,* often on Sunday mornings or afternoons, I try to make the case that the show is sympathetic to sincere faith, if not to organized religion. On these occasions I will often conclude by asking those in the pews or the social hall to give the show a chance. Invariably when I do this, the episode airing that evening will be raunchy in the extreme, with nothing positive to say about religion. With *South Park,* I would never urge a congregation member to watch the show. And don't wait for a *South Park* Sunday school study guide from me or from the publisher of this book.

On balance, I think the newfound freedom created by *The Simpsons* to portray religion is a good thing, but not everyone agrees. "I think there is tastelessness out there," Ron Buford, a lay minister with the United Church of Christ, told the Hackensack *Record.* "Even though people might have the license and the freedom that permits free speech, it is unfortunate when the use of religious symbols shows a complete disrespect for the culture and the people." Not that Buford endorses legal restrictions that would outlaw religious satires, regardless how tasteless. "I can't stand for freedom of speech on my side and not stand for freedom of speech on their side," he told the paper. Robert Hodgson, dean of the Nida Institute for Biblical Scholarship in New York, agreed: "Part of living in Western culture is that in the public square everything can be analyzed, accepted and rejected." Other religious denominations have become inured to the lampoons. "The Roman Catholic response to a television series, for example, is generally pretty mild and pretty timid partly because there is a very long history of representing the Catholic Church and the Catholic clergy in radio and film," Hodgson told the paper.

In a March 10, 2006, column in the *Chicago Sun-Times,* Cathleen Falsani wondered whether everything is now fair game, whether *anything* could be considered blasphemous or sacrilegious. After all, the irreverent quarterly *Heeb: The New Jew Review,* showed a topless Virgin Mary when it took its shot at *The Passion of the Christ*. But the venerable magazine *Wittenburg Door* still draws the line at "Jesus on the cross" jokes, editor Robert Durden told Falsani. So she, too, consulted Hodgson, who suggested it had a lot to do with perception. "Historically, blasphemy has always been identified with criticizing, denigrating, or marginalizing the sacred, and in Jewish and Christian tradition it's connected with profaning the name of God, or persons such as Jesus or the Holy Spirit, or even teaching connected with the God of the Bible," Hodgson told her. "It's the kind of categorical expression for vast disrespect of the most sacred and holy things in our faith." When holy symbols are "put back into popular culture and the media in ways that don't seem consistent with their sacredness, their holiness, that's where blasphemy occurs," he said. "The test of blasphemy is often not whether we as the consumers feel a T-shirt of an icon or a statue is misplaced or misused. The real test is what do members of that community of faith think?"

For better or worse, the genie is out of the bottle, the lid to Pandora's box has been lifted, and religion is now considered fair game for parody, at least in animated comedies. Sometimes it's treated with grudging, if playful, respect; sometimes it's treated with nothing more than childish cheap shots. But in every case this shows that what was once confined to discussion within churches, temples, and classrooms has now entered the unhallowed arena of popular culture. As I suggested earlier, this portrayal of faith and religion—whether in snippets or full-length episodes—provides an opportunity to begin meaningful discussions.

Notes

Where no citation is given, the quotation comes from an interview or personal conversation between the author and the subject.

Introduction

1. Jon Horowitz, "Mmm . . . Television: A Study of the Audience of *The Simpsons*," unpublished paper, Rutgers University, courtesy of the author.
2. Todd Brewster, "How TV Shaped America," *Life*, April 1999.
3. Kurt Andersen, "Animation Nation," *New Yorker*, June 16, 1997.
4. Robert Thompson, quoted in the *Orlando Sentinel*, December 2, 2000.
5. James Sharpe, quoted in the *Star Ledger* (Newark, NJ), June 20, 1990.
6. William Bennett, quoted in the *Seattle Times*, August 19, 1990.
7. Barbara Bush, quoted in "And on the Seventh Day, Matt Created Bart," *Loaded Magazine*, August 1996.
8. Reinhold Niebuhr, quoted in Conrad Hyers, *The Comic Vision and the Christian Faith: A Celebration of Life and Laughter* (New York: Pilgrim Press, 1981).
9. Hyers, *Comic Vision and the Christian Faith*.
10. Gerry Bowler, "God and *The Simpsons*: The Religious Life of an Animated Sitcom," academic paper presented October 1996 at "The Media and Family Values" seminar at Canadian Nazarene College, Calgary, Canada.
11. William Romanowski, *Pop Culture Wars: Religion and the Role of Entertainment in American Life* (Downers Grove, IL: InterVarsity Press, 1996).
12. Beth Keller, "The Gospel according to Bart: Examining the Religious Elements of *The Simpsons*," master's thesis, Regent University, College of Communication and the Arts, 1992, courtesy of the author.
13. Mike Scully, quoted in "The Gospel According to Homer," by Bob von Sternberg, *Minneapolis Star Tribune*, May 30, 1998.
14. "No Sacred Cows for Groening," Associated Press, April 24, 1999.
15. John Heeren, "Religion in *The Simpsons*," in *The Simpsons and Philosophy: The D'oh! of Homer*, ed. William Irwin et al. (Chicago: Open Court Press, 2001). An early version of this paper was presented at the Society for the Scientific Study of Religion conference in Houston, Texas, in October 2000.

16. *The Door*, November–December 1999.
17. David Dark, "The Steeple and the Gargoyle—Celebrating *The Simpsons*," *PRISM*, July–August 1997.
18. David Landry, quoted in Bob von Sternberg, "The Gospel according to Homer," *Twin Cities Star-Tribune*, May 30, 1998.
19. Paul Cantor, "The Simpsons: Atomistic Politics and the Nuclear Family," *Political Theory* 27, no. 6 (December 1999).

Chapter 1: Divine Imagery

1. William A. Dembski, *Intelligent Design: The Bridge between Science and Theology* (Downers Grove, IL: InterVarsity Press, 1999).
2. "Matt Groening: The *Mother Jones* Interview," *Mother Jones*, March–April 1999.
3. Eric Michael Mazur and Kate McCarthy, eds., *God in the Details: American Religion in Popular Culture* (New York: Routledge, 2000).
4. Abraham Heschel, *The Prophet* (Philadelphia: Jewish Publication Society of America, 1962).
5. David Owen, "Crazy for the Simpsons," *TV Guide*, Jan. 3–9, 1998.
6. Mazur et al., *God in the Details*.
7. Keller, "The Gospel according to Bart."
8. Gerry Bowler, quoted in Douglas Todd, "The Simpsons as TV's Holy Family," *Vancouver Sun*, December 1996.
9. Elton Trueblood, *Humor of Christ* (New York: Harper & Row, 1964).

Chapter 2: Personal Prayer

1. Lee Strobel, *What Jesus Would Say* (Grand Rapids: Zondervan Publishing House, 1994).
2. Robert Thompson, quoted in the *Ventura County Star*, "The Gospel of Homer," by Tom Kishen, September 4, 1999.
3. Ibid.
4. Strobel, *What Jesus Would Say*.
5. Mazur et al., *God in the Details*.
6. Heeren, "Religion in *The Simpsons*."
7. Wendy Kaminer, *Sleeping with Extra-Terrestrials: The Rise of Irrationalism and Perils of Piety* (New York: Vintage Books, 2000).

Chapter 3: The Evangelical Next Door

1. Gerry Bowler, quoted in Les Sillars, "The Last Christian TV Family in America," *Alberta Report*, October 21, 1996.
2. Michael Weisskopf, quoted in the *Washington Post*, February 1, 1993.
3. Harry Shearer interview in *The Door*, May–June 1999.
4. Frederica Mathewes-Green, "Ned Flanders, My Hero," on Beliefnet.com, February 10, 2000.
5. David Landry, quoted in von Sternberg, "Gospel according to Homer."

Chapter 4: The Church and the Preacher

1. Matt Groening, *The Simpsons Guide to Springfield* (New York: HarperCollins, 1998).
2. Mazur et al., *God in the Details*.
3. Ibid.

Chapter 5: Heaven, Hell, and the Devil

1. Pope John Paul II, quoted by the Associated Press, July 28, 1999.

Chapter 7: The Bible

1. "Public Perceptions about the Bible in the Twenty-First Century," survey released by Zondervan Publishing, November 15, 2000.
2. Groening, *Simpsons Guide to Springfield*.

Chapter 8: Catholics

1. William Bennett, quoted in the *Seattle Times*, August 19, 1990.
2. Mark Fischer, quoted in the *Ventura County Star*, "The Gospel of Homer," by Tom Kishen, September 4, 1999.
3. Cardinal John O'Connor, quoted on the Catholic League Web site (www.catholicleague.org/faqs.htm).
4. The Catholic League statement of purpose, from the Catholic League Web site.
5. Letter by Thomas Chavez, quoted in *The Catalyst*, January–February 1999.
6. "*The Simpsons* Gets Too Cute," *The Catalyst*, January–February 1999.
7. "*The Simpsons* Offends Again," *The Catalyst*, March 1999.
8. "Rosenberg on TV: Fox Does Have Standards—And Double Standards at That," *Los Angeles Times*, June 2, 1999.
9. Ibid.
10. Ibid.
11. Ibid.
12. "Fox Gets Message on *Simpsons*," *The Catalyst*, July–August 1999.
13. George Weigel, speaking at a conference sponsored by the Ethics and Public Policy Center at Prouts Neck, Maine, September 1999.

Chapter 9: The Jews

1. Jack Wertheimer, speaking at a conference sponsored by the Ethics and Public Policy Center at Prouts Neck, Maine, September 1999.
2. Mel Brooks, quoted in *The Big Little Book of Jewish Wit and Wisdom* (New York: Black Dog & Leventhal Publishers, 2000).
3. Matt Groening, quoted in "Life in Hell," by Alan Paul, *Flux*, September 30, 1995.

Chapter 11. Miscellaneous

1. Al Jean, quoted in Joe Rhodes, "Flash! 24 Simpson Stars Reveal Themselves," *TV Guide*, October 21, 2000.

2. Matt Groening, quoted in Rhodes, "Flash!"
3. Prithvi Raj Singh, quoted in John Dart, "TV's Most Religious Family?" *Christian Century*, January 31, 2001.

Chapter 13: The Creators

1. Matt Groening interview with Andrew Duncan, *Radio Times*, September 18–24, 1999.
2. Matt Groening interview, "Influences: From Yesterday to Today," CBS, August 27, 1999.
3. James L. Brooks interview, ibid.
4. Matt Groening, quoted in "The Making of The Simpsons," by Joe Rhodes, *Entertainment Weekly*, May 18, 1990.
5. Harry Shearer interview, *FilmForce*, April 25, 2000 (www.filmforce.ign.com/chats/harryshearer.shtml).
6. "Matt Groening: The *Mother Jones* Interview," *Mother Jones*, March–April 1999.
7. Matt Groening interview with Isis Sauceda, *La Opinion*, November 30–December 10, 2000.
8. Deborah Groening, quoted in Paul Andrews, "The Groening of America," *Seattle Times*, August 19, 1990.
9. Matt Groening interview with Carina Chocano, Salon.com, January 30, 2001.
10. George Meyer interview, "Taking Humor Seriously—George Meyer, the Funniest Man behind the Funniest Show on TV," by David Owen, *New Yorker*, March 13, 2000.

Chapter 14: Conclusion

1. Francis Chan, in the *Ventura County Star*, "The Gospel of Homer," by Tom Kishen, September 4, 1999.
2. Cantor, "The Simpsons: Atomistic Politics."
3. Jonah Goldberg, "Homer Never Nods: The Importance of *The Simpsons*," *National Review*, May 1, 2000.
4. Barbara Curtis, "Are the Simpsons 'Okily Dokily'?" *Plain Truth*, January–February 2001.
5. Walt Davis et al., *Watching What We Watch: Prime-Time Television through the Lens of Faith* (Louisville, KY: Geneva Press, 2001).
6. Mike Budd et al., *Consuming Environments: Television and Commercial Culture* (Piscataway, NJ: Rutgers University Press, 1999).
7. Davis et al., *Watching What We Watch*.
8. Mazur et al., *God in the Details*.
9. Joseph Bastien, "Humor and Satire," in *The Encyclopedia of Religion*, ed. Mircea Eliade (New York: Macmillan, 1987).
10. Heeren, "Religion in *The Simpsons*."

Bibliography

Books

Budd, Mike, Steve Craig, and Clay Steinman. *Consuming Environments: Television and Commercial Culture*. Piscataway, NJ: Rutgers University Press. 1999.

Davis, Walter T. et al. *Watching What We Watch: Prime-Time Television through the Lens of Faith*. Louisville, KY: Geneva Press. 2001.

Dembski, William A. *Intelligent Design: The Bridge between Science and Theology*. Downers Grove, IL: InterVarsity Press. 1999.

Dossey, Larry, M.D. *Be Careful What You Pray For . . . You Just Might Get It*. San Francisco: HarperSanFrancisco. 1998.

Irwin, William, Mark T. Conard, and Aeon J. Skoble. *The Simpsons and Philosophy: The D'oh! of Homer*. Open Court. 2001.

Mazur, Eric Michael, and Kate McCarthy. *God in the Details: American Religion in Popular Culture*. Routledge. 2000.

Postman, Neil. *Amusing Ourselves to Death: Public Discourse in the Age of Show Business*. Penguin. 1985.

Romanowski, William D. *Pop Culture Wars: Religion and the Role of Entertainment in American Life*. Downers Grove, IL: InterVarsity Press. 1996.

———. *Eyes Wide Open: Looking for God in Popular Culture*. Brazos/Baker. 2001.

Strobel, Lee. *What Jesus Would Say*. Grand Rapids: Zondervan Publishing House. 1994.

Articles

Curtis, Barbara. "Are the Simpsons 'Okily Dokily'?" *Plain Truth*. January 2001.

Dark, David. "The Steeple and the Gargoyle—Celebrating the Simpsons." *PRISM*. July/August 1997.

Goldberg, Jonah. "Homer Never Nods: The Importance of *The Simpsons*." *National Review*. May 1, 2000.

Kisken, Tom. "The Gospel of Homer." *Ventura County Star*. September 4, 1999.

Mathewes-Green, Frederica. "Ned Flanders, My Hero." Beliefnet.com. February 2000.

302

McKenna, Kristine. "Matt Groening: The Genius Who Controls Bart Simpson (Yeah, Right!)" *My Creation*, May/June 2001.

Owen, David. "Taking Humor Seriously—George Meyer, the Funniest Man behind the Funniest Show on TV." *New Yorker.* March 13, 2000.

Sillars, Les. "The Last Christian TV Family in America." *Alberta Report.* October 21, 1996.

Todd, Douglas. "The Simpsons as TV's Holy Family." *Vancouver Sun.* December 1996.

Von Sternberg, Bob. "The Gospel according to Homer." *Twin Cities Star-Tribune.* May 5, 1998.

Academic Papers and Journal Articles

Bowler, Gerry. "God and *The Simpsons*: The Religious Life of an Animated Sitcom." Symposium on "The Media and Family Values" held at Canadian Nazarene College, Calgary in October 1996.

Cantor, Paul. "The Simpsons: Atomistic Politics and the Nuclear Family." *Political Theory.* December 1999.

Heeren, John. "Saints and Sinners in Springfield: Religion in *The Simpsons*." 2000 meeting of the Society for the Scientific Study of Religion.

Keller, Beth. "The Gospel according to Bart: Examining the Religious Elements of *The Simpsons*." Regent University, College of Communication and the Arts. September 29, 1992. Unpublished.

Trammell, Jim. "The Wages of Sin Is D'oh!: An Analysis of the Portrayals of Religion on *The Simpsons*." University of Georgia, Grady College of Journalism and Mass Communication, December 2000. Unpublished.

Acknowledgments

The reason I usually turn to the acknowledgments page of a book is to see if my name, or the name of anyone I know, is there. If that is what you are doing now, I'll do my best to see that you are not disappointed.

I first found the idea of writing books attractive because I liked the idea of working alone, of having the illusion of control in this small portion of my professional life. In contrast to writing for newspapers, magazines, radio, television, and film—all collaborative projects—this time it would be my show. Or so I thought. It puzzled me when, while searching for my own name in the back of books written by friends and colleagues, I would find page after page of names and institutions and expressions of gratitude.

Well, now I know. Even in a book this short, there are many people to thank. First, of course, I must thank my family. My children, Asher and Liza, got me started on this project, as I explained in the introduction, and since then they have tolerated my telling this story about them over and over again. My wife Sallie—the photographer Sarah M. Brown—has been supportive and encouraging throughout the process, and has assisted me in keeping my head from growing too large to fit through the doorways of our home. My in-laws, Joe and Charlotte Brown, good Presbyterians both, were my two most enthusiastic cheerleaders. Maryland Senator Paul Pinsky, my younger brother and one of my heroes, asked some hard questions and taught me, through his example, to recognize an opportunity and seize the moment.

Peter Brown, my good friend and former colleague at the *Orlando Sentinel*, is most responsible for launching this book. What began on one of our regular afternoon walks around the block as a general notion for an essay in his weekly editorial review section became a book proposal thanks to his wise judgment and experience. Our then *Sentinel* book editor, Nancy Pate, was never too busy to advise me about the ins and outs of the publishing industry. Hal Boedeker, the *Sentinel's* TV critic, a frequent lunch companion, and a perceptive sounding board, was also a great help as my valuable pipeline to the Television Critics semiannual meetings. Old China hand Fergus Bordewich, a better writer than I will ever be, was a great resource. My former *Sentinel* editor, Loraine O'Connell, edited much of the new material in the second edition. Thanks also to Jon Steinman, formerly with the *Sentinel* and now with Bloomberg News Service.

Brent Bierman, of Knight-Ridder-Tribune news service in Washington, DC, saw my original *Simpsons* essay and put it on the wire. My Internet friend, David Buckna, of the delightful religious trivia list "Sol O Mann Top 10," was one of the first people to see my *Sentinel* essay on the Internet and to encourage the idea of a book. In the years since then, he was always willing to steer me in the right direction.

I am most grateful to the creators of *The Simpsons* Archive Web site. Their meticulous research was invaluable, in particular their episode capsules. Jouni Paakkinen, Jordan Eisenberg, and Bruce Gomes, among many others, answered hundreds of my questions. When they didn't know an answer, they used their contacts to find it for me. Evan Dunlap, a fan's fan in Orlando, also had some good catches, as did Steve Mathewes-Green.

Even before I was able to sign a contract with a book publisher, Douglas LeBlanc, then associate editor of *Christianity Today* magazine, saw the value in the sample chapter I wrote on Ned Flanders, and tirelessly shepherded it to the cover of the February 5, 2001, issue. I know he had to convince a lot of people that it was the right kind of story for the publication, not to mention that it had been written by a Jew who was well outside the evangelical community.

Gail Hochman, a longtime and long-distance friend and supporter, did me a very large favor on very short notice that I will never forget. Jill Schwartz, my neighbor and friend, and Cecil Ricks, of Costa Mesa, California—the finest employment lawyers on two coasts—also helped me when I needed it. My editors at the *Orlando Sentinel* were gracious in granting me two book leaves and supporting my work.

The academic community, both religious and secular, was extremely helpful. Professors were willing to walk this C student through some very complex concepts and analyses and to allow me to pilfer their scholarship for my own purposes. They include Quentin Schultze and Bill Romanowski, both of Calvin College; my good friend from *Duke Chronicle* days and Columbia J-School, Clay Steinman, of Macalester College; John Heeren, of California State University at San Bernardino; Michael Glodo, Lyn Perez, and Matt Lacey (the latter two also neighbors), all of Reformed Theological Seminary in Oviedo, Florida; Eric Michael Mazur of Bucknell University; Gerry Bowler of University of Manitoba; David Landry of the University of St. Thomas; Tom Rainey of Evergreen State College; and Paul Cantor of the University of Virginia, who also copied some of his own tapes for me. In a category of his own was Martin Marty, the godfather of America's religion writers and the dean of academic observers of church life.

I benefited greatly from the advice of my journalist colleagues around the country, such as S. V. Date of the *Palm Beach Post*, and my cousin, Linda Loyd, of the *Philadelphia Inquirer*. I also benefited from some colleagues whose excellent work on this subject I have cited in the text, but never met, such as Les Sillars of the *Alberta Report*, Douglas Todd of the *Vancouver Sun*, Bob von Sternberg of the *Twin Cities Star-Tribune*, Paul Andrews of the *Seattle Times*, and Tom Kisken of the *Ventura County Star*.

In particular, I wish to thank my colleagues in the Religion Newswriters Association, as collegial and supportive a group of journalists as one is likely to find. These include Gayle White of the *Atlanta Constitution*, Cary McMullen of the *Lakeland Ledger* (Florida), Ken Garfield of the *Charlotte Observer*, Yonat Shimron of the *Raleigh News & Observer*, David Briggs of the *Cleveland Plain-Dealer*, Patricia Rice of the *St. Louis Post Dispatch*, John Dart of the *Christian Century*, and Adele Banks of Religion News Service.

Several other friends read this manuscript and offered many valuable suggestions, including another old friend from Duke,

Rusty Wright, whose renewed acquaintance and friendship helped shape this manuscript. John Valentine, of the Regulator Bookshop in Durham, was an early and enthusiastic encourager of my work. Mark Andrews, a *Sentinel* colleague, offered some keen insights and made the kind of good catches editors often do, and *Sentinel* film critic Jay Boyar made some excellent suggestions. Darren Iozia, also of the *Sentinel*, came through with copies of vital tapes. Rob Waters, of the *Raleigh News & Observer*, the best newspaper editor in the world, provided some of the same wise counsel he has been giving me for the past fifteen years (this time I took it). Durham novelist and dear friend Laurel Goldman had acute observations, whenever I was able to decipher her handwriting. Joe Puente helped me with Mormon references.

The leaders of Central Florida's religious community have taught me much about Christianity, from left to right, mainline to evangelical. Often they have kept me from embarrassing myself in print by taking my phone calls at inconvenient times. I have learned a great deal from them. In particular, I wish to thank these pastors: Jim Henry of the First Baptist Church of Orlando; Howard Edington of the First Presbyterian Church of Orlando, the "Heart of the City"; Clark Whitten of Calvary Assembly of God in Winter Park; Joel Hunter of Northland Community Church, Distributed, of Longwood; John Dalles of Wekiva Presbyterian Church in Longwood; and good neighbor Reid McCormick. Also, Bishop Norbert Dorsey of the Catholic Diocese of Orlando and Bishop John Howe of the Episcopal Diocese of Central Florida, and, especially, Bill Bright, founder of Campus Crusade for Christ.

National leaders of the Southern Baptist Convention, whom I have come to know and respect despite our many differences—political as well as theological—were also of great assistance, challenging me when and where I needed to be challenged. Knowing them, especially Dr. Richard Land of the SBC's Ethics and Religious Liberty Commission, I trust and expect this process will continue. Art Toalston, editor of Baptist Press, the SBC news service, was an early backer of this project.

My own rabbi, Steven Engel, of the Congregation of Reform Judaism, is a gifted and sympathetic clergyman who was kind enough to read my chapter on the Jews and offer his insightful views. Rabbi Sholom Dubov of Congregation Ahavas Yisrael (Chabad) in Maitland, the "rabbi around the corner," not only read the Jews chapter but also helped me put on *t'fillin* (phylacteries) while I was writing the book. Rabbi Daniel Wolpe of Temple Ohalei Rivka in Orlando offered the unique perspective of a *Simpsons* fan who, like Krusty, comes from a family of distinguished rabbis.

In New York, Comedy Central's Tom Fox and others at the network provided many episodes of *South Park* I would have had difficulty locating, and the show's Matt Stone and Anne Garefino made time to speak with me.

David Dobson, my wise and light-handed editor at Westminster John Knox Press, bolstered my shaky confidence as a first-time author from our first telephone conversation.

Finally, I would like to thank the Reverend Robert Short, who blazed this particular trail of religion and popular culture more than four decades ago with *The Gospel according to Peanuts*. He was most generous with his time and encouragement.

Index